D0444971

"In his book, Dr. Blanton shows us that telling the truth is far healthier, easier and more socially acceptable than we may have imagined."

—Phil Laut
Author of *Money Is My Friend*

"Brad Blanton's practice and community building around Radical Honesty is truly remarkable in this world where anything, but anything, is acceptable— except for the truth. And that's why I love Brad's work: Simply telling the truth has the power to break the molds we hold so dear. If you've seen him work, you know that he's gifted with the skill of a master therapist and visionary blended from a deeply compassionate place. Radical indeed. He challenges us all to take a leap of faith into a world where the truth is not whispered. Meet you there."

—Brett Hill
Editor for *Loving More* magazine

"Brad Blanton's books on radical honesty offer the possibility of a new world: A world where truth-telling reigns supreme. I believe Blanton has the vison, brilliance and courage to lead us to the threshold of this new world."

—Arielle Ford
Author of *Hot Chocolate for the Mystical Soul*

"I don't know anyone who's not "Radically Honest" that has a quality of life that comes close to the quality of those who are. Brad Blanton is 100% on target. Honesty is the foundation for what really matters: the truth. Anything else is empty and meaningless. Living honestly is infinitely easier and more rewarding than living a lie. The only requirement is courage."

—Will Richardson
Author and Real Estate Developer

"Practicing radical honesty has been the hardest but most rewarding discipline of my life! It totally turned my life up side down. After 21 years of intense spiritual searching I found this to be the most impactful, intense way to get to my own authenticity and truth. I can live full-out on a day to day basis—and my life is unfolding in a way I never believed possible."

—Marlene Martin
Orange County Newspaper Publisher

Brad Blanton's books and seminars are a call to courage. The courage to tell the truth. The courage to face down our rationalizations, look at the real reasons we don't tell the truth and haul those monsters out of their caves of denial. Brad's book places the scalpel in our hands and teaches us to be skillful surgeons, cutting away the lies that have encrusted our existence. Don't read this book, unless you want to face your demons and change your life.

—Dirk Metzger
Attorney, San Diego, California

Practicing Radical Honesty

How to Complete the Past,
Live in the Present,
and Build a Future
with a Little Help from Your Friends

by

BRAD BLANTON, PH.D.

Author of
Radical Honesty
How to Transform Your Life by Telling the Truth

www.radicalhonesty.com

Published by
Sparrowhawk Publishing
646 Schuler Lane
Stanley VA 22851
800 EL TRUTH
www.radicalhonesty.com

Publisher's Cataloging-in-Publication Data:

Blanton, Brad.
    Practicing radical honesty : how to complete
the past, stay in the present, and build a future
with a little help from your friends / by Brad
Blanton. -- 1st ed.
    p. cm.
    Includes bibliographical references.

    1. Self-actualization (Psychology). 2. Life.
3. Social ecology.   I. Title.

BF637.S4B57 2000   158.1

Copyright © 2000, Brad Blanton

Cover by G Whiz Graphics
Interior design by Brenda Plowman
Printed in USA
First Edition

10 9 8 7 6 5 4 3 2 1

CONTENTS

Foreword

Don' t look now, but the human race is terribly unhappy. Oh, not you, of course. You're fine. It's the rest of us that have bungled it. We have imprisoned ourselves in jails of our own devise. We have sentenced ourselves to lives of quiet desperation in punishment for the violence we have done to our own souls.

We have done this violence by the simple expedience of lying. We meant nothing by it, of course. We were only trying to get through the moment. Yet by making lying a lifestyle, we have missed the moment. And the next moment. And the next. In this way, we humans have missed most of our lives. Worse yet, our cumulative lies have cost others. Namely, those who have followed us. For they have lived the cultural story created by our untruths. Thus, humans have not only sentenced themselves, they've sentenced entire generations to unhappiness.

It all started innocently enough. The Little White Lies of Childhood. White Lies we learned from our parents, and from the world around us. Untruths masquerading as social etiquette. "I'm fine, thank you," when we knew Mommy was feeling terrible. "Gosh, we'd love to come over, but we're just really busy this weekend," when we could see that Daddy had nothing at all to do on the weekend, and simply disliked the Johnsons. We saw others do it—others whom we respected—and so we thought, maybe I'll try that. *This must be the way to get through the moment.*

Only when we ourselves have finally grown up—and then only if we are very lucky—is it clear to us that not only have we missed the moment, we've killed it. We've robbed it of any life it had any chance of holding for us by lying and evading and avoiding our truth at all cost.

Those last three words were well chosen, because it has cost us plenty. Our lives. Our fortunes. Our sacred honor.

It has cost us our very selves. We don't even know who we are anymore, with all the hiding and deceiving we've done. We've lost ourselves in the labyrinth of our own lies. Astonishingly, we can't even admit this. Thus, we commit the highest insult: we lie to ourselves.

And so we carry on—day after day, week after week, month after month, year after year—living our lies as if they were our truth, unable to stop ourselves from lying even when we know we are doing it.

Oh, Neale, stop it. You're making too much of this. You're going on and on.

Really? Look around you.

Our governments lie. Our politicians lie. Our economists lie. Our police lie—*sometimes on the witness stand.* Our educators lie. Our religions lie. Our parents lie. And nobody admits it.

Not only won't the *liars* admit it, the people being lied to won't admit it. *They know they're being lied to, but they won't acknowledge it.* Do you want to be the one to tell the Emperor that he's wearing no clothes?

So not only do we all lie, *we lie about our lying.*

And oh, what tangled webs we weave...

There's a way out of all this. A way to a life of peace and joy and incredibly exuberant freedom.

Tell The Truth.

About Everything.

All The Time.

Big order? It shouldn't be. But let's acknowledge that it is—otherwise we'll wind up lying about *that.* It is a big order. Because we've been lying for so long, it's become part of our way of living. We have to learn a new way to live—and a new way to love. That's what we're talking about here. We're talking about love. We're not loving anybody to whom we are lying. That includes ourselves.

No wonder the world is in the shape it's in.

I think we should change. In the *With God* series of books, I spoke about living a life of total visibility. This means utter transparency. The irony of transparency, I wrote in *Friendship with God*, is that it produces complete visibility. And complete visibility is all that is going to save us. We've got to come clean with each other. At long last. Or we'll never make it. Not as a species, not as groups within the species, and not as individuals. *We aren't making it now – look around you.*

How do we change things? How do we spring free from this trap we have set for ourselves? We adopt radical honesty as our new lifestyle.

I don't agree with every word that Brad Blanton has written here. Indeed, I take exception to some of what he has said, and the way in which he has said it. Yet Brad and I would have it no other way, for we concur on this: the day that we agree with every word of another, without exception, is the day that we have stopped thinking for ourselves. Neither of us are prepared to do that. I am prepared, however, to tell you that I agree profoundly with the thrust of Brad's argument here. This book will give you an incredible ride through the corridors of consciousness, taking you to places not many have had the courage to visit before. That visit could change your life.

—Neale Donald Walsch

Author's Preface

Here's what I want. I want you to be happy about your life most of the time. I want the trail you follow in your life from reading this book forward to be mostly happy. When you finish this book I want you to jump up and holler and fall down and laugh. To get to that "Hoohah!!" kind of joy may require a trip through some sadness and some anger and some thinking the likes of which most of us don't often do. That sadness, and that anger and that joy and that brand new thinking, comes from growing, which keeps us alive.

To grow, and to continue growing throughout life, and to contribute to the personal and collective growth of humankind in the great conversation about what it is to be human, we need two things:

- the ability to have a transcendent perspective, and
- the ability to transcend.

A transcendent perspective comes from *thinking* and from processing a lot of information (which has to be accurate information, not lies). Transcending is done by *noticing* and *experiencing* – particularly, our resistance within (the individual self) and without (other people and other social structures).

For example, many people believe both that it is possible for them to love more than one person, and that they shouldn't. People often do love more than one person, however, even though married and in a monogamous relationship. If both married people tell the truth to each other, they may encounter difficulty loving their partner who is also loving a third party. In most cases, this type of love requires more personal growth than either of them can stand, particularly if sexual involvement with another person arises as a possibility. According to reliable surveys, more than a third of all married people do have sex with people other than their mates. They don't tell each other about it though. They choose instead to lie to each other, have affairs in secret, and avoid the suffering of personal growth in favor of the suffering of lying. If they commit to work their way through jealousy honestly, and stay with each other and share all the resentments, appreciations, pleasures, and pains and break through to a transcendent perspective, eventually they are able to love and value each other for the shared struggle of personal growth and can deepen their lives together. They may or may not screw around with someone else, but their lives together are deeper and more intimate and each feels included in the life of the other and a participant in the decisions the other makes.

This is not usually the case. In most conventional marriages the ideals are clear but the practices fall short. Because of withholding, the bliss imagined becomes the perspective that mocks the real experience. Visions of heaven become the source of hell.

In another example, most people will tell you that they are not in favor of war, while war persists. Defense budgets deplete a gigantic proportion of the world's resources, and warfare is still frequently used as an attempt to settle disputes. War and preparation for war remain a completely acceptable exception to collective personal preferences against violence.

Other examples are abundant. All point to the same dilemma. *We can go places with our minds that our psyches can't yet reach.* We don't have the heart to grow into what we know is possible. Many of us are now learning that growing is, in fact, worth the struggle.

Those of us who have decided that growing is worth the trouble need an ongoing supply of two things. We need information about new perspectives and we need to process the information personally with friends to really be able to apply it. This is why I don't just write books, but also lead workshops and trainings, train trainers, and do consultations: *We human beings do not revise perspectives without a fight.* Experiments in personal growth, and working through our resistance to giving up old perspectives, provide us with more information, but they are hard work. This then helps us to revise the old perspectives or come up with entirely new ones—and so the process continues. Ideas are useful only when modified in the guts of the living.

This book is about a few new perspectives:

- the need for honest and accurate information—how to give it and how to get it,

- the work needed to bring about "the getting" of new perspectives into our bones and into the world,

- how to support each other in the process of shedding old perspectives and building new ones, and

- creating a larger context politically and economically for the growth of human knowledge, thus expanding our ability to survive and thrive.

Beyond these perspectives, this book is about a perspective on perspectives. The perspective I am advocating in this book is to view perspectives themselves from a transcendent standpoint. That standpoint is that all perspectives are relative. No perspective is absolute except this one.

One first gets the relativity of perspectives intellectually. After a long time and a lot of work, one gets the perspective on the relativity of perspectives practically, "feelingly," usefully, psychologically, structurally, interpersonally, and whatever other "lys" pertain to the *actual bringing into being* of the perspective of detachment from perspectives itself.

How many Zen Buddhists does it take to change a light bulb? Three. One to change the bulb. One to *not* change the bulb. One to *neither change the bulb nor not change the bulb.* The ultimate detachment includes detachment even from the ideal of attachment. This is the kind of thing that can make you lose your mind …and come to your senses.

The training programs developed by my colleagues and me at Radical Honesty Enterprises, Inc. are designed to help participants process and integrate information about new perspectives. We help people come up with new perspectives and use them and adapt to them and dispense with them. We introduce people to others who are interested in ongoing personal growth. Our own courses are not the only ones we recommend. There are a lot of good teachers and good courses in personal growth these days. Our programs are just part of what is available, but a certain amount of discrimination is required to sort the airy fairy from the authentic learning.

We sort through what is available using certain standards. We use *honesty, sharing,* and *practicality* as our guidelines for judging the value of training programs and books. When you read this book, or if you take any of our programs, please be self-ish. Make sure you get the benefit of a more useful perspective as well as practice in applying it. Good luck.

— *Brad Blanton, Sparrowhawk, March 2000*

Part One:
True Individuality

The Decline of Individual Psychotherapy and the Rise of Therapeutic Community

Let's talk straight here for awhile. I think being honest helps, even though it can be depressing to start with. Let's start with the depressing truth about low level depression. Aren't almost all the adults you know, and most of your friends and acquaintances, less than happy, not living up to their full potential, sometimes lying and sneaking around, getting by with what they can, and generally, furtively, looking here and there for a little relief or pleasure or freedom? Don't they waste a lot of energy more or less desperately pretending that everything is all right? Don't you? Aren't most of us just completely resigned, or trying too hard, or feeling depressed at a low level a lot of the time? If you happen to hear somebody singing the blues about how life is—like, for example, the song that goes: "I got the steadily depressin' low down mind messin' workin' at the carwash blues...", don't you want to say "Amen! Ain't it the truth!" Doesn't it make you feel better to hear someone singing about it?

If you walk down the street and just look at people's faces, or if you drive in traffic and watch people in their cars, and make a quick judgment, one face at a time, do any of them look happy?

If you encounter two out of ten that actually look happy, you've had a good day, haven't you? Most of us, at a glance, just from our faces, look mildly distracted or frozen or furious or sad or completely masked or desperately tense or in a big hurry or just plain worried, most of the time.

Many of us live in the United States of America, one of the richest, most powerful, greatest countries in the world, but by the time most of us grow up, we are not really happy. Most of the people I know and I think probably most of the people you know, including yourself, are not dealing with a full deck, not firing on all cylinders. I mean, really, isn't this the way most of us are actually living most of the time?

I think our whole culture is, in many ways, insane, and this insanity is taking over the world. We have all gone crazy together. We are crazy over money. The whole world is involved. The best and most nurturing cultures are succumbing to the influence of multinational corporations for the sake of toys advertised on TV. More and more of us directly or indirectly are working for "the Man." The average work week in the United States in 1954 was seventeen (!) hours *shorter* than in 1994. On average, we are all working seventeen hours per week longer than people did in 1954! (Korten, *When Corporations Rule the World*[1]) Not only that, if you take into account the real value of the money made in terms of purchasing power, the current captains of industry have two workers for the same price they paid for one in 1954! It's a great thing that women can work and compete in the marketplace, but it is incredibly stupid for men and women to have children together and both keep working fifty-five to sixty hours a week. This is particularly true when children are young. It is also absolutely ridiculous for single parents to be working all the time to care for children they are not actually, in reality, caring for.

In the Western world (the model now being copied by the rest of the world), we have recently come to value money and the material it provides more than being with our children. We're abandoning our children when they are very young and leaving them to caretakers other than ourselves, using the rationalization that we have to do that in order to take care of our children. That is a terrible mistake. These caretakers do the best they can, but for the most part, do not love the child like parents who bond with their own child upon its arrival. We give birth in hospitals, where often everything that can be done is done to block initial bonding. So many parents miss even this — the best and first real opportunity to bond with their children.

In spite of missed opportunities to bond at the very beginning, parents generally still love their children. They do the best they can, but within an extremely ill-fitting and inappropriate parenting and educational system and culture that has become increasingly dysfunctional since its inception. The more a lot of us think about this, the more our depression seems to turn into anger. I think that is a good thing. I think it's time we get mad about cultural ignorance instead of depressed because we can't make ends meet.

It is time for a revolution. I don't mean a phony Republican revolution with welfare reform that impoverishes another one and a half million children to protect the poor helpless rich people. I don't mean a phony Democratic revolution where the drop in the bucket of having "paid leave" for parents when children are sick is hailed as a great leap forward. I mean a revolution, a turning of the wheel, that comes from waking up and seeing the stupidity of what we have all been doing.

Many of us are working at home now, and many more will be doing so in the next ten years. We hope that by doing this we will get to spend more time with our children and our mates and our friends, but often we won't. Even if we do, and we are in our minds, rather than in touch, we might as well not be there. We have hope that a kind of symbolic "being there" will substitute for real contact with children, friends, and mates. It doesn't. We are, all of us, most of the time, simply operating from a commonly shared belief system that is quite dysfunctional.

I think this all has to do with lying.

Individual Psychotherapy in a Dysfunctional Family Doesn't Work Unless the Family Changes

For twenty-five years, I have been a practicing clinical psychologist in Washington, D.C., specializing in individual, group, and couples psychotherapy. I have helped thousands of average, normal, miserable people become less miserable, normal, and average. I helped them to quit lying the way they had been taught by nearly every person and institution they had been in contact with all their lives. When they quit withholding, hiding, manipulating, performing, or lying outright to everyone in their lives, their depression went away. Anxiety disorders disappeared. Psychosomatic ailments were cured.

Most of my work with people has been about repairing the damage done by their education and parenting. Their parents and teachers communicated that the highest value a person could hold was to perform well, or at least to appear to perform well. They had learned never to be satisfied with anything less than perfection and always to pretend that everything is okay and improving. Who you are, they were told, is your performance. With such a stress on performance, their whole lives became an act. Then, maintaining and enhancing the act captured all their attention and they began slowly starving to death for lack of the nurturance that comes from commonplace experience.

Almost all of us have been poisoned by such pretense, and few of us grow beyond that. We lie like hell all the time to maintain our systematically indoctrinated image of who we are. We Americans live privileged lives in a wonderful country with fantastic opportunities *and* we have been brainwashed since the day we were born. In fact, we are so used to the brainwashing we hardly even notice it any more. We are used to being poisoned on a regular basis, from within ourselves and outside ourselves, that we don't even notice we are feeling sick anymore. As a result, we live in a kind of well-decorated hell together. Telling the truth can help you start to notice how you poison yourself, how you feel as a result, and how you maintain the social structures around you to keep from noticing the nausea that comes from maintaining the act. Once that occurs, all hell breaks loose.

Based on my experience as a psychotherapist, workshop leader, and consultant, I have come to the conclusion that what most dramatically transforms lives from normal misery to unreasonable happiness is telling the truth. When I talk about telling the truth, I mean giving a blow-by-blow description of what happened, what you thought about what happened, and how you felt at the time it happened, as well as what you are doing, thinking, and feeling about it right now. It is important that you tell these things to the people from whom you are most inclined to hide this information. *Tell the truth about what you have done, what you think, and what you feel.*

Telling the truth is hard to do, because it is so contrary to our conditioning. People might get their feelings hurt, or get offended or shocked or unbearably relieved. But if neither you nor they run away, and you stay with your experience, on the other side of that short-term breaking of the taboo is great freedom and love for each other. Telling the truth is hard, but covering up is harder on you and harder to live with than the truth. Being isolated within our own internally-judging minds is what most of us suffer and die from. The rescue from our mind's oppression comes through authentic contact and honest sharing with other human beings. Not only does the quality of our lives depend on this contact and sharing, but as Dr. Dean Ornish has demonstrated in his recent book, *Love and Survival: The Scientific Basis for the Healing Power of Intimacy*[2], life itself depends on this authentic contact with others.

Two recent movies, *Secrets and Lies* and *Courage Under Fire*, illustrate the transformation that follows from telling the truth. In both movies, when the main characters finally muster the courage to tell the truth, the difficulties they face as a result are less damaging to everyone than the lies they had been hiding behind. That same kind of transformation has been experienced by hundreds of real-life graduates of my workshops and psychotherapy clients. In each case where this extraordinary level of honesty occurs in real life, there is an authentic sharing of emotion, a rebirth of intimacy, and a renewal of relationship and psychological healing—in many cases not only for the truthteller, but also for those hearing the truth. Here are a few examples of the transformations accomplished by participants in Radical Honesty™ workshops.

- A husband who was having an affair, and not for the first time, told his wife the truth when he described in detail the number of times he had seen his lovers, what he had done with them and how he felt during the liaisons. The initial conversations were really hard, and both he and his wife lived through a lot of fury and hurt and fear. They were coached by other friends and me who simply held constant for them the goal of being explicit and clear about what they felt, what they thought, and what they had done. Eventually, she forgave him and they chose to continue living together. The result was not only forgiveness for hurts and transgressions from the past, but great joy and renewal of the whole family. The perspective and the conversation and the closeness that developed out of that renewal continues to this day, as they work to consciously design and create together the future life of their family.

- After withholding information from her fundamentalist parents for years, a daughter told them the truth about an abortion she'd had while in college. She went back and told them everything, including how she got pregnant, what she'd done when she found out, where she went for the abortion, and how she felt about not being able to tell them. She was sure her parents would disown her. Her parents expressed their sorrow at her having gone through that experience alone, and their desire to be there for her even if she violated their expectations and values. She and her parents now have a more authentic and open relationship. Dozens of times, I have coached women to make similar revelations, with like results. Out of this experience they can, for the first time, make plans for the future of their own love relationships and the families that proceed from them without being blocked by undone knots from the past.

- A young man wanted a better relationship with his parents but felt that certain things were "unspeakable" as a part of the family code of silence. He had a five-hour session with his parents in which he shared specific resentments and specific appreciations for things they had spoken and done in the past. He spoke in detail about things that were implicitly not talked about in his family. Afterward, he began to realize that the "family code" was partly in his imagination. He also became more open to who his parents really were, just as they became more open to who he was. Now they all acknowledge that a new family of adult friends has been born, made up of people who work together on joint projects and support each other in separate projects. (There are many millions of people in the world who never really get to know their parents as adults. For others, this simple process of declaring "I am grown" and "This is what I resent about you and appreciate about you from the past" and "This is who I am and what I value now" often leads to complete renewal of the whole family and stands in stark contrast to the norm.)

- A woman diagnosed by physicians with arthritis told the truth to her husband about an affair she had been hiding for a long time. They eventually split up, but her "arthritis" went away. Her next relationship was one of more honesty, less pain and illness, and more creativity in a shared life together.

- A man with chronic sleep-onset insomnia started falling asleep peacefully every night after cleaning up his act by telling the truth at work and at home. He risked his job by telling his boss his specific resentments and as a result, instead of getting fired, he was given a raise in pay. He risked his relationship with his wife by telling her the truth about what he felt, thought and did, and instead of her leaving, they fell in love again. As a side effect, he can sleep now. He now has work and love in a community of friends rather than a life of isolation.

There are scores of such examples throughout our own radical honesty community of friends. The common thread across all these stories of successful deliverance from the mind is *the revision of an incorrect belief, on the part of each individual, about who they are.* When we discover that we are not our reputations in the eyes of our parents or bosses or spouses, we also discover the same thing about other people. We find out who we are behind the mask of false identity, and simultaneously begin to glimpse the same in those close to us. Once this gets straightened out, authentic conversation can begin. Sometimes it begins with a person admitting that they are a liar and accusing their friends of being liars as well and then sticking with the discussion until they all can laugh at their own and each other's pretentiousness.

Deliverance from Mistaken Identity

When I wrote *Radical Honesty*[3], a number of concepts had become apparent to me, through working with hundreds of people suffering from depression, anxiety disorders, and stress-related ailments. These concepts follow.

1. Lying is the primary source of most human stress.

2. Stress is caused by the mind of the individual suffering from stress, not by circumstances.

3. Most suffering is generated by the tendency of the mind to moralize and judge, and to mistake belief for reality.

4. Most of us suffer from the fundamental problem of mistaken identity—we tend to identify with our judgments and

criticisms of ourselves and believe our judging minds to be who we are.

Freedom from the foolish notion that our fundamental identity is a judge and critic gives us the possibility of living our lives according to our *preferences* rather than the "shoulds" our minds generate. Once people complete the undoing of their past lies and get "current" by telling the truth, they must continually reground themselves in the present moment with the use of daily practices that help them *stay* current.

The daily practices, as the world's great wisdom traditions have always taught, all have to do with *noticing*. Meditating, telling the truth, practicing yoga, being aware with the senses, and many other practices lead to a new way of identifying oneself. This new identity as the Noticer rather than the Performer grows on you. The Noticer takes charge of the mind rather than the reverse. Belief is distinguished from reality. An individual is born.

In addition to daily practices to maintain and sharpen noticing, something else is equally important: the mind has to be given new work to do, to keep it from backsliding into its habitual patterns. The judging mind is like a teething puppy; it needs to be given a bone or toy or an old rag to chew on. That new work for the mind-dog, that "something bigger" to chew on, is the work of creating one's life as an artist. Getting free and staying free from the jail of the mind, identifying oneself as a noticing being, and using the mind rather than being used by it are practices at the heart of how honest people create the good life in a community of friends.

Approaching Life Problems

Once belief is distinguished from reality, a whole new approach to life problems emerges. We stop wasting energy protesting and simply accept that life comes with problems, whether we are honest or engage in spiritual practices or not. Problems are best handled by confronting them openly rather than keeping them secret; by telling other people what problems we have and working them out in the public arena. As it turns out, not all problems are miserable. A lot of problems are fun. Even those that were once miserable can become fun through a change of perspective and a change of heart. People who stop resisting life problems become a community of support for each other's practice of honesty, awareness, and creating life by intentional design. The most wonderful thing about this whole process is that people's contributions to the lives of others become the primary means of getting the results *they* want in their own lives.

After Liberation from the Jail of the Mind — Conscious Creation

My clients have all been average, functional, tax-paying, voting citizens — normal people — with problems that were getting them down. Out of the work they did with me and my colleagues, however, they became *abnormal* people — abnormally successful. They didn't settle for just getting over something or resolving their problems. They began to create. When that happened, my job changed. I became a coach for creating. As the Radical Honesty Workshops evolved, my job shifted from encouraging liberation from limiting beliefs to supporting "designer beliefs" — beliefs consciously invented to bring about certain results. The function of the mind shifts from maintaining an image to imagining a future and then to creating a future. Beliefs that are just functional and not a substitute for reality can be *useful*.

The future that emerges from conscious planning and conscious use of the mind is absolutely not predictable by inference from the liberated person's past. Energy that was once expended on self-criticism, conflict, and suffering has instead nurtured projects resulting in multimillion-dollar businesses, startups of new enterprises, marriages after years of inability to partner up, children born and adopted, homes built, careers changed, indebtedness resolved, and reunion with alienated friends and families accomplished. Take, for example, Melody Harris.

Depression and Liberation

The first moment I met Melody Harris she started crying. She came into my office for a psychotherapy appointment, introduced herself, sat down, said, "My sister-in-law told me to come see you because I'm depressed..." and started crying. I just watched her and waited and didn't say anything. She dug a bunch of tissues out of her purse, blew her nose, looked at me, and started talking again. Over the course of that first hour we spent together, I found out that she was in her forties, lived alone with a five-year-old child she'd adopted just before her husband left her, and worked as a secretary in a law firm. She hated her job, even though she liked the lawyers for whom she worked.

There was a history of depression in her family, and she had been on anti-depressant medications of various sorts for several years. At the time, although Melody was taking Prozac, she still cried frequently and felt hopeless a lot. I also learned that she loved to read, had read lots of good literature and self-help books, and that she had a sense of humor.

Toward the end of the hour, I asked, "Did you hear the joke about the computer programmer who died in the shower?"

Melody said, "No."

I said, "She read the label on the shampoo. It said, "Wet hair. Lather. Rinse. Repeat.'"

Melody looked blank for about five seconds and then laughed—a great big guffaw of a laugh. She got it. She got that the computer programmer, caught in the "do-loop" of the instructions and shampooing herself to death, was just like herself in some way. She got the joke and she got that the joke was on her at the same time. I liked her and thought she was smart and funny and she felt the same about me. That was about three years ago.

Melody and her eight-year-old daughter came to our house to visit for the weekend not too long ago. We spent most of the time laughing, singing songs, and talking about her plans to quit her job, sell her house, and move out to the country. My wife, Amy, and our kids and I love her.

Melody is no longer victimized by depression, and over the last six months has been able to slowly reduce the amount of medication she's been taking so that now she is off it altogether. She may or may not stay off medication, but the choice will be made by her according to what she notices about her life and her moods, not according to some physician's best guess about the state of her neurotransmitters. She recently told me she hadn't started the day by crying in the morning for over six months. She is way happier most of the time than she used to be.

Melody learned how to be happier and no longer victimized by so-called endogenous (genetic, biochemical) depression. She was worse off than you probably are. Yet she stopped being a victim and became a creator. She stopped being a victim of circumstance and became the creator of her own life.

It didn't happen overnight. She still has relapses. But she herself and anyone who knows her will tell you, she is more in control of her life than she used to be. She did it systematically, over about a three-year period, through individual and group psychotherapy, participating in workshops and groups designed and conducted by me and other people I have trained, and by spending time living among and playing with other honest people.

She came to Mexico with us in early February for the last couple of years with about fifty-five of our closest friends, to attend the Annual Unconvention of the Futilitarian Union Network, which is the name of our "cult." She quit her job and moved to the country with her daughter and until recently has been living with us while preparing to build a little house nearby. She is consciously designing a way to make a living in some less miserable fashion by working with us and carving out a new career.

Dual Relationships

There is a term among psychotherapists for the kind of healing that involves creating together and being friends: it's called "dual relationship" and you lose your license to practice psychotherapy for it. A dozen or so therapists a year lose their licenses and their listing in the National Registry of Health Service Providers in Psychology for conducting "dual relationships" with their clients. These rules were made when the model we were operating under was the doctor/patient or teacher/student model. This model was set up to protect the patient or student from being taken advantage of sexually or financially by the caretaker and to prevent the caretaker from having undue influence over a patient or student's life because of the position of authority held by the caretaker. Seeking to avoid any possible Bill Clinton and Monica Lewinsky events or cult leader advantages, licensed therapists made rules that say we are supposed to play doctor and our clients are supposed to play patient and so we shouldn't hang out with each other at all. As is the case with the evolution of most rules and regulations in the minds of most people, what starts out as an impulse toward fairness and consumer protection eventually becomes moralism and ignorance. In the context of honesty we are equals from the start. Whatever expertise gets shared comes from another flawed human being.

Currently, all my relationships to all my clients are dual relationships. The evolution of psychotherapy and teaching to the stage where the therapist and teacher are demoted and the power of the client is promoted has occurred in the context of honesty to the point where we are presumed equal because, in fact, we are. As beings we are equal to start. As minds, we are both screwed up whether we are playing trainer or trainee, and either one of us may be more screwed up than the other at any given time. Most of the psychotherapists I train nowadays admit this equality of being and most form friendships with their clients. That kind of sharing is actually critical to creating the kind of therapeutic community that gives rise to the psychological growth of all its members, including its so-called leaders.

This book explores the same path Melody and others have followed and includes most of the content of the training groups that teach a new egalitarian model for living called *radical honesty*. Melody is now busily engaged in the process of consciously designing her life. She has accomplished her main goal of no longer having her mood determine the results she gets in the world. Ironically, this detachment from mood has had a subtle but unmistakably positive effect on her mood. She is now in training to be a trainer to run groups that teach radical honesty. My family and friends and fellow therapists and trainers and other "dual relationship" clients are working away at modeling and teaching this way of "living out loud" and "living with no apology" that we have learned from each other.

How Does One Live Honestly?

First of all, Melody took permanent responsibility for the moment-to-moment quality of her own life. Then she learned a number of practices that keep her grounded in the present; noticing her experience and distinguishing between *noticing* and *thinking*. She meditates and exercises regularly, communicates her feelings all the time whether she is scared to do so or not, practices yoga occasionally, speaks honestly with other people about her life and theirs, and seeks coaching from friends about work and child-rearing-related problems and perplexities.

As a result of our coaching and conversations and encouragement, she also contacted and completed unfinished business with people from her past, most notably her ex-husband from whom she had been alienated for seven years. She found him and met with him in person. Face-to-face and out loud, she told him what she resented him for and what she appreciated him for. After she had traced him down and met with him to clearly experience and live through all the anger, hurt, and appreciation she had avoided for all those years, she found that her life changed. In all the rest of her life, she now has the power to make things happen differently from how they had happened before. She completed what had been avoided and left incomplete, in the real world, with real people in her real life. And she has had more power in relation to every person she has come in contact with since then.

In addition to what Melody learned by facing those major things she had avoided, there were dozens of other small things that she learned to do as a result of her openness and availability. As both advisee and advisor to her friends in our local radical honesty community, which is made up of people who are also taking charge of their lives, she has continued to become more skillful at listening and communicating. Everyone in this community has tried both avoidance and taking charge and they have found that making things happen is more gratifying than whining and complaining and blaming and making excuses for all the bad things that have happened to them that were beyond their control. We all remind each other of that now and then. Those of us who have discovered our own authority in our lives have compassion for those who haven't, but we don't buy into their tales of woe-is-me. We often make fun of each other as much or more than we feel sorry for each other. When we get over the stories about the past that we have been living in, what used to be tragic often turns out to be more funny than tragic.

As a result of communicating with honest friends over a period of time and completing what she had avoided in the past, Melody no longer believes a number of things she used to believe. She used to think she was a *victim* of depression and many other accidents of fate, and that there was nothing she could do about it except to stay on medications at high dosage levels that had negative side effects (no sexual interest, dulled sensations, weight gain, and more). She used to think that she had to keep working at a job she hated no matter what.

Through coaching and practice in noticing sensations in her body, from one moment to the next, Melody came to recognize that a global category like "depression" didn't precisely describe each individual moment of real feeling. She became skilled in distinguishing the difference between limiting beliefs, such as "I am a depressed person," and actual experience, such as "I feel pressure in my chest right now and I am crying." She developed skills for designing step-by-step blueprints to build the future she envisions for herself and her daughter. Furthermore, she has the continuous support of a community of people who love her and consider themselves to be in the same boat with regard to making their lives work.

By telling the truth about what we have previously avoided, we progress from living within the restraining context of limiting beliefs, to *noticing* real experience, to *conscious design* of the future with the help of a community of friends. This is accomplished through a series of learnings. This book is a detailed description of that series of learnings.

Of course, it's not just folks who have worked with me who are making these great transformations. There are other therapists and trainers and consultants and teachers and philosophers who, out of discovering their own individuality, make immense contributions to others by assisting them to find their own individuality. It's more like a movement. This book is dedicated to that movement. Those of us fed up with pretense and lying are gaining ground.

A revolution is happening. It is called the revolution of consciousness. It involves:

1. Liberation from the traditional jail of the mind;
2. Constant engagement in the practices of meditation, awareness, and radical honesty to maintain contact with being alive and with others; and

3. Consciously designing the future with the help of friends —
   being a creator in a community of creators.

The Revolution of Consciousness

As I have traveled across the country speaking and doing book signings and leading workshops on radical honesty, I have met hundreds of people who are members of a great revolution in consciousness presently taking place in America, and in much of the rest of the world, fomented by individuals who want to improve not only their own lives, but also to change the way society educates us about what is important and valuable. The leftovers from Judeo-Christian fundamentalism and stoicism — the belief instilled in most of us that we *must* suffer all kinds of unhappiness just to survive — still determine for most of us our automatic approach to life. We who have grown beyond that have learned two very important things: we don't know much about how to leave ourselves alone, and life can be so much easier than how most of us are willing to let ourselves live. Life can be so much richer when we shift the focus from increasing the *quantity of our accumulations* and concentrate instead on the *quality of our attention.*

There is a way out of the desperate, driven way of living we have all been taught, and we can only create it, simultaneously for ourselves and each other, through an honest dialogue about how our lives are and how we want our collective future to be. I am writing this book to make it possible for readers to benefit from the same processes and practices that have helped my clients, workshop participants, and me not only to get over our suffering, but to begin creating a less dysfunctional world family.

Through all these years of working closely as a psychotherapist with people who were screwed up by how they were parented, instructed, and acculturated, I have been asking myself:

"What makes people happy and free?"

"What is functional and what's dysfunctional?"

"What is an average functional person, and how does a highly functioning human being operate?"

The answer to all these questions has something to do with continuing to grow. And continuing to grow seems more and more to require shedding one's mind and one's outdated culture like a snake shedding his skin each time he outgrows it.

A fulfilled life is going to be something different for every person, but there are some qualities, skills, and abilities that are essential. In addition to being willing to take responsibility for one's own life, and maintaining an ongoing engagement in practices that keep one grounded in the experience of being and noticing, one needs to find work that seems like play. What used to be work becomes play because it is based on the future you envision and want to bring into being simply because you love the idea of it. To make all this possible, you need skill in maintaining strong, nurturant, loving participation in a community of friends who support you in an honest and creative life. Rather than using your mind simply to react to the events in the present that vaguely remind you of your past, as most of the miserable people in the world do, you use your mind instead to create a future for yourself and your friends.

Practicing Radical Honesty is about the re-attainment and rediscovery of what Nietzsche called "that seriousness of a child at play." This book shares insights, practices, and exercises that work. Done in sequence, they allow you to move all the way from feeling overwhelmed and depressed to feeling, most of the time, as if your whole life is playing and having fun and contributing to other people. To move along the path from being a victim of overwhelming circumstances to becoming a masterful creator at play, you must constantly practice noticing with the senses to escape domination by the mind.

The Workbook Section

The revolution of consciousness is the organizing principle for the workbook section of this book. The path goes like this:

first we recognize and then transcend the limiting beliefs of our own minds. Then we stop being victims of our own and our cultures' ignorant and outdated prejudices. Finally, we accept full responsibility for the quality of our present and future lives.

Once we get beyond the paradigm of beliefs that has been limiting us, and are restored to our true identity as beings in our bodies right here and now, we have to put our minds to work doing something other than worrying and criticizing. We do this because we have learned that if we don't give our minds work to do designing the future, they will convert remembered experience into limiting beliefs all over again. To keep our concepts about reality from recapturing the here-and-now space of the experience of reality, we assign our minds the task of bringing about a future we envision. Unless the work we give our minds keeps them busy, we will go back to judging ourselves according to the old-fashioned and inappropriate values of the past and believing that who we are is the judge-and-victim game. We have to give our minds something to chew on or they chew on us.

Designed to be used by individuals or groups, the workbook section of this book contains exercises and experiments and practical techniques for becoming attuned to the sensations of our bodies and grounded in our experience in the here and now. These practices allow us to *become identified, through practice, with our ability to notice.* The workbook exercises are introduced, one set at a time, according to what seems to be the natural developmental sequence people go through when they begin to grow up. The highlights of the steps are as follows.

First: Get Over It

Nobody is going to be able to make up for how you got treated as a child. No one owes you compensation for your suffering. The scars are not going to go away, and the odds are you can't be fixed anyway. It turns out that no matter how good a listener your therapist is, your whining about how your parents didn't do it right, and how nobody has done a good enough job since then, isn't going to help you lead a better life. You need to accept what skills and scars you have and live in the present and look to the future. Once you accept that being a victim is an impotent protest and a waste of your life and energy, you have a chance to do something about it. One of the first things you do is go back and confront your parents and ex-spouses and begrudged people from the past and complete with them, forgive them, acknowledge them, and turn yourself loose from your *story* about you and them. Express your resentment and get over it. Express your appreciation and get over it. Then, articulate and confirm value differences that are real, and be separate individuals and still be related in the context of forgiveness. Get over it.

Primarily, we are each victimized by one thing only: the limiting perspective of our own minds. Formerly limiting perspectives, once transcended, can be used to construct a better life. You can create the life you want using the equipment you have. Your neuroses, your limiting beliefs, your defenses, your paranoia, and your hypersensitivity can all become useful tools once your perspective on them changes. Examples of this transformation are plentiful.

John Bradshaw, the famous author, personality theorist, and therapist, says he became a therapist because of his codependent relationship with his mother. There is a fellow I know who teaches the rich and famous how to stay safe, a skill he developed from being an abused child and later a thief. He began his training in life by learning to watch for subtle cues in the behavior of potentially violent people and to rip them off first, in order to avoid being ripped off. He now teaches people how to avoid being victimized by people skilled in his kind of survival system. My wife, Amy Silver, a writer, songwriter, and performer, spent her childhood climbing trees and reading books to escape the fury of her hysterical mother and the insanity of her space cadet father and the way they ran the family in her earlier years. After she voluntarily came back to this world, she turned out to be a poet, having learned to synthesize her facility with language and her skills in noticing. She now uses her art to share her vulnerability with others as a singer/songwriter instead of trying to "escape" or "get better."

In all these cases, the very equipment developed to survive as children traps us in a "jail of the mind"—the primary set of limiting beliefs constraining further maturation—as adults. When transformed, these self-same patterns become the instrument of creation. These stories are fascinating, and we have so many of them now in our community of friends that we are currently writing another book together, *The Truthtellers: Stories of Success by Honest People.*

Second: Continue to Develop Your Awareness

The awareness continuum can be divided into three parts:

1. What we notice within the confines of our own skin *right now;*

2. What we notice outside of ourselves *in the moment;* and,

3. What we notice going through our minds *right now.*

I call this *Inside, Outside, Upside Down,* after my favorite children's book (Berenstain, 1982)[4]. There is a progression in the way we *train our noticing* that parallels these divisions of the awareness continuum. Exercises developed in the course of training Gestalt therapists are used to practice and develop skills that involve noticing and describing what is noticed. In the Course in Honesty, we teach and practice these exercises intensively and develop skills in noticing.

When we become skilled in noticing and describing what is going on inside our bodies *right now,* we can then practice noticing what is going on in the world outside of ourselves *right now.* Finally, we develop our ability to pay attention until we become capable of noticing what is going on in our own minds *right now.* In other words, our skill in noticing what is going on within the confines of our own skin, and our skill in noticing what is going on *outside* of our bodies, moment by moment, can eventually be applied to our ability to notice our own thoughts as they arise.

After becoming skilled in noticing, we begin to become *identified with our ability to notice.* Who we consider ourselves to be is the *Noticer,* the perceiver who is consistently there, which includes but is not limited to the perception, thought, or sensation that may arise. We have perceptions, sensations, and thoughts but they are not our primary identity. Likewise, we are not our biography. *We still have a biography but it is not our primary identity.* Though we still perform, we no longer identify with our performance as who we are. Identification with our literal experience of being in our body in the here and now, present to the external world here and now, and observing our thoughts here and now, gives us the opportunity to use our minds rather than being used by our minds.

The power of this quality of attention, free from the distractions of the mind, is demonstrated in the classic Kurasawa film *Seven Samurai.* A samurai takes on the task of defending a village of farmers from raids by bands of thieves at harvest time. He needs more samurai to help him. To interview those willing to help defend the village, he invents a system of screening applicants. He places a samurai with a drawn sword just inside the doorway of the interview room with instructions to behead all who enter. The interviewer faces the doorway to greet arriving applicants. If the applicant, upon entering, notices the person attempting to behead him and blocks the blow, he is hired.

Our trainers who lead Radical Honesty workshops (the Courses in Honesty, Forgiveness, and Creating) and community meetings are skilled in defending against invasions by the marauders of the mind who come to steal the benefits of the work of being. The trainers have been selected based on their capacity to save their own lives from being devoured by their minds.

Third: Spiritual Practices + Planning = Creation

A person who takes full responsibility for how her life is, and what her life is for, can create the life she wants by using a number of spiritual practices within the context of a consciously-designed plan. The life of the spirit is maintained through specific practices like meditation, telling the truth, and yoga. To live the spiritual life, you don't have to be a "spiritual type" or some kind of goody-two-shoes. You don't have to be a religious moralist to be a spiritual person.

As far as I can tell, spiritual and experiential are synonymous. When I am fully engaged in any experience with my full attention, it is a spiritual experience. Spiritual/experiential events come from the heightening, deepening, and widening of the quality of life through the quality of mindful attention. Meditating, telling the truth, yoga, and many other practices enhance the quality of my life and that of my friends because these practices heighten our experience of being. Spiritual practices enhance the quality of our lives by heightening, deepening, and widening our *experience of being* through mindful attention.

As it turns out, spiritual practices not only enhance the quality of life, they also empower you to create. In fact, to bring about the results you imagine you want in your life, spiritual practices are essential. Being holy or righteous about spiritual practices or spiritual beliefs is entirely unnecessary and antithetical to their functional use. In fact, if you are a moralist, sickening daily with the disease of attachment to righteousness, you are as far from spiritual as a person can get.

My friends and I have found something more valuable than the fun of righteousness. It's those amazing moments when we are suddenly productive after being inspired by an honest conversation with a friend, or just after returning from a vacation, or right after meditation. We have learned that we become productive and creative out of spiritual experience. Spiritual practices, both private and public, are regular mini-vacations that refresh your quality of life every day. These practices help keep you mentally focused, healthy, and relaxed, functioning optimally while you implement your plans. Regular spiritual practices help you cope with the tendency of the mind to transform inspiration to obligation and enable you to recapture the space of freedom.

Fourth: Don't Be the Lone Ranger — Do This in Community

Ongoing support groups, which connect you with friends who are doing the same thing you are, end up being project planning and vision sharing meetings that are at least as much fun, if not more, than whining and moaning sessions about who is to blame. We call them therapeutic communities. We could call them creative communities. They are going on in cities and townships all over America right now, and starting up in other places in the world. We have dozens of these groups of friends associated with our work to which we refer people who say they are interested in radical honesty.

The final section of *Practicing Radical Honesty* describes the model for how to develop and live in communities which support honesty and creation. When we belong to a community based on sharing honestly, there are people around who know us and whom we know deeply. These people are the means of support for bringing about powerful results for ourselves in the world, even if other people in the world are against us. Good friends can get us past our own mind-centeredness and hysteria and back into the here and now. Good friends can also help us feel okay when we don't tread the beaten path, and when people with old-paradigm values say we're crazy.

Networking among the communities of support that have developed from the Radical Honesty workshops and affiliating with other communities of support that share our new values are ongoing sources of inspiration for all of us.

Summary: From Victim to Creator

Most human suffering comes from being trapped in the jail of the mind. We are confused by the map and can't find the territory. Like Alzheimer's sufferers, our brains misidentify our surroundings and we become lost and confused. We have concepts that don't fit reality and reality that doesn't fit our concepts. We get further into the soup by trying to explain why the pieces don't fit. Then we make matters worse by trying to get ourselves and others to straighten up and fit in. We end by telling some kind of story that builds a case for ourselves, and trying to put on our best face so we can convince others we are the model for what fits, good and not bad, right and not wrong, capable, adequate to the task, and so on.

Deliverance from the suffering caused by being trapped in the mind comes through sharing with other people how life actually is for us—honestly—rather than lying in the conventional ways we have all learned. We have been taught in school and at home and in the marketplace to anticipate what other people expect and to perform accordingly, regardless of whether it makes sense to us or has anything to do with what we want. There is a strong taboo against telling the truth about how we actually feel and what we actually think, and strong reinforcement for doing what we imagine our peers and elders expect of us. We are convinced that this performance is very important; we are quite attached to our assessments about our own and other peoples' performance and our stories about who is to blame when performances are not up to par. Basically we are performing and judging all the time. Constantly performing and judging wears us out. We get tired from it. Getting tired *of* it is the next step.

Practicing Radical Honesty draws on the major philosophical systems and religious and psychological practices of the world to develop a program that has four fundamental elements:

1. A series of processes for getting "current" and detaching from the past;

2. Ongoing practices to reground ourselves in present-tense experience to help us through obstacles and rough moments and our mind's built-in resistance (attempting forever to make categories seem like reality);

3. A design-and-management system for life-projects; and

4. Information about how to develop honest, sharing relationships with friends in a community of support so that, through making contributions to each other, we bring our individual projects into being.

The road from victim to creator is an ever-opening path into the future. The combination of radical honesty, spiritual practices, and co-creating in community keeps the way clear. The life-altering, community-building, world-changing program we have refined over the last ten years of is presented in Part Three. It includes practices we have developed to sharpen skills in noticing, until identity with the Noticer occurs, and from which a community of people in love with each other comes into existence.

The results you can bring into being with this technology and these practices are almost limitless. Once you lose your mind and come to your senses, you get your mind back. But, because you don't have to use it to defend your image anymore, you can use it for other purposes. You envision what you want and make a plan. Planning is the work of making things happen according to your vision. Your personality, which developed from what happened to you in your past—the very mind system that formerly constrained you and caused endless neurotic suffering—is now the equipment you use for the act of creation. What was once the source of your suffering becomes a tool to create and operate your plan for the future. Rather than the usual psychotherapeutic approach of figuring out what is wrong with you and trying to fix it, this approach advocates the use of your personality quirks and problems as instruments for creation. You take damaged equipment and make something useful. Stumbling blocks become stepping stones.

Honesty about what you have done, what you feel, and what you think, shared on an ongoing basis, creates an intimate connection with and concern for the ongoing well-being of other people. Out of this grows a community of mutual support and co-creation. If you want the good life, a community of co-creators is the place to be.

Chapter One

Living Under the Old Paradigm

Many of us begin to feel victimized by our circumstances because *we try to fit into a model of living that doesn't work for us.* We feel trapped by a sense of obligation to perform our lives in obedience to a way of living that somebody else invented. No matter where we live in the world or what we believe, when we are driven by our obligations—all the things we think we "should" do—we get further and further behind, and that way of living ends up draining us rather than inspiring us. The pressures of modern-day life—to move faster, work harder, earn more, get ahead—weigh heavily on us, and as a result we're working harder than ever at jobs we don't enjoy, and find we don't have enough time to spend with our families or other pursuits of happiness.

We work too much. Strangers are raising our children and we are missing out on one of the most precious gifts life has to offer—being with our own families. *We are living in a paradigm we learned from people who had no idea what our modern lives would be like.*

The parents, teachers, neighbors, politicians, religious leaders, television personalities, writers, musicians, friends, and talk show hosts who were primarily responsible for our education as we grew up had no idea what our lives would be like now. Likewise, we cannot know what our children's lives will be like. It is one of the givens of living in the Information Age that we cannot be specifically prepared for the future that will show up for us. *Therefore, it is critical to our happiness and well being that we get over attachment to beliefs quickly and repeatedly.*

People all over the world suffer like hell from the tenuous relationship of their beliefs to reality. They cannot live happily within the constraints of traditional ignorance. People who have become conscious creators of their lives—like the people described in the first part of this book—not only cannot live, they will not live, within the torturous constraints of these antiquated paradigms.

The largest single economic enterprise worldwide is the sale of illegal drugs—most of them painkillers. That doesn't even count the billions spent on *legal* painkillers of one kind or another from the pharmaceutical industry. According to Breton and Largent, authors of *The Paradigm Conspiracy*[5], *more than half of the people in the world are addicted to some substance or some process! Why* are we so sick and in pain?

Because we *think* that when we can't make life turn out the way it is supposed to, we, ourselves, are just not good enough. It's our fault that we suffer, because we are bad and inadequate and less capable than "successful" people. So we suffer and we assume we deserve the suffering we get. It could be, instead, that we are fine, but just a little too attached to those models of how life is supposed to be—models that don't have much to do with reality anymore.

People come to participate in workshops and psychotherapy with me because they are frustrated, overwhelmed, feeling deeply ill-prepared and inadequate to the tasks they feel obligated to perform at home and at work, and anxious and mildly depressed about the future. Their personal relationships don't satisfy them emotionally, they are isolated from their friends and family, and they feel disconnected from being alive and awake like they were as children. We all share a kind of cultural shift pain, from a world constantly in transition from one model of living to another. Something just doesn't feel right, and we cast about for someone or something external to blame. No matter what we do, we don't seem to be in control of our lives.

We're all trapped in a do-loop we don't seem able to escape. We wonder why we're not experiencing a richer quality of existence. We can remember how, as children, we were eager and curious and had a spirit for living. How did we lose it? Is it possible to regain our passion? Isn't there an alternative to obsessive use of painkillers and alcohol and overeating and overwork and other addictive substances and processes?

The Rediscovery of Our True Identity

The ill-fitting cultural paradigms that live in people's minds create intense suffering. These limiting cultural and family paradigms exist only in the minds of individuals. The courage to "live out loud" is required of each individual before outmoded systems can be revised or dispensed with. This is why telling the truth is so critical.

As it turns out, when you tell the truth and hear the truth enough, you become a revolutionary. As George Orwell said, "In a time of universal deceit, telling the truth is a revolutionary act." I wrote this book to teach people who have suffered from middle class child abuse — that is, normal parenting and schooling — how to create a way out of the mind jail they have built. There is a way out of the desperate, driven way of living we have been taught, and we can only create it simultaneously for ourselves and each other through an honest conversation about how our lives are and how we want our future to be. Through honest conversations, we come to identify ourselves as "the being who notices in the moment" rather than our case histories.

There are thousands of us now, most of whom have never met each other, who are a rapidly growing cult, fomenters of a new revolution, and we plan to change the world. We are going to change the world by modeling a better way to live than all the other cults, particularly the money cult that is currently in charge. We are going to win the competition with multinational corporations and the money cult by outdoing them in the quality of our lives together. The quality of of life that we create is better than the quality of life they create; it will just take a while to let the world know. When people modify what they are greedy for, it radically alters what money is, and what money means. That alteration is what the very last chapter of this book is about. We follow a trail from individual suffering to the examination of dysfunctional families and cultures to the establishment of communities of liberation and ongoing renewal.

Practicing Radical Honesty naturally follows from the concepts in *Radical Honesty*, just like creating with friends naturally follows from the practice of individual radical honesty. The workbook section, with exercises and detailed instructions for designing and creating a vibrant, fulfilled life, gives you actions to take to employ the mind for something other than useless worrying and self-criticism. Plans for the future are the natural next step to transformation. Creating the future intentionally is done in the same way any artist intentionally creates a work of art, only it is done in community and with contributions to others as a part of the work of art itself.

The Old Activist, Old Hippie, Young Dissident Revolution

Many of the people I have met on book tours and talk shows are people like me, who were in the civil rights movement, and the anti-war movement, and in humanistic psychology, and in Haight-Ashbury, and in school buses traveling all over the country for years, and experimenting with drugs and roaming around the rest of the world to find out more about it. We who are awakening, according to a recent survey by the Center for Noetic Sciences, represent twenty-four percent of the population of the country. We are everyone who listens to public radio. We are the people who make hits out of really good movies like Secrets and Lies, and make popular more honest TV shows like *NYPD Blue* and *Roseanne* and *Seinfeld (Seinfeld* was honest by frankly portraying modern life as contrived) and *Ellen* and *Politically Incorrect* and *ER* and a few others.

Ministers of various faiths have written or called me after reading Radical Honesty to let me know that my time as a preacher in the Methodist Church and as a student of existentialists and Buddhists and Sufis did teach me something valued and needed by people in modern times. People in recovery from every drug and process addiction known have thanked me for my work. Unitarian Universalists and Unity Church people and even Methodists have been inviting me to come and preach and sing my songs about this work. *We're all hungry for clear articulations of what we are presently in the middle of doing.*

As many people have learned through Radical Honesty workshops, deliverance from the suffering caused by being trapped in the mind comes through sharing how life is for you with other people. This sharing can occur in psychotherapy and/or some other kind of formal or informal training in life. Any instruction is revolutionary that allows one to be grounded in experience, fundamentally identifying oneself as the experiencer, in order to transcend the mind, and then to use the mind to stay free from the mind. The first, most important transcendence is getting over a particular state of mind: namely, moaning and whining about how your parents didn't do it right and nobody has done a good enough job since then, either.

Once we see ourselves whining in impotent protest, and really "get" that we are wasting our lives that way, we have a chance to do something about it. We come to understand that we are all primarily victimized by one thing only: the limitation of perspective of our own minds. Once we gain a perspective on our own minds we have the possibility of using them rather than being used by them. In addition to this learning about transcendence, an ongoing practice or set of practices (such as meditation) is necessary on a continual basis to keep the mind from recapturing the space of freedom and starting to whine all over again about some other victimization. This work is about how to use your mind to keep yourself from falling back to the neurotic survival skills of the mind and its familiar complaints.

You use your mind to transcend your mind. You use your mind to direct your attention to constantly practicing noticing, and to your vision of the future. In the present, you create work that seems like play because it is based on the future you envision and want to bring into being because you love the idea of it. Rather than using your mind to simply react to the things in the present that vaguely remind you of your past, you create.

The progression of growth for human beings who reach their full maturity looks like this: innocent child in touch with being — raised by well-intentioned but inept and stupid parents to be neurotic — attains adolescence, which is almost psychotic — gets therapy or gets wise some way, and rediscovers being — becomes functional and maintains it by practicing meditation and consciously creating a life as an intentional work of art in the context of a community of friends. Getting this whole picture is critical to being able to apply the benefits of enlightenment to your everyday life. Figure 1 below summarizes the path to maturity.

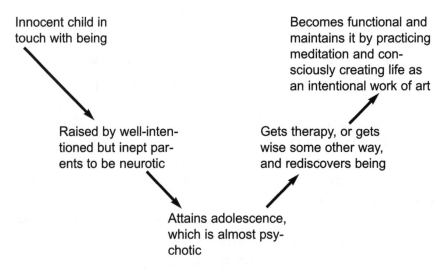

Innocent child in touch with being

Raised by well-intentioned but inept parents to be neurotic

Attains adolescence, which is almost psychotic

Gets therapy, or gets wise some other way, and rediscovers being

Becomes functional and maintains it by practicing meditation and consciously creating life as an intentional work of art

Figure 1. The Growth of Human Beings

Freedom

This is a "how-to" book on freedom. *Radical Honesty* was the cake with the file in it, so you could escape the jail of the mind. *Practicing Radical Honesty* is instruction on how to use the file and where to start filing. This is the information on the practical work of transcendence so we can use our minds rather than be used by them. That is the heart of the new revolution, the revolution of consciousness.

The cultures of the world, living in the minds of the people of the world, are under the influence of the various transcendent, but not transcendent enough, meta-cults of the world, based on money. The corporate/money culture, directed by a very small number of very rich people, transcends cultural boundaries of the world, but fails to transcend its own limited culture which is based on the accumulation and control of resources.

Once the people of the world learn to use the culture that has been using them, by transcending their own culture, whatever it is, the current multi-national corporate rule of the world, based on the bottom line, will almost simultaneously be transcended as well. This may or may not be traumatic, but the way the world is governed will significantly change, and the process will probably not be gradual.

This work, which results in communities of support for transcendence through being radically honest, is designed to help individuals to change, not by trying to change, but by transcending their own minds. This will change the cultures of the world, because cultures are only habitual mind-sets with a lot of emotional attachment.

This community already exists and is growing and I intend to do everything in my power to support it until I die. I expect to help this already existing community become conscious of itself by consistently training trainers to run Radical Honesty¨ workshops and by conducting workshops myself and writing books as our community of conscious co-creators grows larger.

We will live long and prosper as the world gradually turns our way — and then suddenly blossoms into a whole new garden, for which the next generation will thank us, and then, hopefully, plow under to make room for something new we never even dreamed about. We are becoming a movement. We intend to be a movement that keeps on moving. We invite you to join us. Our revolution starts with the understanding of our own minds, how they were built, and how they operate.

What Is a Mind
and How Does It Work?

This is the story of Sally Jean Henry and her life up to age nineteen. She was born in 1980 and she grew up in Cleveland, Ohio, in the United States of America. Before we tell the story about how her mind was built and how it used her, let's talk generally about what a mind is.

I am stealing from some of the best thinkers here. I acknowledge primary recent contributions by L. Ron Hubbard, Werner Erhard, and Tor Norretranders. I acknowledge the source of this conversation in Buddhism, Taoism, Yoga, Vedantic philosophy, and in Western philosophy in the work of Leibnitz, the existentialists, phenomenologists, and perceptual and cognitive theorists in psychology. I am discussing the following questions: What is a mind? What is a mind for? How does a mind get built? How does it work? How can you tame one and keep it from running away with you?

What is a Mind?

The model of the mind provided by L. Ron Hubbard, with a bow to Liebnitz, (who spoke of "monads," which were little Lego™-like units of stored information) includes this definition:

The mind is a linear arrangement of total multi-sensory recordings of successive moments of now. This is a good definition of the fundamental reactive mind: stored records of events that occurred as we got born and grew up. The records that make up the mind are multi-sensory recordings, not just videotapes but recordings that include taste, touch, smell, balance, feeling states, and thoughts.

These recordings are not all the same with regard to how long they last. A beginning of a recorded moment is demarcated by noting some significant-to-you event that stands out at the beginning of a moment, and lasts until you consider it played out. These moments are recorded and stored as records in our brains. They are collected and stored in a linear fashion from early in our life to recently in our life, and they vary in length from a few seconds to several hours. "Moments of now" vary in length according to clock time, they are all in a linear arrangement, and they are total multi-sensory recordings in succession. The sum total of these stored recordings is the fundamental reactive mind.

What is a Mind For?

A mind is for survival. We have minds in order to survive. Human beings, biologically, are a-tube-within-a-tube construction. We have a tube of skin covering up many more tubes inside us, including our veins and arteries and capillaries, and our digestive system. Millennia ago in our evolution, we became independent of the ocean by creating our own ocean inside called the bloodstream. We survive now by putting water and food in one end of the tube and running it through our other tubes. Eventually, everything we put in comes out again through tubes at the other end, when we defecate and urinate, and through little tubes that come to the surface of the skin where we sweat.

A mind is useful for our survival if it helps us be successful at assimilating food and water and running it through the tubes so that we are sustained in being. If we continue to do it long enough and survive to pubescence, we then put a male tube inside a female tube and make another tube. When we do this we have fulfilled our mission to survive and the mission of our species to survive. The mind serves the survival of the being if it is of some use in assimilating things to put in the front end of the tube, and finding other tubes to play with long enough to create more tubes. It's a tube maintenance program.

All in all, this sounds easy. But there is one small problem. We haven't quite answered the question "What is a mind for?" A more complete answer is: "A mind is for the survival of the being, *or of anything the being considers itself to be.*" This addition to the definition of the purpose of the mind engenders a problem. Suddenly we are talking about more than tubes here. The problem is that the tool called *the mind* is what *the being* does its considering *with!* The mind, in considering the survival of the being, comes up with the idea that it also has to survive so the being can survive.

The mind knows it has to be maintained and it is in charge of its own maintenance. The mind is its own mechanic. The mind gets to thinking that its own survival is what it is for! "Because my survival as a being depends on me," the mind thinks, "I must preserve myself at all costs." *And the mind can come to think that its own survival is more important than the survival of the being.*

For example, Jack Benny, a comedian noted for his tightness with money, created on his radio show a skit that took place in Central Park in New York City. A mugger stuck a gun in Jack's ribs and said, "Your money or your life!" With his thumb under his chin and forefinger on his cheek, Jack paused and drawled, "Wel-l-l-l..." The mugger repeated himself and Jack responded peevishly, "I'm thinking! I'm thinking!!" He was having a difficult time choosing which was more important, his money or his life. "What is worth more," his mind wondered, "My money or my life?"

For another example, let's say you are sixteen years old and you were born in Baghdad and you want to be a good Moslem and a good citizen and a good follower of Saddam Hussein. You put on a uniform to preserve that identity and go with 80,000 of your brothers to Kuwait, and the Americans kill you and 60,000 others sharing the same identity. Your identification with your ideal has cost you your life.

When I was eighteen years old, many of my contemporaries went to Vietnam, trying to be "good Americans," and many died trying to maintain that identity. Just like all the pitiful, well-meaning young soldiers throughout history who have died for ill-conceived ideals by the dozens, we can let whom we consider ourselves to be, what our minds say we are, cost us our life. What is more important: our image or our life?

Two phenomenological psychologists named Schneideman and Farberow[6] wrote a book about suicide after seventeen years of research in which they studied 350 cases of suicide. After studying suicide notes left behind and examining all the stories and interviews with friends and families, they found a theme that seemed to apply in all cases. They concluded that every suicide can be explained as "an attempt to maintain or enhance the self." The mind is maintained at the expense of the life of the being. The mind survives by being right. The mind would rather be right and die than be wrong and live.

Teenagers identify with their self-image rather than their being. The internal judge who makes the assessments about life — "It's too hard," "I can't take it anymore," It's not worth it," "Now, this will show them!" — survives at the cost of life itself. Suicide rates are highest among teens.

The mind is for the survival of the being or of anything the being considers itself to be. Sometimes it doesn't preserve the survival of the being while it thinks it is serving its own survival. The mind is not a perfect instrument of survival. The mind misfires.

The mind makes mistakes and cannot always be trusted to maintain survival. The mind's survival depends on being right, whereas the body's survival depends on being fed and kept well and free from harm. There sometimes appears to be a conflict between these two goals, and the mind decides its survival is the most important. In Eastern philosophy this is called the problem of ego.

Once the mind has decided that itself is what must survive, it believes its survival depends on being right whatever the cost. A mind survives by being right and not wrong and by getting agreement, not disagreement, from other minds. This narcissistic preoccupation with itself and its own survival necessitates the defense of all its assessments, judgments, decisions, stories, products, creations, and so forth. The mind's primary job switches from survival to defending itself.

How Does a Mind Get Built?

The records of the mind are formed and stored continually as each individual grows older. All the records of total multisensory recordings of successive moments of now can be divided into three types. That is, we can sort all the records of the mind into three groups. They can be thought of as records stored on three spindles. Imagine three spindles for three different kinds of records of the mind: Spindles A, B, and C. The criteria of selection for storage on one spindle as opposed to another are as follows.

Class A Events

Spindle A stores records of events involving *a threat to the person's survival, pain, and a partial loss of consciousness.* These stored records are called Class A events. For an example of a Class A event, let me reintroduce you to Sally Jean Henry and pursue her story starting when she was a young child.

Sally Jean Henry: Scene One. Sally is four years old and is playing with her brother, Tom, who is five and a half. They are sailing a toy sailboat in a small pond at the playground in a park near her house. Her mother is there, talking to a neighbor lady.

It's a sunny day and the wind is blowing through the trees and Sally is busily engaged pushing her toy sailboat back and forth across the little pond with her brother. Her dog, Rags, is there playing with some other dogs and children.

Suddenly, her brother snatches up the boat, says "My boat!" and starts running away with it. Sally knows that the boat is hers and she starts running after Tom yelling, "My boat! My boat!" Rags chases both of them. As they approach the other side of the park, her brother runs down three concrete steps, but just as Sally gets there, Rags gets tangled up in her feet and she falls headfirst from the top of the first step. She misses the steps but lands hard on her shoulder, arm, and head on the concrete sidewalk at the bottom of the steps. She scrapes her left arm and shoulder and bumps her head as she falls and the wind is knocked completely out of her.

The next thing she knows, she is coming out of a fog, rolling over, trying to catch her breath. Her mother comes running up and kneels in front of her. The sunlight reflects off her mother's glasses into her eyes, making her squint. Her dog Rags is licking her face. Tom is saying, a little anxiously, "She's not hurt; she's not hurt!" in the background. Her arm and shoulder hurt and she feels nauseated. Her mother picks Sally up and carries her home, cleans her cuts, puts on battle ribbon Band-Aids™ and gives her some M&Ms™. That's the end of the event.

The moment of record started when her brother grabbed Sally's boat and ended when her mother gave her the M&Ms. It is a Class A event, in which she experienced pain, a partial loss of consciousness, and a threat to her survival. Sally makes a total multi-sensory record of it at four years of age. The record may or may not remain conscious, it may become buried, it may be partially forgotten, it may be modified in conscious memory, but in some complete form it remains as a total multi-sensory recording of a Class A event. We all have many of these events in our lives and therefore we have many records of them. One of the first of these recorded Class A events is our own birth. The trauma of childbirth for the baby meets all the criteria of a Class A event. Getting born, for most of us, involves pain, shock, a partial loss of consciousness, and a threat to our survival.

Class B Events

Class B events stored on Spindle B involve *a sudden shocking loss, with strong emotion, usually negative, and something in the event related to a previous Class A event.*

Sally Jean Henry: Scene 2. Sally is seven years old now. She's running on a sidewalk behind her brother Tom, next to the stadium. Rags is running behind her. Suddenly, her brother cuts to the right and runs across the street. She follows him. Rags follows her. There is a screech of brakes and a thud. She looks back. Rags has been hit by a dump truck. She runs back. She bends down to look at Rags and touches him. Her hand feels sticky and she smells blood. She realizes he is dead and begins to cry.

This is a Class B event—a sudden shocking loss, with strong emotion, usually negative, associated with a previous Class A event. Rags was running in the park, got tangled up in her feet, and licked her face in the previously stored Class A event. His sudden, shocking loss becomes a permanent Class B record in her mind. We can't grow up without experiencing these kinds of events and storing them. We all have a bunch of Class B records of loss.

Class C Events

Class C records are anything at all that occurs in the experience of a person which can be associated with Class A or Class B events. Anything in the world that is associated with spindle A and B events can be separately recorded and is called a Class C event. For Sally, any earlier or later records of trees, sunshine, breezes, ponds, toy boats, parks, grass, sidewalks, steps, eyeglasses, falling, being near the ground, brothers, dump trucks, dogs, fur, wet sticky things, M&Ms, and so on are all events that can be stored separately but with their association with A and B remaining intact. *So by the time we are seven or eight years old, and have stored a number of Class A and B events, EVERYTHING IN THE WORLD is associated with a threat to our survival!*

The mind is essentially a paranoid instrument. We have records in our memory of threats to our survival, and of loss, which we are to avoid in the future in order to survive, and they are associated with every other recording of everything we have experienced. Every new stimulus from outside ourselves after about seven or eight years of age just triggers a whole chain of associations. We are on guard, looking out for trauma and trouble at all times — and that's what a mind does. It's like an accountant or a lawyer or some other kind of deal killer who is hell-bent on anticipating the possible recurrence of some tragedy that has happened before, or one very much like it, and trying to avoid that happening.

How Does the Reactive Mind Work?

Here's how the associative/reactive mind works when we are adults. Let's say it's twelve years later and that same little girl, Sally, has grown to be nineteen years old. She is a pretty young woman and she is a freshman at George Washington University in Washington, D.C.

Sally Jean Henry: Scene 3, Option 1. Sally goes to a park on a picnic with her boyfriend of several weeks, Gary. It's a sunny day and the wind is gently blowing through the trees. They've had some wine and cheese and a few bites of food; Sally leans back against a tree and Gary comes over to sit beside her. As he leans over to sit down beside her, he squeezes her knee. "Ouch," she says. He replies, "You're not hurt; you're not hurt," and some vague discomfort comes over her. Then, just as he bends over to kiss her, the sunlight glints off his glasses right in her eyes and she squints. He kisses her and she kisses him back, but she feels nauseated and mildly anxious and slightly uncomfortable. After the picnic they go home separately. When he phones, she doesn't return the call. She never goes out with him again.

If you ask her why she quit dating Gary, Sally has all kinds of rational explanations: he's not her type, he doesn't have a good sense of humor, she is just a freshman and wants to "play the field" and doesn't want to be tied down right now, and so on. These rational explanations, however, have nothing to do with why she dropped Gary. She dropped him because her associative mind identified him with her partially forgotten Class A event from when she was four years old. His saying "You're not hurt; you're not hurt," and the tone of voice in which he said it, combined with the glare of the sun off his glasses making her squint just when he kissed her brought back the pain and nausea and the threat to her survival she experienced when she fell and hurt herself. Her Class A record was reactivated in association with Gary, and she avoided him thereafter.

Sally Jean Henry: Scene 3, Option 2. Let's say the same events occur on the picnic with a slightly different outcome from the same associative chain. Sally leans back against the tree; Gary comes to sit next to her and squeezes her knee. She says, "Ouch!" He says, "You're not hurt; you're not hurt," and as he leans down to kiss her the sunlight glints off his glasses, but this time when he kisses her, instead of nausea, she feels an insane urge for him to lick her face! As he pulls back at the end of a French kiss, he accidentally, just barely, licks the very edge of her lip. She marries him!

If you ask Sally why she married Gary, she will have all kinds of valid reasons for marrying him: his family is wealthy, he's going to go to medical school, they are the same religion, and so on. But her associative mind chose him prior to all those reasonable rationalizations. She married Gary to bring her dog Rags back to life. (A lot of us married our dogs, at least the first time around.)

The Illusion of Control

The rational, thinking, reflective mind *thinks* it is in control, but it isn't. As writer Annie Dillard says, "We are most deeply asleep at the switch when we fancy we control any switches at all." Our rational decisions really aren't decisions at all, but rationalizations to justify the choices already made by associations of the reactive mind. The reactive mind works according to associations — links between records formed in previously experienced events. Control is an illusion provided by the quick thinking (but not quite quick enough to actually be in control) reflective mind. The reflective mind just tags along closely behind the reaction and generates explanations to maintain the illusion of control.

The Reflective Mind

On top of the reactive mind, the reflective mind is formed. That is, we have records of yet another kind stored in our minds. These records are made based on comparisons of replicated experiences. In George A. Kelly's *The Psychology of Personal Constructs*[7], volumes I and II, is a more thorough explanation of the development of what we are here calling the reflective mind. Basically, from very early on in life, we begin to form thoughts by comparisons based on replicated events. The minimal requirements for a thought to exist are three: a similarity between two things, something that is different, and an overriding construct of relatedness. If A and B are males and C is a female, they are related by an all-encompassing construct we call "gender." In linear time, events that are repeated and remembered as similar get compared to a contrasting event along a common dimension of relatedness. Concepts are formed from these minimalist requirements starting from very early in life. The reflective mind is an interlocking hierarchy of subsets of these three concepts.

An example of formation of an initial idea may be as follows. The baby has repeated experiences of being nursed. The baby has repeated experiences of being hungry and crying. The baby builds a little memory of feeding events and compares them to a non-feeding event. The overall relatedness may be just "events." Then a little concept emerges based on distinguishing feeding and non-feeding events from the ocean of experience. In a short while, the baby feels hungry, cries, gets fed, and confirms her little hypothesis. As she matures, she distinguishes in the same way the breast, then mother, then her crib, then daddy, then her room, and so on. With a second order of association, using replicated events, the mind we call the reflective mind is born.

Sit with this for a minute. I'm not asking you to believe this idea instead of whatever you now believe. Just try it on for size; use it as a temporary model; imagine it to be true just for the time being. If this is considered to be true, even temporarily, it is kind of disorienting. We fool ourselves into believing that we are in charge of our lives through having concepts about life. But the concepts about life are not what our "decisions" are based on. Our "choices" are reactions. Our thought processes are merely rationalizations of reactions of a paranoid reactive mind. If you think you know why you got married or why you didn't, or why you got divorced or why you didn't, or picked a certain path in life or didn't, or got remarried or didn't, or had children or didn't, or moved to another location or didn't, and so on, you are seriously deluded. Your belief that you are in control is a complete illusion.

If we make this model of the mind temporarily true just for an experiment in this moment, several things that follow from it are quite obvious.

1. All the beliefs you have defended were merely for the sake of providing you an illusion of control. Every thought about what was right or why you were doing or had done anything were just after-the-fact rationalizations for choices you had already made by reaction. All the reasons you have come up with for anything are suspect. All of what you might call "values" are fundamentally rationalizations for behavior you were not in control of.

2. All the theories you have expounded explaining your motivation for doing thus and such are a waste of time.

3. The truth is you're not in control at all, and all your attempts to explain in order to fool other people only show who was really fooled all along. You!

The only thing one can do to be in control in any way, shape, or form is to stick with merely describing what happened. For any event in the world that any human being participates in, there are always at least three levels from which to report the event, one level of description alone and two levels of abstraction from experience. There is what occurred, the story made about what occurred, and the meaning made out of the story about what occurred. The most abstract level, the meaning made out of the story that occurred, is the sales pitch that most of us are calling reality. What most of us call reality is just a story about reality or a story we have about the story.

Rationalizing the Choices of the Reactive Mind

We keep reacting to events from our past that are triggered by what happens to us in current relationships to people. Our spouse hits a certain note in their tone of voice or says something a scolding parent said in a Class A or B event and an argument ensues about something in current time. *Most arguments between partners in a couple are reiterations of records of feelings and events from the past triggered by each other.*

We start to make explanations to pretend we were in control at an early age. When my son, Amos, was about four years old he explained to me in great detail how his Big Wheels were faster than the other kids' Big Wheels because his wheels were more "sharp." Explanations become important as proof of being oriented and in charge at about that age. Any explanation will do. Sometimes these explanations themselves become part of what is stored as a record. In our particular culture, because of the surrounding Judeo-Christian shame and blame context, we become more sophisticated in learning how to blame ourselves for anything bad that happened to us (from about three or four years of age forward).

Whenever we make mistakes, particularly, we make little resolves in our developing linear reflective minds, intense resolves to avoid replication of certain experiences. We make these intense resolves many times between ages two and sixteen years and we hold on to them tightly as guidelines for life for the ensuing years. We said to ourselves, quietly within our own minds, "I will never, ever, ever, let this mistake happen again."

In my own life, when I was about ten years old, I experienced the following intense event: My younger brother (nine years old), my little brother (one year old), and I were in the back of the car. In the front seat my mother and stepfather, who both had been drinking, were in a loud shouting argument. We kids were all scared. I kept saying to myself and my brothers, particularly to the baby who was crying at the top of his lungs, "We'll be home in a few minutes....We'll be home in a few minutes."

When we got within a mile of home I said to myself, quietly within my own mind, "Okay, we're here. It's just over this hill. We're home." But just then, my stepfather hit my mother in the face, slammed on the brakes, and began beating her more. It was a two-door sedan and we were trapped in the back and the car was sliding sideways on the gravel road. She was screaming and hitting back. Blood splattered on us. We were trapped in the back seat. When the car finally came to a sliding halt, I held the baby tightly in one arm in a total panic while I hit the back of my mother's seat with my body as hard as I could, pushing her forward into the windshield. Then all-in-one-motion I grabbed the door handle, pushed the door open, and jumped out of the car with the baby in my arms and my other brother right behind me. We began running up the road. As I ran, carrying the baby and crying, I said to myself: *"Always remember! You're never there until you are there! You are never home until you are home! Nothing is over until it is over! Don't ever make the mistake of thinking you are there until you are there!"*

This resolve, to be continually on guard and not take anything for granted, to be wary on behalf of my brothers and protect them by not making false assumptions, became a theme in my life. It was a resolve *based not only on that experience but on previous experiences triggered by that one* and it had the emotional force of a lesson based on previous trauma. I preserved an illusion of control by blaming myself for being caught off guard and not doing a good enough job of caretaking, and by swearing I would never do such a careless thing again. Out of this, caretaking became my method of preserving an illusion of control.

Such resolves only further delude us into thinking we are in control. The next time, we say to ourselves, we will be in control like we should have been this time.

Is Actual Control Over Our Life Really Possible?

Even when we are not simply reacting unconsciously and rationalizing the reaction, our partially conscious memory of our linear mind's early resolves to preserve an illusion of control seems to be what we usually call "thinking." As it turns out, "making up our mind" may be more like "making up" any other story. It appears to be just an exercise of imagination. What we are doing, then, is reviewing the lessons of old that were themselves an illusory attempt at an earlier time to preserve an illusion of control. Isn't that just pathetic? Aren't we just unbelievable pitiful fools?

Is it possible to keep our own reactive mind from determining our life based on very old data? Is it possible to actually have any real control over our lives when we have such a vested interest in preserving an illusion of control based on what we imagine other people think we should think and on childhood resolves? Before we attempt to answer those questions, let's add in one more idea.

The Being Beneath the Mind

You are now looking at ink on a page or pixels on a screen. The light reflects off the page and goes to your eye, through the lens to the back of the eyeball, and there, a certain chemical reaction is triggered. This reaction throws off an electron that causes another chemical reaction that throws off an electron that causes another chemical reaction and there is an electrochemical transmission up the optic nerve to the visual cortex. There, in the visual cortex, a chemical reaction occurs, and you see the words, immediately interpreting both what you see and what it means.

The place where you are creating seeing the words is in your brain. You experience the words on the page, outside of your brain. You are creating the perception of the words on this page in your brain and experiencing them as outside of you. You create the whole world in your brain by a chemical reaction, but where you consider the world to be is outside of you. You do this electrochemical act of creating many, many, many times per second. Just like a movie projector provides an illusion of real action by rapidly displaying slightly changing images, you keep everything out there looking constant. You are creating the room you're in or whatever surrounding you have around you, all the other people in your life, and everything in view of you at all times.

You do the same thing with sound. If someone makes noises with their voice box near you, the vibrations reach the hammer, anvil, and drum in your ear, a chemical reaction occurs causing an electrical transmission to your brain, and you hear the sound. You integrate the sight and sound and other sense data in your corpus collosum, and you also make meaning out of the words being heard or read probably using your frontal lobes. This is all completely effortless. It requires no strain or effort or trying on your part. It happens automatically simply because you exist as the perceptual organizing machine you are.

This creation by perception is the most magnificent thing you will ever do, yet you give yourself no special credit for it because it doesn't count, because everyone else does that too, so it doesn't make you special in any comparative way. It is not important to who you usually think you are, yet it is ongoingly, millisecond by millisecond, the most magnificent thing you will ever do in your life.

Nothing you ever achieve with your mind or your life will come close to matching the miracle of creation of the world by your involuntary nervous system, effortlessly, just by being here, right now. We all know that doesn't really count. What counts—we all know, don't we?—is all that hype we have been taught, that has to do with our performance and our products and our appearance of being in control. Who you really are, however, is *the creator of the world.*

I think whenever one of us creators dies, the world comes to an end. I think that who you are is the creator of the world and who I am is the creator of the world. I think when I die the world will come to an end. I think when you die the world will come to an end. And for all practical purposes that appears to be true. You die. The world ends.

So I want you to consider these two ideas at once now. You are the creator of the world and you have no control. You are out of control. Control is purely an illusion of your reflective mind, to protect you from discerning that you are helplessly at the beck and call of your reactive mind and of circumstances beyond your control. Yet, at the same time, as a being, you are the creator of the world. And when you die, for all practical purposes, the world comes to an end. Just consider both of those things true at the same time. *You are the creator of the world and you are not in control.* You are out of control. All control is an illusion, yet you are the creator of the world.

What is the View of the Illusion of Control from the West?

There is a story told about all the Greek gods sitting around on Mount Olympus. They were all-knowing and all-seeing.

They knew all the past and all the future. So, very soon, they became bored. To entertain themselves and pass the time, they started inventing and playing games. One of their favorite games soon became one called, "Let's pretend that what is not here is more important than what is here." This game, pretending that what is not here is more important that what is here, became the common obsession, and after they played and played, after quite a while of playing the game, they forgot it was a game. They forgot it was a game for a long time, in fact until right now. It's my job now to remind you. So, I am reminding you, God, it's just a game. *You are the creator of the world. You play a game that something that is not here is more important than what is here. It's just a game.*

I am speaking to you directly now. The idea that something that is not here is more important than what is here is just a game. It is just pretending. It is just a pretense. It was just something you got in your mind from your upbringing that made you forget that you were God, and it made a modification of how you lived. We human beings, because we have minds, forget that playing toward the future is just a game and that our fundamental identity as creators in the moment, in the flow of creation, is reality. We are creators without any real control.

What is the View of the Illusion of Control from the East?

We are not talking about something new in history, just something relatively new in western history. Yoga, which means yoke or union—that which connects together intellect and spirit, or being and mind—is primarily concerned with exactly the topic we are now considering. In the millennia-old philosophy and practice of yoga, as summarized in the Yoga Sutras of Patanjali, countering the mind's distortions is given the highest priority.

In Sanskrit, there is a form of embodying all there is to be known about any area of study in one hundred *sutras*, or verses.

These are short phrases, limited to about a two-line statement, organized in a specific form. The structure of one hundred two-line statements precedes the content. The first sutra says what the set of one hundred sutras is about. For example, if we were to put the whole body of knowledge we call physics into one hundred statements, the first statement would be, "These are the sutras of physics." Then we would have ninety-nine statements left to cover all of physics. The second sutra is designated, traditionally, as the most comprehensive overview of the whole body of work and all the practices of the area under consideration. In our example, we would be expected, in the second sutra, to say in one statement what all of physics is about.

After Yoga had been around for 2,500 years, Patanjali wrote the *Yoga Sutras.* By the time he wrote them, many different methods for the practice of yoga had been developed while the teachings of yoga spread over most of the continents in the world. These methods include Karma Yoga, Bakti Yoga, Tantric Yoga, Kundalini Yoga, Hatha Yoga, and so on. These yogas of service, love, sex, work, physical health, and the philosophy of yoga had all undergone literally thousands of years of development through many languages in various geographical locations in the world. There had been thousands of teachers of Yoga, hundreds of sects, and hundreds of practices. Thus, the second sutra had to encompass the unitary theme that made sense of all these developments. The second sutra of the *Yoga Sutras,* the one that most comprehensively covers its subject, is: "The objective of all yoga is to bring about an *inhibition of the modifications of the mind.*"

Notice that Patanjali says that the objective of all yoga is just to *inhibit* the modifications of the mind. He doesn't say it is to destroy them, or do battle with them, or obliterate them, or over-come them—just inhibit them. Just hold them back a second or two. Just decrease or delay the effects of the little suckers a millisecond or two.

How do you do that? With yoga. What kind of yoga? Any kind. Whatever works! Creating art or music, loving, performing physical exercise and stretching, being present with a child, meditating, lovemaking, working—anything you can attend to for a sustained number of seconds or minutes without the modifications of the mind!

The modifications of the mind are all those records, memories, principles, conclusions, morals, and beliefs we have stored from the past. When we *inhibit* the modifications, as the yogis instruct us to, we discover what is here in the world of present tense reality, other than the mind.

What is the Current Cultural and Scientific Synthesis with Regard to Being and Mind?

Telling the truth is the particular yogic practice necessary *in our time* to inhibit the modifications of the mind. We are all engaged in a gigantic experiment to discover and invent what a human being is. We need each others' data. Our only hope to keep from being interrupted to death by our own minds is by *using one mind to inhibit the modifications of the other.* "The objective of all yoga is to bring about the inhibition of the modifications of the mind." The mind includes the reactive mind that is based on stored memories of Class A, B, and C events and the reflective (logical or linear) mind that comes up with the explanations. The reactive mind is just an accidental random chain of associations of stored memories. The reflective mind is the rationalizer who makes up good reasons to justify the associations of the reactive mind and makes up these reasons to be consistent with resolves made by a child. These minds are the smoke and mirrors that keep us from attending to the reality of being. Authentic spiritual practices are done for the sake of experiencing reality directly.

So, if we assume that the reactive mind truly determines how we live and what we do and what attitude we have about it, and the reflective mind preserves the illusion of control through explanation and interpretation, and that the fundamental identity of ourselves as human beings is the *being* part that creates the world, is it possible for a person to be consciously in control of his or her life?

Wait. It Gets Worse

Tor Norretranders, author of the recent book, *The User Illusion: Cutting Consciousness Down to Size*[8], says, among other things, that, "In recent years, scientific investigations into the phenomenon of consciousness have demonstrated that people experience far more than their consciousness perceives; that they interact far more with the world and with each other than their consciousness thinks they do; that the control of actions that consciousness feels it exercises is an illusion. ... Consciousness plays a far smaller role in human life than Western culture has tended to believe."

George Johnson, in reviewing Norretranders' book in *The Washington Post*, summarized some of his main points about consciousness in this way: "Most revealing of all are famous and controversial experiments by Benjamin Libet and other psychologists. Subjects wired with measuring electrodes are asked to move a finger. A half a second before the decision is made to flex the muscle, an electrical signal is detected in the brain. Astonishingly, the "decision" seems to be made by unconscious neurons before the self becomes aware of its desire to act.

"Consciousness portrays itself as the initiator, but it is not," Norretranders writes. "Consciousness is a fraud." Norretranders compares consciousness to a concept invented by the computer scientist Alan Kay: "the user illusion."

"Sitting at the computer, (controlling a mouse), dragging documents into folders or into the trash can, the operator is under a machine-induced hallucination. Inside the computer chips there are no documents, folders, trash cans, words or letters—just voltages and charges representing the ones and zeros of binary code. Instead of overwhelming the user with a flood of useless information, the computer projects a simple array of metaphors: icons that can be manipulated to get things done. In a similar way, the brain, throwing away unneeded data, generates its own user illusion: the interpretation called consciousness. In the consciousness section, in a chapter entitled "The Half Second Delay," Norretranders concludes that,

"Consciousness cannot initiate any action, but it can decide that it should not be carried out. ...Consciousness is not a superior unit that directs messages down to its subordinates in the brain. Consciousness is the instance of selection that picks and chooses among the many options nonconsciousness offers up. Consciousness works by throwing suggestions out, by discarding decisions proposed by nonconsciousness. ...The notion of consciousness as a veto is a very beautiful, very rich one. Its kinship with Darwinism and natural selection is not its only parallel in the history of thought."

This view of consciousness as veto power over the options of all that is nonconscious becomes even more interesting when compared to the second sutra of Patanjali's *Yoga Sutras*[9]: "The objective of all yoga is to bring about an inhibition of the modifications of the mind." The objective of yoga is to inhibit the primary function of consciousness—its veto power! What is left when thinking is inhibited? What is there to notice? Is there noticing without consciousness? Clearly there is, at least, noticing without thought. We sometimes call this "being conscious of...," but even that, even noticing, is a half-second behind!

When, in the movie *Little Big Man*, the main character, played by Dustin Hoffman, is being taught by his sister to be a gunslinger, she says, "Draw and shoot before your hand touches the pistol." It is possible that we can act before we register acting. Who is it then, who acts? There are plenty of people who testify to this. Joe Montana, former quarterback for the San Francisco Forty-Niners football team, says, "When I go out on that football field, I am not conscious." He means he is not self-conscious, not thinking, not aware of himself. He is not thinking and deciding what to do with the ball. He is acting without thinking. Tim Gallwey, the great tennis coach and author of *The Inner Game of Tennis*[10] (and *Golf,* and *Music,* and *Business),* says that we all have two selves, self one and self two. Self one is the one who knows everything there is to know about playing tennis. Self two is the one that can play tennis if it can get self one out of the way.

In my book, *Radical Honesty,* I repeatedly contrast "being" and "mind." I suggest that, over time, when we become more identified with being than mind, we regress to being in touch with the source of our experience, our bodies, in the moment, rather than the adolescent/adult identity of the mind that tells stories about experience and explains how it was in charge.

Our minds do not initiate anything. They associate and rationalize and maintain the "user illusion" that the mind is in charge and initiating action in the world. Quite the contrary, the mind is always behind. As Marilyn Ferguson said, "The mind is like a reporter at a funeral." It runs around asking questions like "Who died? Are you mourning? Where is the grave? How long did you know this person? How long have they been dead? How long did they live? When will this funeral be over?" The mind is obtuse, behind, frenetic, insensitive to feeling, blocking presence to life. It asks questions desperately to find out what is going on, while blocking the noticing of what is going on. As I have said before, a mind is a terrible thing. Waste it! Or at least just inhibit it for a few seconds!

You create the world by perceiving it and your perceptions are more reliable than your conceptions. But even that is not simple—it's an interpreted perception, based on past experiences of distinctions in perception that you use automatically but are not conscious of having learned. Those perceptions themselves are at least a half-second behind in registering what occurred from the impingement of the bandwidths of impact on the senses from the world, most of which we are never consciously aware of. This is when you are functioning at your best, before you begin thinking. If you think, you are interpreting interpretations—representing representations—that will put you further away in time from your experience and further away from the data of the least representational form of your experience. Put simply, we are always dealing with second-hand information and, usually, it is used second-hand information.

If All This is True, How Can We Live?

What are the implications of this? What are the minimal inferences one can make from this model of the brain/mind? If this is true, what should one do? Well, first of all, a few immediate things are clear.

1. Give up the illusion of control. Your consciousness, or what you usually call your self, is not in control. Your sense of agency in the matter of being sure that you are reasonably in charge is all nonsense. Forget it.

2. Know that you are already sufficiently taken care of by your involuntary nervous system, which keeps you alive without having to think about it. Perceiving is superior to interpreting, though no perceiving occurs without some degree of interpretation. *The least degree of interpretation is the most reliable.* Noticing is a better mode of orientation than thinking, even though you can't keep from thinking.

3. Tell the truth about what you think and how you are interpreting things, but do not value it as reality. Also, don't see your interpreter as your whole identity, and don't imagine that what you think is very important. It's all stuff you are making up. A lifetime spent protecting your "story" is not a good lifetime. Besides, the rest of us need your data. An intentionally well-wasted life is somehow less tragic than an unconsciously wasted life.

4. Identify with your being. Be aware of being a moment-by-moment creator of the world. Surrender your life to your involuntary nervous system. Develop skill in noticing every-

thing you can about what is going on within you and outside you.

5. Focus on becoming "organismically self-regulating." That is, live by paying a lot of attention to immediate physical needs as a way of orienting yourself in the world. If you are thirsty, drink. If you are hungry, eat. If you are tired, rest.

6. Practice noticing. Notice even your mind. Notice thinking. Notice sensations in your body. Notice the outside world. Notice noticing.

7. If you are a being with a mind (I am, therefore I think) rather than a mind with a being (I think, therefore I am) as your culture has taught you all your life, a whole new world of possibility opens up.

8. You could possibly become a conscious creator of your life by using your reactive and reflective minds instead of being used by them. You could dream up a future based on what you remember really liking in your life, make a plan about how to get there, follow the plan to create what you envision, and use up your mind and body consciously on the trip from here to the tomb.

I highly recommend all eight of these options. But how on earth can you live like this?

The best way to start is to constantly do things that help you to identify with the being you are, who notices, rather than the mind you are, who thinks. Then put your mind to work in service to your being. It helps greatly to begin the practices that help you to notice being here. These practices include but are not limited to: meditation, yoga, honesty with others, and sharing your experiences and your plans with others. Instead of keeping your mind in the foreground in charge of your being, switch figure and ground, and put your being in charge of your mind. The details about how you do that are the focus of the rest of this book.

Existential Anxiety

This place is scary to actually live from—this not being in control. Tibetan Buddhists have been talking about it and working with the fear that is triggered from the knowledge of not being in control for a long time. In an interview in the *Shambala Sun* in March of 1997 reprinted in the *Utne Reader* in June the same year, a Buddhist teacher named Pema Chodron said,

"We have so much fear of not being in control, of not being able to hold on to things. Yet the true nature of things is that you are never in control. You're never in control. You can never hold on to anything. That's the nature of how things are. But it's almost like it's in the genes, part of being born human, that you can't accept that. You can buy it intellectually, but moment to moment it brings up a lot of panic and fear. So my own path has been training to relax with groundlessness and the panic that accompanies it. Training to allow all of that to be there, training to die continually. To stay in the space of uncertainty without trying to reconstruct a reference point."

I believe Pema Chodron unflinchingly faces the truth of her experience and reports honestly how it is for her. This makes her a great teacher, because we are moved to emulate her courage. We can take what comfort there is from sharing in the despair of attempting to control our life with our mind.

From that space of uncertainty, when it is not something to be avoided, but in fact quite rich, you can begin to play. Go ahead and read the summary of this chapter and then start playing with the exercises at the end of thie chapter.

Summary

Because of the way the mind is made up of recordings of unconsciously selected previous experiences, and a rationalizing internalized judge who thinks she is in charge, we all have illusions about having control of the world and our lives. We use methods of survival based on association with early childhood events and we rationalize actions based on these associations with theories that we made up as children. We are only occasionally conscious of these childhood-formed sets of associations, assumptions, and beliefs. We vaguely feel that because childhood beliefs worked when we were younger, they should work now and we keep trying them over and over and ignoring any new evidence about their usefulness in current time. These associations, assumptions, and beliefs, which are championed to maintain an illusion of control, limit our adult lives.

By overcoming our culture's blind faith in the mind, and adopting a transcendent and non-defensive perspective, we can see how these old beliefs affect what we think, feel, and do. Once we have perspective from which to view these limiting beliefs, we can stop wasting effort on hiding our true selves, struggling to survive, and can start living freer lives based on noticing before thinking. Luckily, the same illusion-making capacity of the human mind can be harnessed intentionally to create a vision of a future life and bring it into being.

Exercise

How do you get in your own way? The first step to discovering and inventing an answer to this question is to acknowledge how you DO get in your way. How do you block yourself or interfere with yourself? How do you shoot yourself in the foot before the race is over? How do you talk to yourself, coach yourself, warn yourself, worry yourself from within your own mind? Think about your favorite way or ways of limiting yourself or stopping yourself. Write them down. Do this now.

What are your favorite "limiting beliefs?" From what automatic reactions of carefulness did you formulate those beliefs to justify placing those limits on yourself? (For example, you might believe that if you are good, life will treat you right, and if life is not working out, it's because you were bad, concluding that you should redouble your efforts to be good. How old were you when you started doing that "careful to be good" racket?) What are your main methods of maintaining your illusion of control? Do any of them involve self-blame and intense resolve as though you should be held accountable for being in control of your life? Write those down.

Save what you write because you will need it for exercises in the workbook section of this book. Think about this. Work at this. After you read the next chapter, you will be sent back to revise and edit your initial draft.

Dysfunctional Family University, The World-Famous School Within Which We Grew Our Minds

"...all experience hath shown, that mankind are more disposed to suffer, while evils are sufferable, than to right themselves by abolishing the forms to which they are accustomed."

– *The Declaration of Independence of the United States of America*

We have lost touch with our simple, instinctual, common sense function of *noticing* what is needed to take care of ourselves and our own, and then simply doing what we've noticed is needed. In our culture, we lead with our minds rather than with our noticing—a distortion of the happiness we were born with.

The Dangers of Belief

All the major scientific discoveries of the twentieth century have been based on shifts in perspective. Einstein invented the theory of relativity, tried it out in space and with subatomic particles, and it worked. He looked at the world differently than had Newton, whose model also works. If you want to build a dog house, use Newton's theory. If you want to design a bomb, use Einstein's (but use Newton's again to actually build it).

We have discovered that *perspective* is a matter of invention and that different perspectives yield different information, and that all the information is to be judged with regard to its usefulness rather that whether it is "right" or "wrong." In physics, psychology, linguistics, economics, sociology, theology, philosophy — the list goes on — all the advances are in the direction of the relativity of models. Models of all kinds are subsumed under what I call the Kleenex™ tissue model; you use one and throw it away. When the full implications of this are finally integrated into religion, education, family life, government, organizational development, group psychotherapy, and individual psychotherapy, the world will be quite a different kind of place; and very suddenly. All beliefs are relative. All models are just functional or dysfunctional toward certain ends.

All models are dysfunctional when we attempt to use them where they don't serve. Nothing is sacred except that nothing is sacred. All shoulds are relative. All obligations, mindsets, ideas, and gods are mere structures of belief for certain ends. All personal life stories are just stories. All concepts are fictional. All constructs are imaginary. Nothing is absolute. Possibility is not determined by belief. The greatest intellectual advance of the twentieth century is that, through the integration of Eastern and Western thought, the growth of science, and the ability to make comparisons of religions and cultures, it is now possible to question *all belief.*

The transcendence of moralism, *the main sickness of our time,* allows us to gain detachment enough to see cultural moral values as mere beliefs. *The use and abuse of belief is the fundamental issue for the twenty-first century.*

The Integration of Knowing and Believing

Western philosophy reflects a faith in thinking, while Eastern philosophy reflects a faith in noticing. The human groups of the world have slowly begun to learn from each other that thinking and noticing are both important. We have also learned, however, that thinking often blocks noticing. Nowhere is this more obvious than with regard to the limitations of cultural beliefs.

A Unitarian minister named Randle E. Vining, in a published sermon, said, "The opposite of belief is experience. If you experience something then you know it is the truth, but the same thing believed is a lie. *If you experience something then you know it is the truth, but the same thing believed is a lie!* But, you say, we can't function without beliefs! Well, I agree that we can't function without theories and ideas. We do need a mental framework to help us interpret our experience of the world. But ideas are not like religious beliefs, because *we wouldn't claim any certainty* for them. They are working hypotheses—I call them notions. A belief is a hardened notion, and a believer is someone who's suffering from hardening of the notions."

Mr. Vining is talking about the tendency we all have to categorize our experience and then, when we recall the category, we think we have recalled the experience! We have recalled a picture of the experience only. This picture can trigger a new experience *but it often doesn't, particularly if we concentrate too hard on getting the picture right.* For example, many of us have had the peak experience of suddenly being delivered from the burden of intense worry and avoidance and the delivery into a new experience of freedom like that described by people who have been "saved."

We get free from our mind and notice the joy of being really connected with and aware of another person we love. We then think, "That was a wonderful experience and I should never forget it and everyone should have it." This originally generous impulse quickly becomes a belief and a "should" and a moralistic value to be imposed on others whether they are interested or not, including the person we were in love with. Then we join up together with other believers and we are off to the races.

The world is still suffering mightily from believers. True believers usually value their beliefs more than they value other people. Other people are expendable as long as the beliefs can be maintained. Their own children are expendable. Pakistanis and Indians, Arabs and Jews, Catholics and Protestants, Serbs and Croats, Moslems and Christians, Serbs and Albanians and so on can all vouch for the ultimate importance of being right and how it justifies the perennial murder of each other. *As long as people are less important than belief, the world will continue to go to hell in a handbasket.* How's that for a belief? That's what I believe and I am quite attached to it. Anyone who disagrees ought to be shot!

Hiding From Experience by Believing

Seriously, if you really want to hide something, put it behind a belief — preferably a belief about what it is you want to hide. If you want to avoid the experience of love, hide behind a belief in love. Then romanticize love and watch a lot of soap operas about love and make a lot of soap operas in your real life about love. Go to war in the name of love if you can. If you want protection from any uncontrollable feelings, make up some belief about them and hold on for dear death.

Heretics Who are Beyond Belief

There is a significant and rapidly growing minority of people in the world who realize personally the relativity of belief. We have discovered and invented ways to learn detachment from belief. We have let up on our demand that belief be given the status of reality. *We don't want our children raised that way anymore.* If you read beyond this point, you are one of us.

I am also writing another book, *Radical Parenting: How to Raise Creators,* which is a training manual about how to raise heretics. You can learn something by reading my books, but I recommend that you not believe a thing I say. Just hold the insights lightly, without attachment. Be inspired. If you are, be grateful and expressive or angry and expressive, even be an advocate or an enemy, but don't *believe.* Become a friend to me and my friends, or become our opponent, but let's not be believers.

There is some really good news in the current Zeitgeist as well. The overbalanced stress on thinking by Westerners has been modified in the minds and hearts and actions of people all over the world. The most unlikely people are now practicing meditation, exercise, contemplation of and with the senses, and contact, communication, and openness to people with different beliefs. Slowly the wisdom of the heretics is integrated into the culture, but then the danger is always that new perspectives become merely another set of beliefs, with wisdom defeated again.

It appears that the maximum beneficial use of the human machine requires a constant reintegration of *noticing* and *thinking*. Thinking involves categories developed from previous noticing. The constant update of thought only occurs when the continuous recurrence of noticing is possible, not limited by the previous set or "belief."

For this reason, lucky for us, every belief system that cannot rapidly modify itself is falling apart. For this reason, communism is falling apart. So is fundamentalism of all kinds. So is capitalism, and a growing number of experts can see that now. In our lifetimes, most of us will witness many downfalls as a result of the coming to an end of the long-honored human habit of reification and blasphemous worship of organized belief systems.

We have worshipped belief for untold millennia since our genetic pathway diverged slightly from our brother chimpanzee. *We are going to miss holy reification of belief terribly, but it is time we grew beyond that.*

The Mind, the Culture and the Possibility of Recreating Both

Now, what we have said so far is this: We all have minds and we all are beings. If we assume that we are beings within which the mind resides, rather than minds within which the being resides, we experience a big difference. We humans in the West made a slightly aberrant turn back there when Descartes said, "I think, therefore I am." Unfortunately, that was a mistake. After a few hundred million useless deaths and a couple thousand years of damaged suffering lives, we now know that was wrong. "I am, therefore I think" is a better premise. It makes all the difference in the world. To learn from being is more fruitful than to be from learning. A grounding in being, as children have, is also the best trait for adults to have, at all times and no matter how old they get. What we learn from studying how we be and how we have been is of value. What we learn from studying what we have already learned is not worth much unless it is done from a transcendent perspective, centered in being.

Exercise

Now revise and edit what you wrote about getting in your own way, at the end of Chapter 2. Take into consideration what you have just read. Save what you write for later use in the workbook section coming up.

The Truth About All Cultures

Cultures operate consistently with a mythology that allows them to focus the energy of their members toward certain ends. The benefits of this include creating things, conditions, and institutions to benefit the people of the culture. However, this focus limits what we can notice outside the mindset of the myths we live by. Our culture, as cultures do, has taught us to be ignorant.

I imagine you are engaged in the middle of life with other people, including children, doing your best to responsibly care for your children and raise them right. I'm sure you're well-intentioned. But well-intentioned people mislead and mistreat their children every day because of highly valued and unquestioned cultural ignorance, moralism, righteousness, paranoia, obsessiveness, and other charming human characteristics. I'm sure you have plenty of them; I certainly do.

Cultures live in the minds of individuals. You have a mind within which the culture we live in, lives. It is a mind full of hopelessly obsolete subsets of ignorant prejudice that compete with each other for dominance. I know this from personal experience with lots of parents and with lots of neurotic adults like yourself. I also have made plenty of mistakes of my own and produce my fair share of misleading data every day. We live in illusions that direct our attention to certain things and also block our view of what is out there in reality, other than what we are looking for.

The reason I know you are living in an illusion is because we all are, all the time. It's just that most of us don't know it, and for that reason we are living out a script written years ago that determines almost everything we do, including how we raise our children and how we treat each other. Illusions can be our friends if we can just get one point: illusions are for creating, not for self-assurance.

Living in a story is what we all must do because we are human. Human beings live in the real world, but always in a way consistent with some story. Most of us live in stories that were created for us by the conditions we started out in, and survived with, as children, and the cultural prejudices we were born into. Some of us grow beyond that and, as adults, actually design the story we live out of. There are not really a lot of us, but those of us who have transcended our raising have found that living in a story of our own conscious creation is a lot less miserable than living in the survival story we came out of childhood with.

Most of us live our entire lives trapped in a story we desperately contrived so we could endure circumstances of middle, or lower, or upper-class child abuse in the culture in which we were raised. When we shed the delusional system that tells us life has a particular meaning, or that we must be careful to avoid symbolic dangers, or we should compete to overcome our adversaries, or be polite above all else, or maintain our belief in God or God will die, or any of the thousands of outdated, misleading, and actually damaging beliefs of any kind that people have been selling as reality in our culture for centuries — when we get over attachment to the image or the illusion of who we are, then we get to create some new illusions for the future. We don't have any choice not to live by illusions, but we can choose which illusions we live. It is our given destiny to be delusional. *It's out of these illusions of a possible future that we live the creative and intentional life,* and that we heal the damage done by our previous attachments to beliefs that don't work anymore and haven't for a long time.

Creation of the future with conscious illusions (called visions) works best if the illusions meet two criteria: they have to involve making a contribution to other people in some way, and they have to closely match the survival skills from our past. Because we've already developed upkeep and maintenance skills for these, this habit structure can be used.

A person who understands the use of illusion from a position of transcendence or detachment (that is, a person who uses illusions, but doesn't believe in them) has a much happier and fulfilled life. If I am disappointed about an image I just dreamed up and am not attached to, it's quite different than feeling like dying because somebody was disappointed with, or rejected, the image of whom I truly believe myself to be. All those folks who jumped out of the window when the stock market crashed were doing so to escape the negative meaning of the crash in a very limited view of life.

When people can use illusions to design their future in a playful and creative way, they can also design a life and education for their children in cooperation with the children themselves, and at the same time model for the children what creating with illusions consists of.

Radical Being

In *Radical Honesty,* I said, "We come into existence as beings and grow minds, which eventually come to so dominate the experience of being that there is little time or space left to attend to any aspects of life other than thought."

The books I'm writing are all dedicated to attempting to undo damage already done by overly moralistic parenting. For the child raised by the standard "attached-to-cultural-belief" parent, the mind becomes a jail. Being in jail is worrisome and depressing. One major thesis of these books is that the primary cause of *most anxiety* and *most depression* is being trapped in the mind, unable to *notice* because we're constantly thinking. We stay trapped in our minds because of various kinds of lying—outright lying, hiding, lies of omission, pretense, little white lies, withholding, yadda yadda yadda. Lying keeps you trapped in the jail of the mind, and most of us lie habitually most of the time.

My clients over the years have reflected the culture they grew up in. They had all been taught systematically to lie by the way they were parented and educated. The only thing that could rescue them from the jail of the mind was to start telling the truth about everything they had done, everything they felt, and everything they thought. Telling the truth gets you back out into the real world, where you can deal with other people and feelings to some degree of completion before you recreate the next mess in your life out of the unfinished business from the last completion you avoided.

Human stress is caused by the mind of the individual suffering from stress. Suffering comes from being trapped in the mind, unable to escape the categories you have made up for yourself and others from previous avoided experience, the emotional attachment to ideas you invented to protect yourself from feelings in the past, and the ranting and raving of the mind. I call this fundamental dis-ease of being trapped in the mind moralism. Moralism is characterized as extreme attachment to moral principles—being trapped in a valuational continuum where judgments about right and wrong and good and bad are given excessive significance and emotional charge. These principles become more important than life itself. We all have the disease of moralism, and the secret of the good life is learning how to manage the disease like one manages herpes or diabetes and other incurable, but somewhat controllable, diseases.

Most of us keep repeating the same kind of behavior in relation to other people and ourselves; begging, berating, and scolding ourselves and each other and our children, trying to convince everyone that if we would all just live up to our expectations we'd be happy. In our neurotic way, we do this over and over again and expect a different result each time. We get the same results: anger, discomfort, depression, anxiety, and somatic ailments due to stress. Most parents believe that the primary responsibility of parenting is moralizing intensely! This is the worst piece of delusional data extant today. This is the core source of middle class child abuse.

Old-Timey Parenting as Cultural Instruction

How do most of us become repetitively self-limiting and self-torturing in our standard, garden variety neurotic ways? It clearly starts with how we were parented. Your parents did the best they could, given that they lived in the dark ages, where male intellect was thought to reign supreme, with no respect for the continuum of genetic learning from which we came. You've probably survived well enough to go on to have children of your own, but your method of survival still probably limits you much more than necessary. You are very likely to be more worrying and worrisome than necessary, trying to fill up emptiness with good behavior to get brownie points along the way as a pathway to happiness. You might already know that being trapped in performance mode is pretty screwed up, but you're raising your kids the same way anyhow.

Keep reading; there are some ideas that can be a big help. *The main thing seems to be to grow beyond* the limitations imposed by your culture.

About Growing and Not Stopping with Up

Human development is a continuum of growth of the mind out of the being (when we are babies), through a period in which the mind captures all our attention (adolescence), and then to a time in which the liberation of the being from domination by the mind occurs (maturity). The full path of growth from birth to maturity consists of the birth of being, the growth of the mind, a period of domination of the being by the mind, and finally, a mind used by the being who has escaped domination by the mind.

How capable we are in keeping body and soul together as adults is directly contingent upon staying in touch with the experience of being in the body — noticing, moving, playing, and manifesting energy doing things other than thinking. Happiness and freedom depend upon not losing touch with being in the body and in the world, as one grows a mind.

As a psychotherapist, my main therapeutic method (for people who have been torn loose from contact with being and are trapped in their minds and kept out of contact with being) is coaching people to tell the truth. When people begin telling the truth about what they have done, what they feel, and what they think, they free themselves from the jail of their own mind. It's lying that keeps one from gaining freedom from domination by one's own mind.

When a person who was once divided against herself, and out of touch with the joy of living, becomes whole again through psychotherapy, it is the result of beginning to notice things in the world all over again, including her own body, and running her life more in obedience to what she notices, rather than in obedience to interpretations she has worked hard to brainwash herself with. She reports her mind's machinations to others, simply to share with others (including others she's thinking about), but she doesn't have much faith in her mind as a source of directions. When one who has been damaged by how they were raised begins to heal and become whole again, the healing is a result of establishing balance out of imbalance, a reunification of being and mind. A person who has become whole again makes the best parent.

When a person "loses their mind and comes to their senses" in psychotherapy, there is a period of troublesome disorientation. Reorientation occurs through getting back in touch with gravity, sensation, and what Wilhelm Reich and Fritz Perls called "organismic self-regulation." To become grounded in experience again is not just changing some opinions. Opinions do change, but that is after the reorientation to experience has occurred. You start living from what you notice you want rather than what your mind says you should want.

Thinking itself becomes merely something else to notice and use, once one has become reoriented to experience. Thinking loses its prior status as a primary ruler and jailkeeper of being and becomes more like the chauffeur. The mind becomes background and the being in the body is in the foreground. So when you're thirsty you get a drink, when you're hungry you eat, when you're tired you rest, when you have to go to the bathroom you go, and so on. You notice other people's expressions and tone of voice and changes in coloring and pace of speech, and whatever else helps you comprehend their communication to you. You are centered in the world of noticing as the foreground and your opinions are in the background — *and changing constantly!* This includes cultural values of all kinds, and is threatening to those whose world depends upon belief. Practicing radical honesty with every human around you is the first step in this transformation.

In this view of human development as a continuum of growth of the mind out of the being, and then the liberation of the being from domination by the mind, the most obvious question that arises concerning child rearing is: "How can we allow minds to grow without losing touch with being?" The most important question before all the nations of the world at the turn of the century is, "What is the best way to raise children so that they don't have to be torn loose from their grounding in being?" Even though young humans must go through a long period of growth of a mind, and parenting and teaching must assist them in this task, can they do it without losing the nourishment of commonplace experience? Can they learn about the values for sale by the culture they are dumped into without having their spirit crushed?

In All Cultures: Let's Quit Brainwashing Our Children to Be Moralists

Luckily, through sharing honestly, some of us have learned from each other a few things that we know don't work. We know that moralizing constantly with children at an early age makes chronic liars out of them in their adulthood. We know that enforcing rules with a vengeance damages people and makes for a miserable life. Stringent moral instruction at an early age doesn't create a happy, whole adult; it creates miserable, self-righteous, phony, and manipulative people.

Intense early religious and ethical instruction makes chronic liars out of people in their adulthood. Unhappy parents and teachers, enforcing rules with a vengeance, damage children. This instruction results in a miserable childhood with children mistreated in the dysfunctional ways of the tradition. Many among us know that stringent moral instruction at an early age doesn't work, but too many of the teachers in charge of our children don't have a clue about the damage they do. There are plenty of fine teachers whose hearts are in the right place and who love children, but they are operating within a system that is impossible to survive in without being agents of misery. There are teachers in the educational system who know that stringent moral instruction at an early age doesn't work. There are also teachers who don't yet recognize this, and most of them are completely unaware of the damage they do with their shoulds and their conditional love and their misplaced moralism. Because the grading, comparing, coaching, pushing, and moralizing that is already in place, provided by the structure of the system itself, is so poisonous, the people of compassion too often quit. Even when they do stay, their primary function is to be outlaws within a corrupt culture, and slightly block the damage done.

Even parents who know better often continue to damage their children in spite of what they know. We find ourselves, in trying to help our children, acting "on automatic" based on how we were raised. Out of love for them, mixed with anger, expressed through stringently enforced cautionary rules, taught at too early an age for the child to comprehend, we teach them the same anxieties that were trained into us. In addition to that we send them to schools, make them do whatever homework is assigned, and encourage them to be successful in a system that is killing their spirits.

Calling all Cultures!

How might we design a better way for children to be raised so they don't have to suffer so much? What if children were allowed to discover how to take care of themselves? What if parents had faith enough in themselves and their children to simply protect children while they unfold as they were genetically programmed to do? What if, instead of forcing them, with punishment and shame, to be worried and afraid, and to memorize rules "for their own good," parents allowed their children to learn from experimenting and learned with them? What if love and encouragement and an even-handed permission to experiment were given to children based on assuming they are okay to start with, rather than assuming they are evil little pleasure-seekers who need to be taught how to behave?

If love and encouragement with freedom works, and I say it does, it could become the norm, and we could reorganize the whole human community and create the possibility of a lifetime of play and service for every human being on the planet.

What if parents were in a therapeutic community in which their tendency to take out their misery on their children in the name of love was compassionately interrupted? What if the world became such a therapeutic community? Changes in the way we all live together can happen through a radical change in how we raise our young. Without radically changing how we raise and educate our children, homo saps will increasingly be unable to enjoy the greatest benefit of life, that of living freely and fully in the moment, cherishing every sensation and connection with life and with other human beings. If that change in how we raise our young doesn't happen, we are finished.

Cultural Blindness: Trying to Teach Too Much Too Soon

One of the primary causes of the disease of moralism is the forced training of children with abstract concepts they are developmentally too immature to comprehend. Children are forced to act as if they understand abstract cognitive principles (like right and wrong, good and evil, the existence of God, the concept of fairness, and so on) before they are capable of abstract cognitive thinking.

Children do not learn the ability to generalize and abstract until about ten or eleven years of age. They learn quickly, however, to focus on avoiding punishment for not understanding and by acting as if they are trying hard to understand. Children don't know how to generalize quite like adults, but they learn to be afraid of what is required of them, and to feel stupid and inept. They learn this quickly, and carry it with them for a long time. They learn how to cower and falsify "sincere" effort. Once a child learns this phony pretense of understanding to avoid punishment, along with being afraid all the time, any further learning is blocked. After the child has attained the age of eleven or twelve and develops the ability to do abstract thinking, they use it to make only a few permanent defensive generalizations, one of which is: "If I put on a show for the sake of the teachers and my parents to keep them off my back, maybe I can have another life in secret, protected by pretending to be good." The problem with too much force in training in abstraction in any culture whatsoever is that human children can't do the abstracting required prior to ten or eleven years of age, and if forced to act like they have, they continue to play like they understand when they don't, for the rest of their lives.

The Fundamental Assumptions That Come with Feeling Whole

People who are happy in life, regardless of the culture they grew up in, learn how to feel connected with the continuum of life they encounter as they roll out of bed each day. Because of that feeling of being present in their bodies and present to the life around them, they wake up into an assumption that something interesting, something challenging, something good, something fun is likely to happen today. Wouldn't it be great if the next generation of people, raised by us, could wake up in the mornings with an expectation that is vague but always there, that this day is to be looked forward to? Feeling whole is a fundamental necessity for being a creator.

Children learn first, as a natural consequence of their development, to locate themselves in the real world of sensate reality in the moment. Then, because we are usually in a hurry, we train them out of it. For example, a child might notice and comment, "That toothpaste smells good," when she's brushing her teeth. A parent who is attentive to the child as a constant guru of living in the moment would themselves notice the smell of toothpaste, something they hadn't noticed for a long, long time, and say, "Yep. It sure does," in a grateful tone of voice. A parent who is in a hurry to get the kid off to school so she can get off to work to get to the next place she has to go to, to get through the day and get the day over with, would say, "Hurry up, honey. We're going to be late." This little difference in parenting can make all the difference in the world.

The systematic teaching of hysteria about time is a part of the curriculum for the day, on most days, for most of the children in our culture. The parents of millions of children wake up into a frenetic assumption: "I have to make everybody get there on time." They resentfully force themselves to push the kids to get ready in time, resenting children for "dawdling" while being afraid of what the boss will think if they're late again. Somehow, we have to interrupt that interruption. Every time a child interrupts your mental agenda to point out something they have noticed in the moment, follow their lead instead of overriding their discovery because your agenda is more important. Your agenda isn't more important. Your culture has given you a bad agenda. You've been torn loose from the continuum of being and captured by intellect. Most of us are psychotic with regard to time and money.

Children who are "spoiled" in the old paradigm way of thinking are actually the ones who have been raised the best. They have been taught to expect that the world is a place of nurturance and love, and as they gradually, over about twelve to sixteen years, take full responsibility for their lives, they develop their skills in taking care of themselves in the context of an assumption of each day bringing a new and interesting adventure. Children do a lot of fantasy play to develop their imaginations. Our job is to play along with them by helping them develop their ability to envision the future and live into their visions.

Marilyn Ferguson says in her great book, *Radical Common Sense* (which hasn't been published yet because of complications with international corporations who own almost all the publishing companies), that in her extensive study of visionary people she found that, "…consciously or unconsciously, they have learned to be good parents and teachers to themselves." I think this is more than likely related to them not having had their natural born optimism stomped out of them at an early age by parents and teachers hysterical about time and money.

How Would We Treat Children If We Weren't Working so Hard to Teach Them Something?

Let them lead every now and then. Just do whatever they do or ask you to do. You'll learn how to play with them the way they like to play at whatever age they are. Play with them. They will teach you again to be a visionary, thereby allowing you to envision how to raise them. We could just start learning with them.

Radical parenting means staying connected as an older being with your child as a younger being. To be present to a child's presence to you, to notice that you are being noticed and to give your full attention with no particular agenda, is one of the great joys of parenting. You and your child can play with your developing minds together, bonded as one noticing being noticing the other. As Kierkegaard said, "A person who relates to another person and relates also to that relationship relates thereby to God." My understanding of this is that you discover yourself as God and the other as God at the same time. Children are rich with the fullness of being, and the nurturance you get from nurturing them is the best there is. This is more valuable than money. Play with your kids for hours instead of making more money.

Seeing Problems as Opportunities to Play

I believe that people can work out their problems in life by sharing with other people. I have a lot of friends who share that belief, and we act on that belief by telling each other what problems we have and working them out. Life doesn't come without problems. Problems are life. We don't expect life to be problem-free and we don't expect problems to disappear through hope or positive thinking or the magical recitation of "affirmations" or any other form of magical thinking. Those ways of thinking are the leftovers from having been brainwashed into playing like we understand something we don't, and playing that pretend games are the same as reality. Those of us who have grown beyond that handle our problems by confronting them openly and sharing them rather than keeping secrets. Not all problems are miserable. A lot of problems are fun. Miserable problems can become fun through the transformation of perspective on the problem. Reality cannot be changed by thinking or daydreaming. Perspectives on reality can be changed easily. When the willingness and inspiration that come from a change in perspective show up, transformation can occur. Repeated, ongoing, recurrent transformation is the alternative to moralism.

My friends and I all "did our time" in the prison of the mind during quite an extended adolescence. We eventually escaped the pretense of our reputations to ourselves. We finally got clear that our imagining of who we were in the eyes of other people, and our performing whatever lies were necessary to maintain that image, were a waste of time and the source of more problems than got handled. We decided that, somehow, we didn't want our lives used up by such a story. As a way out of the story, we started really talking to each other about our own pretenses. We told the truth about our phony performances to each other, and that took away the need to keep it up.

We now get to invent, for ourselves, what our lives get used up by, rather than having them used up by the method of survival advocated by our trainers; that is, playing to the audience to control their view of who we are so we can get what we want. That got boring and felt futile and we thought, "there must be more interesting things to do in the world." We ended up turning to the task of creating a new world together and it is more fun than the old life was. We decided that because life always involves problems, why not be in charge of inventing some of them, and why not invent one big enough to be worth working on? What we have invented to use up our lives is building a heaven on earth by honestly sharing who we are. Saving the world and improving the lives of all human beings on the planet through sharing is the problem we have invented and taken on for our own sakes. A lifetime of play and service for every person on the planet is the possibility we invented to live for. We would like to spend our lives working on ending human suffering, using ourselves up to end it. Working on the solutions to this problem is much more challenging and fun than a life of just keeping up with the current style.

To bring about a solution to the problems of human suffering and planetary extinction and make a world that works for everybody, rather than just the rich folks, we need to work on a lot of minor sub-problems; namely, the end of hunger, the end of economic injustice, the end of armament, the end of authoritarian governance of countries and corporations, the end of war, the end of enslaving educational paradigms, and the end of genocide. This almost gives us enough problems. This is almost enough to substitute for whining about how you don't love me as much as you love somebody else or whether to get the Ford or the Chevy.

We are taking on the central problem—and we ask you to help—of raising a generation of human beings the world over who are prepared to love and share with other human beings. What you can do to help the world become a much better place is to take delight in your children, and, viewing them through the eyes of delight, work consciously to have them love life, and learning, and other people. Do this more by example than instruction.

So let's get to work. The good life is shared problems. Solving big problems together is the best game on earth. If parents and teachers stop teaching whining and complaining and start teaching the fun of playing with problems, help is on the way.

All in all, our immediate forebears have not done that great a job of loving their children. We can tell by looking around at the world we live in. We can tell by all the damaged children who are our friends. We can tell by looking at our current, mostly sick institutions (the legal system, for example). Most of us are depressed or anxious or angry or distracted or sick or just not happy. We were raised in a way that didn't work, and we are raising our children, for the most part, in the same way. So we have to do some work on ourselves to change how we treat our children.

Cross Cultural Transformation: Learning to Tolerate Joy

Some of us have worked through anger and shame and sexual inhibitions in the course of growing beyond just growing up and were surprised at what came next. We were surprised to discover that we are more afraid of joy than we are of any of the other emotions. The joy and celebration of freedom together that emerged when we got free from most of the mind's taboos was so unfamiliar it was too much to bear.

Many of us have this built-in mechanism to guard against being overwhelmed by love—being unmanned and unwomanned and undone from our identity as survivors. Here is how the mechanism works: we fall in love and feel love for another person and for a little while it is just wonderful; more wonderful than we can allow ourselves to experience.

So our minds, whose duty it is to make sure we are not overwhelmed by any experience, save us from that experience of love by associating the current experience of love with earlier records of having lost this same kind of love. We close down the love with anxiety, to prevent the intensity. We experience love and immediately turn it into nostalgia for lost love because we cannot bear letting love come and go. "I have lost it before," our minds say, "and it was terrible, so don't do that again." Our mothers and fathers and teachers and other big people loved us conditionally and we never quite got the conditions met. We lost their love and thought it was our fault for not being careful enough. We didn't stay in control.

This time we will be careful—so careful we block the feeling with the memory of the loss of the feeling. Love becomes blocked by mourned lost love and romanticized nostalgia to satisfy the mind's need to preserve the illusion of control. It is our mind's job to protect us. We think that who we are is our mind. Our parents and teachers taught us that who we are is our minds. They were dead wrong. Who we actually are, is a being,

in love. We already knew this when we were little, but we did-
n't know we knew it. In the course of growing up, we got trained
out of it by people who thought that developing our minds and
identifying with them was more important. Once we get this
again, and get that we have always known this in our bones, our
life changes from making-do-the-best-we-can (survival) to making out quite happily in the world.

This love of being alive comes with the territory of being
human. The future of humankind depends upon how well we
learn aliveness and love of life over again from our children, and
how well we let love for them be the heart of how we organize
ourselves in the world to take care of them. This book is to help
us learn to teach each other to be beings in love.

We All Have a Common Desire

Wherever I have been with people—jails, mental hospitals,
universities, corporations—I have never found a human being
who didn't want to contribute to the well-being of other people.
Regardless of how distorted their mind or how twisted their
thinking, all human beings fundamentally want to help each
other, be with each other, contribute to each other. Human
beings want to celebrate being alive with other human beings
who are celebrating being alive. This is fundamental to our
nature as human beings. I believe that the world of human
beings can eventually become conscious of, and operate according to, this fundamental love of human beings for each other and
their desire to celebrate being itself, if the mind's resistance to
this doesn't destroy us first.

Our minds resist the risk of surrender to celebration of the
joy of being alive with other human beings because we have
learned that human beings are dangerous. We learn this in the
course of growing up. Most of us overlearn this paranoid fear of
other human beings because of the poisonous moralism and
parental abuse of power in the culture in which we are raised. I
believe that the will of human beings to contribute to each other

is stronger than the resistive forces of their minds. I also believe that one day the force of being will be more in control of how humans live than the forces of the mind's resistance. The key to this is how well we love each other and how well we love our children.

I hope you are inspired by now, but you may be offended instead. If you are offended by anything I've said so far, check to see what moral you are attached to and see if you can forgive me. If you are not offended so far, or are offended but still interested, continue reading this book. We hope it will help you a lot in raising your kids and loving your neighbors and having fun doing it, attentively, playfully, and in no hurry, casually saving the world.

Conscious Community and Conscious Child Rearing

Members of a culture that is asleep are characterized by unconscious attachment to a cultural subgroup of values based on how they were raised, or in rebellion against how they were raised. The most important gift we can give to our children and to humanity is to teach them to grow beyond limiting beliefs continuously. Loving our children unconsciously is not enough.

The gift is to love our children consciously with a clear intention to help them stay in touch with the glory of being alive in their bodies as they grow, so they can transcend the jail of their own mind when they grow up. Nurturing their spirits is important for their freedom. The being of the parent loves the being of the child, consciously, and two free persons grow and grow and grow. The first generation, ever, of independent people not enslaved by their own minds is born. Beings are in charge of their own minds, rather than minds in charge of their own beings. This is the dawning of the age of enlightenment. It has to do with giving up the provincialism of culture itself. Let's do it. Let's enjoy it.

This book is a basis for honest conversation between generations about taking responsibility for the next new generation. I am talking to all of us: Everyone in the home schooling movement, experienced parents and grandparents, single parents, friends of single parents, newlyweds, young couples, first-time parents, first-time grandparents, over 100,000 people who will have bought Radical Honesty by the time this book is released, and all the graduates of the Radical Honesty Two Day Workshops, The Course in Honesty (8 Day), The Course in Forgiveness and Creating (4 days). I'm talking to all the graduates of trainings involving existentialist and Buddhist approaches such as the Landmark Forum, Life Spring, Insight Training, and those conducted by Tony Robbins, Kathlyn and Gay Hendricks, Neale Donald Walsch, Pema Chodron and literally hundreds of other compassionate people and good teachers. I am talking to everyone who has ever been in a 12-step program in AA or in Al-Anon or many co-dependency groups. I am here to speak with the 40 million Americans who embrace "New Paradigm Values" as reported in a survey conducted by Paul Ray reported in Noetic Sciences Review in 1996. I am also appealing to people who are not parents and don't plan to be, but who are interested in new paradigm values and in making a contribution to the people of the world.

I am speaking to everyone who has read *The Continuum Concept* by Jean Liedloff, which has been in publication for almost twenty years now and is a masterpiece. It compares our lives with the lives of primitive tribes with regard to happiness of the adults, and examines the child-rearing practices that make us who we are in each culture. This conversation is with and for everyone who has read the following books and others like them:

- *Summerhill* by A. S. Neill
- The interest-led learning books by John Holt
- The books of John Taylor Gatto
- *The Teenage Liberation Handbook* by Grace Llewelyn
- *The War Against Children* by Breggin and Breggin
- *Spiritual Parenting: A Guide to Understanding and Nurturing Your Child* (Harmony, 1997) by Hugh and Gayle Prather

- Deepak Chopra's new book about parenting, *Seven Laws of Spiritual Parenting,*

- Jon and Myla Kabat-Zinn's book and workshop *Mindful Parenting: Nourishing our Children, Growing Ourselves,* and

- *Love and Survival: The Scientific Basis for the Healing Power of Intimacy* by Dean Ornish, M.D.

I plan to review all of these books and a few more in my upcoming book *Radical Parenting.* But, read Dean Ornish's book as soon as you can, because of his brilliant analysis and evidence of the relationship between wholeness and health and healing and his clear understanding of the uselessness of moralism without love. The people in this world are waking up from a long sleep. We are all helping. This is a great time to be alive because compassionate people are coming into their own power.

All these people, and many more you and I don't know about, are growing beyond the cultural limitations of whatever culture they were born into. I have mentioned just a few leads to contribute to the network that is hooking up all over the world. We will come to recognize each other as time goes on, and when we do, we will change the world.

The Road from the Mind Jail Back to Being— The Sufi Levels of Consciousness

We have just started the conversation about the developmental path from centeredness in being to the growth of the mind in a culture, to the eventual recentering in being for using the mind and the traditions of the culture. Now we want to review what happens when we assume that a person in a culture wants to outgrow the limitations of that culture. What can we do if our starting place is now, and we are trapped in a mind? I'm using the Sufi system called *the levels of human consciousness* as a model for our mutual instruction. This model was first taught to people in the West around the turn of the century by Gurdjieff.

Let's assume we are liars in the acculturated way we learned in whatever culture we were raised. If we were stringently instructed to learn abstractions at too early an age, we live in our minds so much we hardly have any experience of anything and we can barely contact reality enough to walk through a doorway without bumping into the doorjamb. We need to get back into the world of experience and stop obsessively thinking. We would like to get to where we feel happy and in charge of our lives rather than feeling like we're running around in circles putting out fires all the time. We want to "inhibit the modifications of the mind" and become present to experience. How do we do that?

The Level of Belief

We must start by recognizing where we are in the first place. We are at a level of consciousness that the Sufis called the "level of belief." This means we think that to escape our mind we must figure something out. We think we need to figure out what to believe and then act accordingly. The problem is that *we are trying to think our way out of thinking.* Our entire focus is on figuring out what we should believe and acting accordingly. This is the lowest level of human consciousness, called "the level of belief." The Sufis say that ninety-eight percent of us spend ninety-eight percent of our time at this level. (At least we know we are not alone.) Lots of other people in the world share this level of consciousness with us most of the time. This level has an alternative name. It's called hell. It's the inescapable do-loop prison of the interminable warning buttons of the reactive mind and the useless rationalizations of the rationalizing mind. It's hell. It's being strongly attached to the cultural quagmire we got dumped into that I discussed in the beginning chapters you have just read.

Let's say we live in hell for a long time. We grow older, get a job, get married, and so on. When we reflect on our life, we realize life isn't quite living up to its billing. We don't want much. We would just like to work when we feel like it and not work when we don't. That's all. We believe we can't do that but we wish we could. Our job, our kids, our family, our bills, and our other obligations dictate what we do and there just isn't any time left. We just never can, really, relax. It is not all intensely painful, some of it is even enjoyable, but we are basically on duty all the time, dreaming of a day when we won't have to be on duty all the time. We want out of hell.

The Level of Social Contracts

In this level, we have done some work on ourselves, some therapy, some schooling, some honest conversations, some degree of telling the truth, but we are stuck with obligations we just have to respond to. The "level of social contracts" is one notch above hell, but only one notch. It is a slightly higher hell than the level of belief because it at least recognizes that other people out there exist independently from our own mind's pictures of them.

That isn't true at the level of belief, where other people are just categories like "converts" or "heathens." The lowest level, the "level of belief," is where insulated, isolated fundamentalists live. The next level up is where many first generation immigrants live. It is where we live when we are concerned about acceptance and living up to other people's expectations.

So let's say that now we have advanced from the level of belief to the level of social contracts but we are still severely constrained. Plus, many times each day we drop back into the level of belief, where we are trying to figure out what to believe and then do what that belief dictates. Although our contracted obligations to other people constantly "rescue" us from the hell of belief, the rescue is hardly worth the work. Whereas, at the level of belief, we aren't even related to other people except as triggers for other beliefs on our part, we now recognize the independent existence of other people that places constant demands on us. Our marriage, kids, paying taxes, paying bills, and honoring other commitments to other people deliver us from the frying pan of self-torture into the fire of the torture of obligation.

The Saint Ego Level

Eventually, through hard living and experience, we get to know that there must be more to life than showing up to work on time and having a split level house with a two-car garage and two-point-eight children and keeping the mortgage paid and doing our duty to others who are doing their duty to us. There has to be more to life than maintaining our obligations. At least we have learned that. Most of us are in our forties before we learn that. When we do realize that there is more to life than fulfilling obligations, we realize at the same time that knowing that makes us superior to others who haven't learned that yet. We also know that there is more to life than being an obedient, well-behaved citizen for whom living within the guidelines of convention is the highest goal of life.

The Sufis, according to Gurdjieff, who first introduced these levels of consciousness to the West, called this level of consciousness the "Saint Ego level." We begin to understand that we are better than most of the other fools in the world. Some of us modern day Sufis call this the "Muhammad Ali level," because Muhammad Ali in his prime was such a great example of proclaimed superiority. "I am the greatest!" he said, "I float like a butterfly and sting like a bee!" "I am beautiful!" He refused to go to Vietnam and kill his dark-skinned brothers and sisters because the human bunch who claimed he belonged to them told him it was his duty. He was not obedient to the beliefs and the social contracts they claimed he should be obedient to because he was superior to that.

When we attain the level of consciousness known as the Muhammad Ali level, we still make frequent visits back to the two lower levels of consciousness known as belief and social contracts. We still have beliefs and we still have to deal with social contracts, but we tend to not be as attached to beliefs and we handle social contracts so we can spend more time at a higher and less worrisome place. We want to spend more and more time at this higher level because we have a larger perspective that subsumes more information, a perspective of superiority from which to view beliefs and social contracts.

Since I have been hanging out at that level for some years now, let me give you an example of the level by excerpting from a letter I wrote a few months ago to my literary agents in response to their suggestion that I needed a co-author, ghost writer, or editor before I could have a best-seller because my language is too offensive:

"So here is the way it is. I'll write whatever way I want. I know what I am talking about and what I have to say. I will not change what I have to say to suit the market or what so-called experts about the publishing field claim to know about the market, including you two. I will not change how I say what I say if, in my view, it changes in any way, shape, or form the point of what I have to say. I will not surrender any authority over what goes out under my name. At the heart of what I have to say is the general attitude of disrespect for minds. The fundamental integration of Eastern and Western philosophy that I have synthesized, which I both represent and live by, transcends local knowledge, and I am not going to change that for any mere agent or publishing company."

"I don't want a co-author or even a heavy-handed coach about what the mind of the expert thinks the minds of the people think. I have been doing psychotherapy with miserable intellectuals for more than half my life. I don't intend to cater to the sickness I have learned to heal in myself and others. I will work, on a give and take basis, one paragraph at a time, with an editor whom I respect, with me having the final authority over what gets published..."

"The very essence of what I have to say is radical. I am talking about the overthrow of the government of the mind. That includes all minds. Your own mind is not your friend; it is Big Brother inside of you. It considers itself to be who you are. I don't consider your mind or mine to be who we are. I consider the being who grew the mind, the one who notices first and learns second, the observer-in-the-moment-alive-right-now-only being to be who I am and who you are. I do not cater to the minds of what your mind calls 'the market.' I serve their beings instead."

"A fully alive, healthy person raises hell all the time, is not polite, offends people, hurts people's feelings, and also stays with people while they work through the feelings—committed to their being and at war with their minds. He or she doesn't submit to the minds of others or even to his or her own mind. He or she rules his or her own life and creates a life from *being*, which is to say, out of love, *using* his or her mind; not being used *by* it. I do not cater to expert opinion even if it is my own. This is what I am expert in. For the love of being I am a destroyer of minds; incessantly, endlessly, and perhaps fruitlessly, but it is my own sweet damned choice."

"I am in love with hundreds of people and they are in love with me. This is not romantic love or nostalgic love but simply the love of one being for another. The way we did it is through the way of being I have just described. A lot of the people I love and who love me were offended by me in the first place because I threatened the illusion of control provided by their minds. That is what I am about."

As you can see, living at this level is more fun than the previous levels. I continued my rant at my poor agents.

"Once, when Frank Lloyd Wright was being sued by a client, the lawyer for the client began his cross examination of Mr. Wright, who was in the witness stand, by saying, 'Mr. Wright, it's been said that you are the world's greatest living architect.' Frank Lloyd Wright responded, 'That's a bit conservative.'"

"I admire that arrogance. I think Wright showed an honorable disrespectfulness of all human assessments and comparisons and evaluations other than his own. I am proud to be arrogant in that same way, and I think in an important way it is prerequisite to being the creative genius that I am. I don't have much faith in minds at all, but if I am going to place my faith in anyone's mind at all, it will be mine.

"I would like to title my next book *A Mind is a Terrible Thing! Waste It!*" but after reflection and good coaching from some people who love me I am willing to change it to *Practicing Radical*

Honesty: How to Complete the Past, Live in the Present, and Create a Future with a Little Help from Your Friends.

"I intend to teach by modeling, both in how I live and how I write, the life of an individual who is not controllable by moralism. I wish 'mere anarchy' as T.S. Elliot said, to be 'loosed upon the world' and I will do everything I can to make it so. What do we need moralism for if we have the integrity of being? When we break loose from the stupid illusion of control we have trapped ourselves into with the help of the entire culture and educational system and the crippled humans we were raised by, we don't go 'out of control,' but we *do* go beyond control. We are beyond control by political force, whether it be government or office politics. We then discover a new use for the mind — namely, as a creative instrument in service to our true identity, the being within which the mind resides.

"I am a leader in the revolution of consciousness. You don't do that by catering to lame-brained experts. You don't do that by catering to minds' attachments."

That tirade is a fine example, if I do say so myself, of a person at the third level of consciousness, the Muhammed Ali or Saint Ego level. Luckily my agents are used to it, and being superioristic egotists themselves, they understood me, and didn't quit, but figured out a way to continue to support me without controlling me too much. Unfortunately, we didn't find a publisher who wanted to give me a whole lot of money for being the superioristic jerk that I was there. I have had to grow a little more since then but I still have ended up publishing my own damned book now and I'm glad I have. (I like this level.)

Another example of someone who spent time in the Saint Ego level is General George Patton. The movie *Patton* has a scene where, after successfully invading Sicily, Patton is giving a press conference as he's walking through a field. He uses some profanity, and a lower-ranking reporter, trailing along in a carefully pressed uniform, comments on the general's language.

George C. Scott, as Patton, delivers this line: "If I want it to stick, I give it to 'em loud and dirty, and then they remember it."

The Level of Philosopher/Charlatan

After a while at the Muhammad Ali level of consciousness, a being may have a dawning revelation that leads to the next level of consciousness. We recognize that bragging about being superior by virtue of the inferiority of others is not very superior, and even if it is, so what? We are equal as a being to other beings. When we brag about being better than, smarter than, or superior to other people, it is not our being we are referring to, it is our beliefs. We come to understand that the beliefs we have generated from our own life experience are just more beliefs. This includes our belief in our own superiority. We start losing faith in our own ego. We begin to see through our own mind. So what that we are superior to fundamentalists? What does that mean? We know that their attachment to their beliefs doesn't work, but we are still attached to a few we call our own, one of which is about our so-called superiority.

At this point, partly out of desperation, we begin to enroll other people in our hard-earned beliefs (that is, we start selling our beliefs to others). Hopefully, a whole bunch of others will pay to read these beliefs at about fifteen bucks a book. (Ha!) Yep, this is my main level these days. It's called the "level of Philosopher/Charlatan." The beliefs I have generated from my hard-earned experience are, I know, just more beliefs, but I'm selling them to you nevertheless. Most of us have had a taste of all these levels, though we still remain generally entangled at the levels of belief and social contracts. So it is easy to go up or down two or three levels in a very short period of time. But the place you spend most of your time in is "your level" these days.

You know what I am talking about here. You may not spend a lot of time at this level, but you've experienced it when you were trying to sell other people on the virtues of your beliefs. If not, you wouldn't be reading these so-called self-help books. At this level, you acknowledge that you know more than most, you know that doesn't mean much, and you try to sell what you can to make the most of it even though your general opinion of yourself as superior doesn't do much for you anymore, given your knowledge that a superior person and a regular person aren't recognizably different.

The Level of Despair

Here we are, unfortunately, becoming superior to being superior. We are on the cusp of a very high level of consciousness, the next rung on the ladder, known as the "level of Despair." Despair comes from root words in both Latin and Greek that mean "down from hope." We no longer hope. We have no hope. We have nothing to hope for. We are hopeless. We have nothing left to believe in, including our own hardearned beliefs.

We have come to understand that all beliefs, even our beliefs based on our own experience and our beliefs about who we are, are worthless. We get that we are compulsive meaning-making machines who endlessly make meaning out of everything, and it is all a waste. We realize that life is meaningless. This is a very high level of human consciousness. Werner Erhard said, "Until you know that your life is utterly meaningless you don't know anything at all." At this level, you get that the preacher Koeloth in the book of Ecclesiastes in the Old Testament is right when he says, "All is vanity, and a striving after the wind, and there is no profit in it." We are worth exactly nothing. We are not of significant negative value (a popular ego trip), or of significant positive value (all the hype about self-esteem and positive thinking, and all the previous levels of consciousness, and so on). We are of no value. Zero. Nada. Zilch. Nothing.

Now, at this level, we're really getting somewhere. Then it dawns on us that becoming more conscious is not necessarily correlated with becoming happier. There are no guarantees about nothing, and that's not bad grammar and it's not just a pun. Now what?

Well, if we don't run away to lower levels of consciousness as quick as we can (which, of course we do, the first thirty or forty times we reach this level) we get born into the next, very high level of consciousness, known as the "level of Suicidal Panic."

The Level of Suicidal Panic

At this level, we either kill ourselves or we don't. We are desperate for something to believe in. If we don't kill ourselves, we eventually run out of panic. We are at a very high level of consciousness, known as "Suicidal Panic," and then we don't kill ourselves and we are no longer in a panic. That, then, is the next level. But before we name and describe that level, let's focus a bit on what the panic at this level is about. The panic is from not having a single thing to believe in at all, not even despair. We get that not only is our life utterly meaningless, but the fact that our life is utterly meaningless is also utterly meaningless. We can't even get off on being an existentialist philosopher any more! We can't get meaning out of preaching meaninglessness any more! We are left with nothing.

All we have is what the Buddhists call "suchness," the present experience of being, right now, whatever it is, and nothing more. All that is left is just what is in front of us and within us to experience right now. We face the hard Buddhist saying, which is written on the wall of my office: "If you understand, things are as they are. If you do not understand, things are as they are."

The Level of Here and Now

When the panic is gone, we arrive at the next level, which is called the "level of Here and Now." At this level we are present to being present. We are grounded in noticing. We have "lost our minds and come to our senses." If someone else is there, we are present to being present to them. The being we are notices the being in them—the being they are. Our presence to their being salutes their being's presence to us. This is what Kierkegaard was talking about when he said, "When a person relates to another, and relates also to that relationship, they relate thereby to God." Here, at this level, is where love becomes possible. Not a belief in love, but love its own self.

This level is the focus, certainly, of Buddhism and of most spiritual practice and psychotherapy and group process work when the leaders actually know what they are doing.

The level called "Here and Now" has three aspects.

Here and Now but Still Wishing for Something to Believe In

When we first enter the here and now, it has a negative quality. We still wish we had something to believe in and are sorry we don't. We yearn for the former phony security of our belief in meaning beyond the moment. We are present to what is going on in the moment but we wish there was more to expect than just more moments.

Neutral Feeling Here and Now

After a while, we become completely neutral about not having anything to believe in. We are present. We don't feel bad that all we have is this. It's not great. We don't feel good about it; we don't feel bad about it; we are completely neutral.

Positive Feeling Here and Now

Then after a while, we still have no hope and nothing to believe in—nothing but "suchness,"—and that is just fine with us. We begin to feel good about it. There is nothing to believe in, only the present experience of being alive in the moment, which includes everything (all of the past and all we can imagine of the future, including our own death), and that is just fine.

There are actually six levels above this one, but I am only going to describe one more, the next one. If you want to learn about the other levels of consciousness, do our Course in

Honesty or find out from Oscar Ichazo or the Arica training or Gurdjieff or someone else who knows more about the traditional way of teaching this model than I do anyway. My version has been modified based on real-life experiences of my friends and myself for the past twenty-five years.

The Level of Pure Reason

The next level after the "level of Here and Now" is called the "level of Pure Reason." Isn't that something!? We've gone to all this trouble to escape from the jail of alienation our minds create, and the first thing that happens after we get grounded in our experience is we get our minds back! What a difference, though. We now have a mind that is not bound to the defense of our ego. We have this wonderful instrument we worked so hard to grow, and now we can use it! It turns out to be a fantastic instrument for creating! Daydreams become amenable for action! Fantasies become visions! Escapist hopefulness and desperate attempts at reassurance about our self-worth and the entanglement of self-image promotion and maintenance become just possible scenarios to play with. We don't need that mind for our identity anymore! Our identity is the *being* we are, in the here and now! Our identity precedes our mind! We take ownership of our mind and take it out for a test drive! Hoohah!

This is the part where you start to consider the life of the creator. At "Pure Reason" we can think like we have never thought before. We become truly a free thinker. We see the possibility of a lifetime of play and service. As Kris Kristofferson says, "Freedom's just another word for nothin' left to lose."

The experience of living for a while, grounded in your experience of the here and now, leads to thinking about that experience. Sitting in that place, we come to understand things we never understood before. We get that the source of our historical being and the source of our present being is like a generator that has been running reliably ever since it started. Getting back to our source is the first step to transcendence. When we pay attention to the being we are, we withdraw attention from the dilemmas of the mind.

This is at the heart of Buddhism, Yoga, Vedantic philosophy, Christian salvation, and other forms and practices of enlightenment. When a Zen Buddhist sits and looks at a wall fourteen hours a day, seven days in a row, he does it to be able to sit and look at a wall. To be able to sit and look at a wall and just sit and look at a wall is enlightenment. To sit and look at the story of your life like you would sit and look at a wall means you have recontacted your source in the same way as the Buddhist in front of the wall.

Summary

Well, this is what we have to go through once we have a mind, to get back to identifying with our experience in the here and now as who we are. We did this when we were little but we grew out of it. If we can remember, it was a lot of fun. Now we get to do it again, only with better toys and more appreciation of what we've got!

This is our story. All of us.

The poet and artist e. e. cummings, who knew that the source of love is in the here and now, and who was above all else a creator, wrote this poem about our mutual journey. As you read it, pretend that there is a boy named "Anyone" and a girl named "no one." Pretend they met and loved each other and lived for a while and died. Pretend they are both each one of us.

anyone lived in a pretty how town
(with up so floating many bells down)
spring autumn summer winter
he sang his didn't he danced his did.

Women and men (both little and small)
cared for anyone not at all
they sowed their isn't they reaped their same
sun moon stars rain

children guessed (but only a few
and down they forgot as up they grew
autumn winter spring summer)
that noone loved him more by more

when by now and tree by leaf
she laughed his joy she cried his grief
bird by snow and stir by still
anyone's any was all to her

someones married their everyones
laughed their cryings and did their dance
(sleep wake hope and then) they
said their nevers they slept their dream

stars rain sun moon
(and only the snow can begin to explain
how children are apt to forget to remember
with up so floating many bells down)

one day anyone died I guess
(and noone stooped to kiss his face)
busy folk buried them side by side
little by little and was by was

all by all and deep by deep
and more by more they dream their sleep
noone and anyone earth by april
wish by spirit and if by yes.

Women and men (both dong and ding)
summer autumn winter spring
reaped their sowing and went their came
sun moon stars rain[11]

Adults Are Nothing But Large Children Who Have Forgotten How To Play

This chapter title is a quote from the following talk by Tom Robbins, one of the best-loved novelists of our time. Robbins is a tremendously creative author *(Skinny Legs and All[12], Still Life with Woodpecker[13], Another Roadside Attraction[14]*, etc.).

Tom Robbins is a creator. He models what a creator does and how he lives. He is funny, and able to laugh at past and present tragedy and the pretentiousness of belief systems for all the world. He is a model creator who lightens us up before we launch into the hard work of life design and community building. This attitude of play and irreverence for all past tradition is absolutely essential for people who begin to make a life of creating.

He gave this speech to an alternative high school graduating class several years ago. When I asked him for permission to publish it, he responded immediately with a confessional letter, from which the following is excerpted:

"When, back around 1975, I was invited to deliver the commencement address at a small alternative high school in Oak Harbor, Washington, I accepted largely because I was enamored of a young woman connected to the school, and wanted to charm her into my bed. Having to write the speech in a hurry, and searching for a punchy way to begin it, I added to my shame by borrowing—nay, stealing!—the opening paragraph, and the two with which I closed it, from another, now fogotten, source.

"At the time, I was contributing fairly regularly to underground newspapers, and the underground press had a free-exchange policy. Nobody was proprietary and credits counted for very little. Therefore, I felt not a pang of guilt in appropriating three quirky paragraps about life after death from one of the papers, especially since I had no intention of publishing my speech and never expected it to survive the evening that it was delivered.

"Now that it has resurfaced to haunt me (apparently one of the teachers surreptitiously taped the talk and later circulated it), I must apologize to the unknown author whose words I lifted, and say that I'm more than happy to give them back. Please be assured that all of the remainder of the speech was my own original work, and that I never made a dime from it—although I did get laid."

Here is the advice he gave the graduating class:

"I am often asked whether there is life after death. Certainly there is. There is also death after life, and life before death, and death before life. It goes on forever. In fact, you already have.

"As for Heaven and Hell, they are right here on Earth, and it is up to each of you in which one you choose to reside. To put it simply Heaven is living in your hopes and Hell is living in your fears.

"In the traditional image, where hell is down and heaven is up, one escapes from hell by digging a hole in the ceiling. Though in an age of downers and uppers down and up no longer make sense, it is still possible to think of in and out. Think of hell as in and heaven as out. To get out of hell you expend your soul until it is pushing on all the walls from the inside all the way around. If you just maintain a steady pressure, your soul will gradually filter out into limitless heaven beyond.

"One problem with the notion of Heaven and Hell, however, is that, although they are exact opposites, an astonishing number of people seem to be confused about which is which. For example, all over the United States on this very evening, commencement speakers are standing before audiences not greatly unlike yourselves, describing Hell as if they were talking about Heaven.

"Their speakers are saying things such as, "Graduating seniors, you have reached the golden threshold of maturity; it is time now to go out into the world and take up the challenge of life, time to face your hallowed responsibility."

"And if that isn't one Hell of a note, it's certainly one note of Hell.

"When I hear the word "maturity" spoken with such solemn awe, I don't know whether to laugh or get sick. There circulates a common myth that once one becomes an adult, one suddenly and magically gets it altogether and, if I may use the vernacular, discovers, where it's at. Ha ha. The sad funny truth is, adults are nothing but tall children who have forgotten how to play.

"When people tell you to "grow up," they mean approximately the same thing they mean when they tell you to "shut up." By "shut up" they mean "stop talking," by "grow up" they mean "stop growing."

"Because as long as you keep growing, you keep changing— and a person who is changing is unpredictable, impossible to pigeon-hole and difficult to control. The growing person is not an easy target for those guys in the slick suits who want you to turn over your soul to Christ, your heart to America; your butt to Seattle First National Bank and your armpits to new extra crispy Right Guard.

"No, the growing person is not an ideal consumer, which means, in more realistic terms, he or she is not an easy slave. Worse yet, if he or she continues to grow, grows far enough and long enough, he or she may get too close to the universal mysteries, the nature of which the Navy and the Dutch Reform Church do not encourage us to ponder. The growing person is an uncomfortable reminder of the greater human potential that each of us might realize if we had the guts.

"So society wants you to grow up. To reach a safe, predictable plateau and root there. To muzzle your throb, to lower the volume on the singing in your blood. Capers all cut, sky finally larked, surprises known: SETTLE DOWN—settle, like the sand in the bottom of an hour glass, like a coffin six months in the ground. ACT YOUR AGE—which means, act *their* age, and that has, from the moment they stopped growing, always been old.

Growing Up Is a Trap

"As for responsibility, I am forced to ask, "Responsibility to what?" To our fellow humans? Two weeks ago, the newspapers reported that a federal court had ruled that when a person's brain stops functioning, that person is legally dead, even though his or her heart may continue to beat. That means that 80% of the population of the Earth is legally dead. Must we be responsible to corpses?

"No, you have no responsibility except to be yourself to the fullest limit of yourself, and to find out who you are. Or, perhaps I should say, to *remember* who you are. Because deep down in the secret velvet of your heart, far beyond your name and your address, each of you knows who you really are. And that being who is the true you cannot help but behave graciously to all other beings—because it *is* all other beings.

"Yet, we are constantly reminded of our..."responsibility." Responsibility means obey orders without question, don't rock the boat, and for God's sake, get a job. (Get a job. Sha na na na.) That's the scary one. Get a job. It is said as if it were a holy and ancient and inviolable law of nature. But the *fact* is, although cultural humanity has been on Earth for some 2 million years, the very concept of jobs is only about 500 years old. A drop in the bucket, to coin a phrase. And with advent of an electronic cybernetic automated technology, jobs are on the way out again. Jobs were just a flash in the pan, a passing fancy. There is no realistic relationship between jobs and work—work being defined as simply one of the more serious aspects of play any more than there is a realistic relationship between jobs and eating. It is curious how many people believe if it weren't for jobs they couldn't eat. As if it weren't for Boeing their jaws wouldn't chew, if it weren't for the Navy their bowels wouldn't move and if it weren't for Weyerhauser, that great destroyer of plants—plants wouldn't grow. Technocratic assumptions about the identity of humanity, society and nature have warped our experience at its source and obscured the basic natural sense of things. Rabbits don't have jobs. When was the last time you heard of a rabbit starving to death?

"Ah, but we must be responsible, and if we are, then we are rewarded with the white man's legal equivalent of looting: a steady job, secure income, easy credit, free access to all the local emporiums and a home of your own to pile the merchandise in! And so what if there is no magic in your life, no wonder, no amazement, no playfulness, no peace of mind, no sense of unity with the universe, no giggling joy, no burning passion, no deep understanding, no overwhelming love? At least your ego has the satisfaction of knowing you are a responsible citizen. Responsibility is a trap.

"As a matter of fact, the entire System into which you were born and which now, upon completion of high (high?) school you must perhaps face more directly, is a System designed to trap you—and manipulate you as a co-operating slave, a System designed to steep you in Hell.

"Hell is living in your fears, and it is through fear, both subtle and overt, that the System traps you: Fear of failure, fear of social rejection, fear of poverty, fear of punishment, fear of death.

"For example, we once were taught to fear something called Communism, and millions of Americans have gone to sleep each night wondering if Mao Tse Tung is under their bed.

Conversely, on the other side of the world millions of Russians and Chinese have gone to sleep wondering if Henry Kissinger is under their bed. Our Totalitarian government used the hoax of the threat of Communism to control and enslave us, just as the totalitarian communist governments used the hoax and the threat of capitalism to enslave *their* people. It's an extremely old and obviously effective trick.

"You see, the powers behind Communism and the powers behind Capitalism are virtually the same people. We might also include the powers behind the Vatican and the powers behind Islam. Their main function is to mystify the popular mind by creating illusions of omnipotence and omniscience with which to command docility from their subjects, while at the same time creating illusions of health, happiness and fulfillment for their subjects—although it does not require much thorough investigation to discover that few of the peoples of the world are healthy, happy or fulfilled.

"But never mind, there are ways out of the trap, ways, as I earlier suggested, out of Hell.

"The only advice I have for you tonight is not to actively resist or fight the System, because active protest and resistance merely entangles you *in* the System.

"Instead, ignore it, walk away from it, turn your backs on it, laugh at it. Don't be outraged, be outrageous! Never be stupid enough to respect authority unless that authority first proves itself respectable. And, unfortunately, there is no officially sanctioned authority today, from the President of the United States down to the cop on the beat, that has earned the right to your respect.

"So, be your own authority, lead yourselves. Learn the ways and means of the Ancient yogi masters, Pied Piper, cloud walkers, and medicine men. Get in harmony with nature. Listen to the loony rhythms of your blood. Look for beauty and poetry in everything in life. Let there be no moon that does not know you, no spring that does not lick you with its tongues. Refuse to play it safe, for it is from the wavering edge of risk that the sweetest honey of freedom drips. Live dangerously, live lovingly. *Believe in magic.* Nourish your imagination. Use your head, even if it means going out of your mind. Learn, like the lemon and the tomato learned, the laws of the sun. Become aware, like the jungle became aware, of your own perfume. Remember that life is much too serious to take seriously. Remember to never forget how to play.

"In times of doubt and chaos, it has been the duty of superior persons — artists, poets, scientists, clowns, and philosophers (certainly not statesmen or military heroes) — to create order in the psychic vibrations of their fellow beings. But in times such as ours, times that are too carefully ordered, too strictly organized, too expertly managed, thoroughly programmed and carefully planned, times in which too few control too many, it is the duty of all feeling, thinking, humanitarian people to toss their favorite monkey wrenches into the machinery. On second thought, you do have some responsibility to your fellow beings. To relieve the repression of the human spirit, it is your sacred duty to screw things up royally.

"Looking at you tonight, I know you're going to do just fine.

"Let me wrap this up with a few short questions I am often asked.

- Will we be eaten by bugs and worms?
  We ought to be. We have eaten, and we ought to be eaten. This is the Justice, and there is no stopping it. If you have your body burned, starving the earth to glorify a memory, you are asking for trouble.

- Does your soul fly out of your body at the moment you die?
  No, this is a foolish superstition. Your soul is constantly flying out of your body in just the same way that energy is constantly flying out of the sun. At the moment your body dies, the soul stops flying out.

- Is Jesus coming back?
  Yes, all the time. And so are you. All the souls echo forever

throughout the universe. I hope you have a wonderful trip."

Part Two:
Community and Compassion

Getting Over It

Now that we have articulated what a mind is and how it works, and the cultural context in which most of us have grown our minds, and have pictured a model of how one grows beyond the limitations of cultural prejudice that is a natural part of growing up in any culture, we are ready to talk about how we can help each other create a new kind of community of individuals. This next section is critical to individual peace of mind. It is also critical to world peace. It is about how we get attached to belief and then how we transcend belief, and it is not an easy thing to do. This is about saying goodbye to the "home mind" you grew up in and joining a new community of friends who will help you, as you help them, let go of the past.

This section consists of four chapters: Community and Compassion, Radical Honesty about Anger, In Praise of the Old Paradigm and Creating Your Life. These chapters are about openness to the being of other human beings, letting go of anger by experiencing it and getting over it, and letting go of appreciation by experiencing it and getting over it. This letting go of resentment and appreciation for ideas and ideals from the past is the alternative to living in a soap opera created by emotional attachment to beliefs. Instead, you live a life of creating, which is sourced by your compassion.

This coaching about letting go is like going to a funeral. You have a more forgiving and compassionate view of friends once they are dead, you forgive old grudges and appreciate them more for how they lived, and you review your life with them from a new perspective. In fact, you look at your own future life with that same new perspective.

This funeral turns out to be your own, and the more compassionate view you evolve is for yourself. As at a funeral, the friends who console you and whom you console are ready to celebrate what life you have left together, and to appreciate each other more until you die. We all get motivated at funerals to love and live life together in gratitude and with a will to help each other have a good life until we die.

Chapter Eight

Community and Compassion

In his book *Eimi* (Greek for "I am"), e. e. cummings reports an argument he had in 1931 with a Russian dramatist, a true believer in the communism du jour. This is the conversation that was relayed through an interpreter. He was proposing a toast.

Cummings: "Tell him I drink...to the individual."

A pause.

Dramatist:"He says that's nonsense."

Cummings: "Tell him I love nonsense and I drink to nonsense."

Pause.

Dramatist:"He's very angry. He says you are afraid."

Cummings: "Tell him I'm afraid to be afraid. Tell him a madman named noone says, that someone is and anyone isn't; and *all the believing universe cannot transform anyone who isn't into someone who is.*"

Once we have ceased to identify ourselves with our stories and consider ourselves to be only *the being who notices in the moment,* who has stories but is not attached to them, we need a community of other people who have achieved that same psychological accomplishment. Without the support of other people who have rediscovered their true identities as *beings who think* rather than thinkers who be, we will easily fall back into our old acculturated identity and thought patterns. As we engage in noticing and sharing what we notice, we find ourselves reaching out more to each other and creating a community. Then, we find ourselves creating *together* as a community.

Out of this experience of community, we then become a force that can re-form the institutions of our society. We learn from experience that service to others is enlightened self-interest. We don't live in isolation; we live in community, and we begin to see that unless we support the development of a new paradigm that allows for a shift in primary values from "I think, therefore I am" to "I am, therefore I think," this lemming race is headed for the cliff.

Compassion

Both e. e. cummings, whose poem, *anyone lived in a pretty how town,* concluded Chapter 7, and Tom Robbins, whose talk to a high school graduating class made up most of Chapter 8, were born and raised in America. They are both independent individuals. Although he was not appreciated by some of his contemporaries, e. e. cummings is one of the greatest poets of all time. His transcendent perspective on human life, which reflects the level called "pure reason" in the Sufi levels of consciousness, allows us to begin to understand the groundlessness of mind and the groundedness in being. The life of the artist is a life of grounding in experience and transcendence of the mind.

Tom Robbins is a creative genius and a brilliant writer. When he thought seriously about what to say to people finishing high school, his recommendations were to not sell out to the rat race, and to throw a monkey wrench in the works whenever possible. That was the best, most honest advice he could give. Artists tend to leave the rat race. This raises some interesting questions, "Why do so many people join and stay in the rat race? Why does the rat race continue?"

We know that being a wage slave, for most people, is not all that good. We have all seen how people who stay stuck there, tolerating it while their life recedes to the background, are not all that happy or even secure. We know that the people at the top, by and large, do want more and more money and have often developed the capacity to not give a damn about people unless it affects the bottom line. Everyone who is not rich and doesn't stay ignorant is coming to know this, and everyone who *is* rich already knows that "security" provided by money is not the answer.

However, even brilliant insights about who is wrong and who is right are limiting. What we know limits our ability to perceive. It is the things that we are most sure of, and are righteous about, that limit our ability to notice. Ram Dass said he has a particularly gross picture of Ed Meese and George Bush and Ronald Reagan laughing (and, I imagine, looking especially greasy, drunk, and smug) at a meeting in the White House. He keeps this picture on his little puja table where he meditates, along with the picture of his guru — so he can work on compassion. He actually works at being able to love and appreciate them for who they are.

If we attempt, from a compassionate perspective, to figure out why people stay in the rat race, some things become clear that are less blameful. People are in the rat race to get money to improve the quality of their lives. Well, money can actually help improve the quality of life. We all know this; we've seen it happen to our friends and us; we see it in advertisements on television all the time. You can have more fun and therefore a better life with more money. The tastes and temptations we see on TV make us hungry for a higher quality of life all the time.

Crane Britton said, in *The Anatomy of a Revolution*[15], that revolutions occur, not when the peasants are maximally oppressed consistently, but shortly after a generation is allowed slight improvements. Revolutions occur when things have gotten just noticeably better. Using a number of revolutions in several countries he pointed out that for several hundred years, generation after generation of serfs served without complaint, but the generation after they got wooden floors, they revolted. When poor folks get a taste of possibility, they want more and they become dangerous to the establishment. In our day, the establishment has become good at continuing to give us hope of improvement and a rate of improvement that is just enough to keep a revolution from occurring. To a certain degree, this does appear to be done with conscious intention through opinion sampling, market research, PR, spin doctoring, poll taking, advertising, and attempts to influence the media. It has almost worked.

The revolution against the rat race, however, has been greatly assisted by one of the toys we were given to keep the money machine going, the personal computer. The Internet is our wooden floor and they are going to have one hell of a time keeping us docile and drugged and under control and thought-policed from now on.

This revolution now occurring, called the revolution of consciousness, is sometimes called a spiritual revolution. At the heart of this revolution is the growing wisdom that we are all focusing on systematically participating in improving our lives materially, and that is this very thing that makes us able to be manipulated by the controllers of the so-called "market economy." (No one even calls it a "free" market economy anymore because it isn't.) It also makes us more and more aware of the fact that we ourselves are under control by an unfair world economy, and that we are like the prisoners of war in the movie *The Bridge Over the River Kwai*. In the movie, some of the prisoners who built the bridge that allowed their captors to advance the war and stay in power, became unwilling to blow up the bridge because of their pride in the bridge they had built. We actually take pride in our efforts to improve the quality of our lives in the rat race by increasing our comfort and our toys, while at the same time keeping the enemy in power and uncountable numbers of other people under their economic control, doomed to lives of malnourishment and inadequate shelter without education and health care, even though the benefits to us of the maintenance of such a system are really quite limited.

Like prisoners of war who together have built our own prison camp, we take pride in what we have built together to survive under the circumstances of imprisonment in the mind, in belief systems that are more advantageous to the limited few than to us and most of the rest of humanity. We are beginning to catch on to the conspiracy most of us are involved in, to take pride in being promoted from "field slave" to "house slave" on the old plantation, while ignoring the issue of economic slavery itself. We are learning that what is really important to the actual quality of our lives is not more stuff; it's more awareness.

We all want the quality of our lives improved because we are constantly exposed to the possibility of improving our lives by watching television, while the quality of our lives is constantly diminished by the amount of time we spend striving and trying to accomplish living in the fantasies modeled for us on television. We do this and it is fun, and when it becomes an addiction it takes away from being present to our experience of being here in the real world while we are here. The quality of our lives is diminished through the schooling we have received and the ongoing adult education programs via television and the media we are constantly exposed to. For many of us the maintenance and upkeep of the semblances of reality become more important than the enjoyment of the experience of reality itself. We try to eat the menu instead of the meal.

We have also incorporated into our own minds, from our upbringing, a constant refrain: "How'm I doin'?" "Am I doin' good enough?" "How'm I doin'?" Our lives are diminished by our own minds imposing some kind of standard or concept or value or idea of how things "ought" to be, or what we "deserve" compared to what we have. We have learned from our education and culture what we should expect and we obediently do so with a vengeance. We impose some picture of how it ought to be on everything we almost experience, thereby blocking the experience. This occurs regardless of the culture people live in, but it is particularly prevalent in this information bombardment culture we are currently living in. All the lonely people, all the desperate people, all the greedy people, all the hungry people, the rich people, the poor people, and most of all the phony people, are sufferers at their own hands, or rather at their own minds.

Some of us now know what the rest of us desperately need to know: *our minds are not to be trusted.* Our minds themselves are merely model makers. As a species of beings, we are model makers, at once unawares and wary. Models are dangerous. They sometimes suffocate their builder. People become lost in belief and never return. Models of the mind cut us off from the nourishment of commonplace experience.

The key to the revolution is to become a conscious maker of models, and thereby transcend the constraint of any single model. This allows for a life of constant creation, which is the best increase in quality of life a person could dream up, but it is tough on the establishment. We can learn to laugh at the beliefs we have been taking too seriously. As we can understand the inside joke of meditators ("Hey! I'm meditating!......wasn't I!"), we can catch ourselves in the very act of moving from experience to category, thereby not being fooled by categories anymore.

Improving the Quality of Life

The secret to improving the quality of life is to learn how you are diminishing the quality of your life with the models you are using, by attempting to force reality to live up to these models, and then to stop doing that. After you identify with your perceiving-witnessing-being-in-your-body as who you fundamentally are, and knowing that your mind is something you own, rather than who you are, you can have even more fun using the mind that once diminished your life. You can use it then to make models to create and play with, and play for the rest of your days. What I have to say, and the practices I teach to help people distinguish between *noticing* and *thinking, are* of vital interest and vital importance to the whole world, regardless of culture and regardless of socioeconomic level.

These ideas are not in any way exclusive. They are clearly not exclusively my own. They belong to all of us and we are lucky to be alive in a time in which the possibility of the over-throw of all sovereigns and the acknowledgment of the sover-eignty of being is, for the first time in history, actually possible.

The sovereignty of the individual is the last step in the chain of history in which, for thousands of years, rulers were sover-eign for life. After that representative government came into being, and elected representatives were sovereign for limited terms. Now we are coming into the age when individuals can be sovereign. Following the vision of the brilliant former senator from Alaska, Mike Gravel, we can eventually arrange for elect-ed representatives primarily to carry out the will of the people expressed in frequent referenda, something we could do right now, using television, the Internet, and 800 numbers.

The individual being who is in charge of her mind is a sov-ereign being because no mind can control her, including her own. All minds serve being or this being doesn't play. An inte-grated individual has integrity of mind and being. An integrat-ed individual is led by noticing and can no longer be manipulated.

The Work of Stanley Milgram

I first heard about a social psychologist named Stanley Milgram when he presented a review of his research at Yale University during a meeting of the American Psychological Association in Chicago in 1965. Milgram was given an award by one branch of the Association while being censured by another branch on the same day, for the same research. Here is how he got praised and in trouble.

Milgram had, several years earlier, read a book by Hannah Arendt about the trial of Adolf Eichmann, Hitler's infamous sec-ond-in-command, who had been responsible for overseeing most of the executions of six million Jews and other people judged unacceptable by the Third Reich. Hannah Arendt, who had covered the war crimes trial for several American newspapers, pointed out that Eichmann's defense was that he should not be held personally responsible for a crime against mankind because he was doing his duty in the social system of which he was a part. His lawyers said that a court might judge that the social system was criminal, but not the person doing his duty within that social system. This argument was rejected. Eichmann's adjudicators concluded that he was *individually* responsible for the crimes he committed, regardless of the social system of which he was a part, and he was executed.

Hannah Arendt then raised another question, which fascinated Stanley Milgram. Was Adolf Eichmann some unusual social deviant, some sadistic exception to common humanity, or was he just a bureaucrat? Arendt had pointed out that only twice in his entire career had he actually witnessed any executions, which, he said, he found "repugnant." What he actually did was shuffle papers in an office and make phone calls and give orders. Outside of work, he seemed to have a normal life with family and friends and associates. Was he normal?

Milgram designed an experiment to see if he could somewhat simulate the conditions in which Eichmann operated. He drew a random stratified sample of males from the community around Yale. (In later versions of the original study he included females, and found no significant differences between males and females in the results of the experiment.) He paid each subject, in advance, seven dollars for participating in an experiment that he told them was "a study of the effects of negative reinforcement on learning."

When Milgram met his subjects, he used a room in a building on the campus of Yale University. Milgram wore a white lab coat and introduced himself as Dr. Milgram. There were three people in the room: Milgram and two subjects, both of whom were apparently drawn from the sample of subjects. Only one of them, however, was a true subject—the second was a stooge, a student actor from the drama department. Milgram said to them, "I am conducting a study of the effects of negative reinforcement on learning. In this study, one of you will be the teacher and one will be the learner. I will flip a coin to see which is which." The coin flip was rigged, so that the true subject from the sample was always the "teacher."

After the coin flip, Milgram led both subjects into a room containing a very large and impressive electric chair, and proceeded to strap the learner (the stooge) into the chair and apply electrodes to his wrists and head. In later versions of the experiment (the experiment was run several times with several groups of subjects before being written up in journals and reported to the American Psychological Association) Dr. Milgram mentioned in passing that the electrode paste was "to keep the flesh from being burnt," and the learner/stooge mentioned in passing that he had a "slight heart condition."

Then the "teacher" (who was the true subject) was led to a room with a one-way mirror so that he could see the person in the electric chair but the person could not see him. He was seated in front of a panel of thirty switches, which were labeled clearly in 15-volt increments from 15 volts to 450 volts. Above the switches were verbal labels in gradations of degree: "shock," "dangerous shock," "severely dangerous shock," and two steps before the last switch was an ambiguous but ominous "XXXX." Milgram said, "I am going to project a list of words on the wall in front of the person in the chair. He will be given several repetitions of the word list to learn it. When he sees a word appear on the wall, his task will be to name the next word from the list before it is projected, based on having memorized the list. If he makes a mistake, I want you to administer an electric shock, and I would like you to increase the voltage of this shock in fifteen-volt increments. Do you understand the instructions?" When the "teacher" fully understood the instructions, the experiment began.

The stooge in the chair was only receiving a mild cue shock every time a switch was thrown, but the "teacher" didn't know that. As the "learner" made mistakes and was shocked, he reacted more and more dramatically. At first he just jumped a little. As the shocks progressed he began jumping and yelling out. Then he started screaming when he was shocked. Then he began screaming and saying he wanted to stop. Then he said, "Stop this! I want out! Whoever is doing this stop! I want to quit!" Then as the voltage got closer to the end, two steps before the end, the "learner" screamed, convulsed, and collapsed completely. When the next word appeared and there was no response, Milgram said, "We'll have to count that an error; shock him again." Then one more time, no response, "That's an error; shock him again." In order to get to the end of the row of switches the teacher had to shock the learner two more times while he was apparently completely "unconscious."

Prior to actually conducting the study, Milgram had given a questionnaire to a similar random stratified sample of people from the community around Yale in which he asked if the respondents "would ever purposely inflict pain on a fellow human being, regardless of the social circumstances." Over ninety-two percent said that they would not. When he actually ran the experiment, *sixty-eight percent of the people went all the way to the top.* The "teachers" sweated excessively; some cried; some went into hysterical laughter. Many, even though debriefed and told that it was an act, reported when interviewed two weeks later that they had nightmares about what they had done. The subjects obviously had a very hard time doing what they did, but nevertheless did it. They resisted, they felt bad about it, they felt guilty, but they did what they were told. Milgram had written down, in advance, four statements he could make in response to objections on the part of the "teacher" — the strongest one being: "The experiment must go on."

Later, Milgram pointed out that this experiment was not really fair to Adolf Eichmann because Eichmann had many colleagues who cooperated in his bureaucracy. So Milgram modified his experiment by adding one more stooge, who was a person in the room with the teacher who pulled down a master switch to "turn on the electricity" each time an error was made. When the responsibility or blame could be shared with just one other person in this way, *ninety-two percent of the subjects went all the way to the top.*

Milgram's presentation was called "A Study in the Legitimation of Evil" and he concluded about the people in his sample, and by generalization, the people in the culture from which his sample had come: "People will generally go against their own individual moral inclinations in order to cooperate with authority."

No sub-group in the sample differed in a statistically significant way from the norm of the whole population. Women did not differ from men, and groupings by ethnic origin, religious orientation, age, and so on were not significantly different. One group approached statistical significance — Catholics — and that difference was in the direction of more cooperation with authority rather than less.

One of the things I like about this study is that none of us knows how we would have fared. We would all like to think that we would have been in the eight percent who said that they would not go on. But obviously, not all of us could have been in the eight percent. There were some few subjects who not only quit but proceeded to go talk to the provost at Yale and to Milgram demanding that he stop. We would all like to think we would have been one of them. Most of us would have cooperated and felt bad about it, but cooperated nevertheless.

I have been fascinated with this work for thirty-two years. I used to report on Milgram's work in speeches I made against the war in Vietnam. Much of my work as a group leader and psychotherapist has been an attempt to discover and reinforce the kind of independent individuality that might allow for those statistics to change.

I think, to demonstrate independence in the circumstance of that experiment, it was necessary for individuals to be able to act according to their compassion—their identification as one being to another with the person in the electric chair. Their compassion made them "feel bad" about what they did, but it was not enough to overrule their training in obedience to authority. Their compassion would have to have been stronger than their need to obey the professor from Yale in the white lab coat. Their sense of individual responsibility and the courage to act upon it would have to be stronger than their years of training from school and church and family to acquiesce to authority. The integrity of their own feelings would have had to be more powerful in determining their actions than their moral obligation to not challenge the constituted authority or rock the boat of the existing power structure.

Eichmann was just an average guy. Average guys are just Eichmanns. So are average gals. Most of us would obey Hitler like most did in Nazi Germany. Most of us still are obeying some questionably constituted authority instead of acting on our own authority most of the time. Most of us have lined up to go to recess and lined up to come back into the classroom and lined up to go to lunch and lined up to come back from lunch and sat in rows and not talked and waited in lines and behaved and waited for the bell to ring and are still doing that. Most of us operate from models of what we should and should not do rather than what we feel, what we prefer, what we feel called forth to do based on our empathetic connections with other human beings. And for the most part, we have organized our world to keep it that way. As the Sufis say, ninety-eight per cent of humanity spends ninety-eight per cent of their time at the level of belief.

Honoring Being

Use your own imagination; don't you think it very likely that society would be quite different if organized around values that honor being more than obedience to authority? What changes might occur in how we operate together if we had a world organized around honoring the being of others rather than mere order? What if we valued child rearing more than contracts, for example? We might set a maximum of $10 an hour for lawyers because legal work is not all that important, and a minimum of $300 an hour for child care workers because encouraging children to remain more in touch with *being* by being loved and honored by another bigger *being* is so much more important than the work of lawyers. Child care workers and parents and teachers, who are more in touch with children because of their love of the being of young beings, would be getting lawyers' fees, and lawyers would generally be getting the minimum wage. The world would be quite a different place if we valued compassion more than obedience and order, and we put our money where our values were.

Suffering is Attachment to Belief

Suffering comes from attachment to beliefs to such a degree that the person is trying to convince himself and others that the beliefs are reality. What is true about all the successful but miserable people I have worked with for years who are functional in a sick system—depression, anxiety, stress—is true on the macrocosmic level for whole groups of people. Whole societies suffer in the same way and for the same reasons individuals within them suffer.

Learning the distinction between belief and experiential reality relieves suffering for individuals and societies. This distinction is now becoming a part of the public dialogue between all the peoples of the world. This distinction is the wooden floor that lets the peasants know a better life is possible. This is the source of the revolution of consciousness.

This is what radical honesty is about. When enough of us have shared honestly, we discover/invent the possibility of valuing our own minds as instruments of creation rather than do-loops of self-worship or sacred institutional maintenance.

That is a revolutionary idea. That terrifies the established mind, as well as the establishment.

The practical implications of this view for *organizations* is, as all current leading edge management consultation firms are saying, that nothing lasts as long as it used to. All modern corporations are now discovering that running a corporation requires frequent restructuring. Frequent restructuring requires frequent re-noticing, and skills developed in noticing by employees at all levels benefit everyone and tremendously affect the bottom line. Personal development of skills in noticing for employees at all levels is more important even than their belief in or adherence to the corporate culture. Corporations are one form of human organization. Human organizations thrive when the humans in them thrive. *Work and The Human Spirit*[16] by John Scherer and all of the works of Will Schutz and the books by Tom Peters and many others deal with the fundamental elements of radical honesty as it pertains to corporate life. What businesses of all sizes must now adopt as fundamental learning, with regard to management, is that all models are relative and temporary, and that all the relative and temporary models in the world are less important than *skills in noticing and grounding in experience* by every employee.

The relevance of these ideas to *educational institutions* is that schools, as we have known them from kindergarten through the Ph.D. level, are now obsolete. Learning is now more valuable than schooling. Your skills for learning and in continuing to learn with enthusiasm, are based on being grounded in your experience, rather than in forcing yourself on with beliefs in perfectionism. Support of home schooling and individualized instruction is where the future lies. I have a whole lot more to say about this in the next book I am writing, *Radical Parenting,* but that's all I'm saying here.

The practical implications for *psychotherapy* are outlined in *Radical Honesty* and are currently making it a best seller that is published in seven languages. I speak about these ideas and their implications to individuals, college and university groups, national organizations, corporations, businesses, associations, organizational management groups, futurists, and religious institutions. Everyone already seems to understand about the relativity of models, but not to have thought deeply about the implications for their own personally held beliefs. We need to support each other in taking this very personally.

I learned from clients in my psychotherapy practice that lying is the *primary* source of most anxiety and most depression. Lying is also the root cause of most psychosomatic disorders. Often, when our decisions are dictated by our obligations and beliefs rather than by our preferences, we live strapped to our pasts and hopeful about our futures; the kind of hopefulness that attempts to put a good face on despair—yet another pretense. The stress of constantly pretending and avoiding being found out, and the wear and tear of perennially inauthentic relationships is an ongoing source of misery, conflict, ill health, and death.

Then we discovered that radical honesty is the necessary first step to escaping the jail of pretense. When I mustered the courage to tell the truth I discovered, along with my friends and clients, that things didn't turn out as bad as our minds had predicted. So we started doing more of it. After we got good, through practice, at living out loud and letting the chips fall where they may, we then had the freedom to create what we wanted in our lives according to our own preferences, as *individuals together in community*, rather than our imagined role requirements and obligations. Living this way is so much fun, we just had to invite other people into it. So we started some workshops, I wrote a book about it, and now I'm writing another one based on what we have learned from the workshops.

The mission of the workshops and of this book is to train and support individuals to tell and hear the truth and to be powerful creators of their lives. The transition from victim to creator of life as an artist is the focus of this work and it turns out a whole lot of people are interested in that. When I wrote *Radical Honesty*, I found thousands of friends who resonated with these ideas about freedom. In the first book, I said that telling the truth was not for any high moral purpose; it is merely for practical purposes of fundamentally interrupting the mind. I said:

- "Nothing interrupts the mind like telling the truth."

- "We are each individually responsible for cutting ourselves off from the nourishment of commonplace experience by substituting our interpretations of reality for reality."

- "A mind is a terrible thing. Waste it."

- "Telling the truth, after hiding out for a long time, reopens old wounds that didn't heal properly. It often hurts a lot. It takes guts. It isn't easy. It is better than the alternative."

- "People believe immeasurable loads of crap for the illusion of security. We believe security comes from principles and from controlling ourselves and other people. But security doesn't exist. The only security we have is in our ability to fly by the seat of our pants."

- "I believe that fascination with the game of creation is sufficient; that, in fact, it's the only game in town."

One thing led to another, and now all my friends and I see ourselves caught up in the extremely exciting revolution of consciousness. Now at the dawn of the twenty-first century, we are all discovering together that, no matter where we live or what we believe, when we are driven by our obligations—all the things we "should" do—our obligations expand and our lives speed up, and our minds take over our lives, draining us rather than inspiring us. We are increasingly participating in a conversation about the possibility of living our lives according to our preferences, not our "shoulds," the possibility of being an artist creating a vibrant life, rather than a victim. We who know this are becoming a movement.

The key to the success of our movement is transcending that sense of obligation to live up to culturally ingrained expectations that is the source of all anger. Being mad and getting over it is critical to the ability to create a new community based on noticing and compassion.

The ability to do this not only ends wars, it starts peace. So it turns out, the key to individuality, integrity, and individual freedom has something to do with forgiveness, which involves getting over anger. That is done in the public domain, in community, and it is the focus of the next chapter and it is the pathway to freedom for individuals and the key to free societies. *It is the way the statistics from Stanley Milgram's experiments get changed.* Learning forgiveness, as an individual skill, by practicing getting over anger in the context of a community of friends, is an absolutely necessary prerequisite to creating a world that works for everyone. To be an individual who operates independently of authority and according to compassion, you need to learn the fundamental skills of getting mad and getting over it. What comes next is hard work and scary. It is also the work that frees you to be an individual.

Radical Honesty About Anger

The main thing that keeps us attached to beliefs at lower levels of consciousness is our inability to forgive—which is our inability to get over *belief* about how things *should* or *shouldn't* be—which is the source of anger. So let's learn about anger.

If cultural transcendence is necessary to contact reality, and culture resides in the minds of individuals, and other participants in the culture disagree with any change because of attachment to the cultural values they have learned, both *internal* and *external* conflict are inevitable. This means anger is inevitable. Anger cannot be avoided; it has to be gone through and gotten over. Getting over being mad, or finding the capacity for forgiveness, is absolutely necessary for both individual personal growth and cultural change. So one of the most critical questions to be answered for any person willing to grow beyond their cultural provincialism is: How do you get over being mad?

Not Catharsis, Just Full Disclosure

Radical honesty is a powerful process by which people can make corrections in the mind's distorted and only partly conscious map of the world. By sharing secret memories, thoughts, and models—by putting into the public domain among friends what had been hidden and defended—we have a chance to break free of the paradigm of limiting beliefs that we developed in the past. These are the beliefs to which we are emotionally attached; the ones our minds defend as though we ourselves are threatened. The paradigms that allowed us to survive as children within the family and within the culture must be transcended so we can thrive as adults. We do not give up attachments without a lot of practice. Central to that practice is the process of getting mad and getting over it.

There is great freedom in releasing the heavy load of pretense — and the uniquely distorted view of life made necessary by the vicissitudes of how we were raised. Not only is there freedom, but space is created for true intimacy with current friends and lovers, through forgiveness of begrudged caregivers from the past. To do that, we have to get mad at them and get over it by going through it with them, if they are alive, or with the assistance of a skillful therapist or trainer if they are dead.

Getting free of the tyranny of the human mind is the first step in the process of becoming a creator. Creators change cultures and families from dysfunctional to functional.

This chapter focuses on honesty about anger because it is the linchpin to learning to be free from domination by the mind. Freedom from domination by the mind for individuals and then families and then small communities and then larger communities is the key to creating a new functional culture. Developing skill in detachment through learning how to get over anger that comes from attachment and consequently loosening the attachment is as critical to social change as it is to personal growth.

Getting Over Being Mad

There is a specific technology for getting over being mad. Getting over being mad is called forgiveness. It is not easy to do. Essentially *you have to get mad in the presence of the person you are mad at, be present to your experience in your body while being mad, be specific and not abstract about what you are mad about, and stay in touch with the experience and the person and the conversation until you are not mad anymore.*

Our minds, as well as a lot of experts, tell us to avoid this at all cost. Most of us, most of the time, would rather just stay mad and think about it and invent categories full of negative judgment for the rotten jerks who made us mad and look for further proof that we are right and they are wrong. It's more fun and it's easier to do.

Unfortunately, the "easy" way is the one most damaging to ourselves and others and it doesn't work. The only way to get over the depression and anxiety and fury and physical illness caused by this way of avoidance is to get a prescription from psychiatrists or other physicians for drugs that help you avoid feelings. The drug companies are always there to serve, with lots of variety and plenty of support and lots of good advice and tons of alternative "mother's little helpers." If that doesn't work, illegal painkillers of various kinds are easily obtained. The old paradigm is powerful in keeping itself in charge and the opiates for the people are plentiful.

Furthermore, there is lots of advice by experts who will be concerned for your welfare and willing to fix your upset with many congenial old paradigm explanations and things you can do to avoid dealing with your anger. You have heard of or tried many of these ways, I am sure. But let me just review a few of the phony solutions to anger.

If anyone has ever told you that you can forgive someone by just deciding to forgive them, that person was wrong. If you believe you can forgive someone by just deciding to, you're sadly mistaken and you have fooled yourself out of getting over your anger. If you think you can forgive someone you are mad at by praying, thinking, writing letters and sending them, writing letters and not sending them, doing "therapy," talking to someone else about it, "acting out" in a protective environment, beating pillows, shouting at other folks, becoming "spiritual" or "attaining enlightenment" or any of the other methods of avoidance of face-to-face forgiveness that millions of minds have derived as a way to avoid the work of forgiveness and the experience of forgiveness, you are likewise, like all of them, still delusional and still angry.

Seriously, the way you get over being so serious about what you are angry about is to face it and face the person you are mad at if they are still on this earth and work through it until it gets funny. If the person is dead, there are other ways to forgive them without digging them up, but those ways don't work if you are engaged in a conspiracy with your therapist to avoid contact and honest sharing of your anger with the living people you are mad at.

Being Specific and Getting Face-to-Face About Resentments

We have been taught all our lives to abstract from our experience to be able to take control of the experience. This absolutely does not work when you are mad. When you abstract from your experience when you are mad, you displace your anger by redirecting it to the emotional support of an idea that makes you right and the other person wrong. If you want to get over being mad, you have to come back down from the principle, to the experience of being mad—away from the general principle and in the direction of the specific events that preceded the abstraction. You have to say to the person's face, what the person did or *said* that made you mad. Forget about explaining why. You don't know why, anyway. Drop the explanation. Just resent them for what they did and don't justify anything. You are petty. We all are. You are crazy. We all are. Go ahead and be petty and crazy and do it out loud and magnify the experience.

Getting through the experience of anger by getting into the experience of anger is accomplished by contacting the other person, while simultaneously being aware of your own experience in the body at the moment of speaking the resentment. Staying present with the person you resent and to the sensations in your body that you associate with resentment, while being completely willing to experience the resentment and communicating it "contactfully" to the person being resented, results in the resentment going away. You use the phrase, "I resent you for..." and name the specific behavior committed or words said (and perhaps tone of voice used) by the person, while looking the person in the eye and *speaking directly to them in a voice with pitch and volume appropriate to the degree of resentment*. In this moment, you are describing something simple that occurred that both of you can remember (rather than an abstract interpretation of right or wrong or good or evil). This allows you to stay focused on your sensate experience rather than paying attention to your own explanation. Your explanation is just your mind's paranoid way of trying to ensure its survival.

As satisfying as righteousness is, we have to give it up. We might have to play it up in the process of giving it up. So if you want to go on a righteous tirade, go on it, but don't quit there. Keep going until you get specific about exactly what got you so damned mad. We have to do this to get to where we can play with each other again. We do this to get over taking our violated expectations too seriously. We do this to be more powerful in creating together a life of play and service for each other. Get mad and get over it. Forgive and go on and create. This process is critical to transcendence of belief. The chapter entitled How To Deal With Anger from *Radical Honesty* describes in detail the methodology of forgiveness. Please read that chapter, or order the audiotape, or do a workshop with us for more detailed coaching on how to go through anger to forgiveness.

Guidelines for Expressing Anger

Just in case you decide to grow beyond being normal, here are some guidelines for you to follow in expressing anger. Reading these guidelines will do you some good only if you are willing to experiment with this approach and see what will happen. This approach may not "make sense" to you. It works experientially. That is, if you try it to see what *it feels like*, you may get the experience of forgiving the person you were mad at.

You may have to experiment with it several times before you get used to the process. It does work, even though it may not make sense. Forgiveness works in the realm of feeling, and the mind, as usual, lags behind and catches up later.

These guidelines are not moral rules to be memorized and obeyed. They are strategies. The purpose of these guidelines is to direct your attention to the process of learning how to express yourself in the moment so that something happens to actual feelings in your body at the level of sensation. Something will happen because of your willingness to pay attention to your experience. These guidelines will make you aware of your moment-to-moment experience of anger or of appreciation. They are to help you be able to discover something about the process of expression itself.

You can use these strategies and they still won't work if you are only attending to the rules and not to your experience. The point is to be aware of your experience while experimenting, not to figure out whether you are "good" at following the rules. Your goal is to be willing and able to acknowledge to yourself, and to report to the person with whom you are speaking, each new experience as it emerges, whether or not it is comfortable. If you refuse to quit, and keep talking to the person you're interacting with until you *feel* complete, you will eventually be complete with him. You'll have no more withheld resentments or appreciations, and you'll be able to experience him newly, as he is, in that moment.

Love is when you let someone be the way she is. When you let up on your judgments of someone, there is a free space in which forgiveness and love occur. Here are the guidelines:

- *Whenever possible, talk face-to-face to the person with whom you are angry.* It is impossible to do any of this work over the phone. The quality of the interaction is different. You need to look each other in the eye and react to each other moment-to-moment. Over the phone, your contact with the other person is much too limited and you are relating to your concept of him, not to your experience of him as he is. You will miss many of his nonverbal responses. Take the time to see him in person. If he is a long distance away, a phone call is better than nothing, because it can start the process of experiencing the feelings. But don't engage in long conversations on the telephone. To do so is usually a waste of time that increases judgments and displaces feeling. This is the reverse of what is needed when you're mad.

- *Start your sentences as often as possible with the words, "I resent you for..." or "I appreciate you for...".* The structure of a sentence that starts with those words ensures that the anger or appreciation is personal; that there is an "I" and a "thou." "I resent you" has a much stronger and more personal impact than "I resent the fact that...". In the latter statement you are saying that you are angry at some "fact." The slight difference in the wording may seem insignificant to you; it is not. Most people resist saying, "I resent you for..." because they don't want to get "personal." They are uncomfortable when they are directly expressing their resentment to someone.

While you will feel more comfortable being less direct and saying, "I resent it when...", that approach won't work. You won't be able to completely experience your resentment and have it disappear unless you are willing to tell the truth. You resent people, not facts or vague "its." Substituting something milder for the word "resent" is another approach that doesn't work. "I am annoyed at you for..." and "I am angry with you about..." are introductions to a story about *anger*. Those phrases deal more with a general description of a state of being than with the *active* expression of anger. The sentence that begins "I resent you" is different, because it is active and transitive, identifying something you are feeling toward another person, in the present moment of speaking, while the person is there. If doing this makes you uncomfortable, fine. If you expect to handle your resentment without discomfort, given how you were raised, you can forget it. Make yourself uncomfortable on purpose. Acting according to what feels comfortable when you are attempting to get over anger is a mistake. It's like drinking Pepto-Bismol to keep from vomiting, staying sick for three hours, and then puking your guts up anyway.

A lot of people are also uncomfortable expressing direct appreciation and have as much difficulty admitting warmth as anger. Appreciations often emerge right in the middle of expressing resentment. Appreciations are to be handled in the same way and gotten over in the same way. Trying to hold on to appreciations works just as poorly as trying to avoid resentment. New appreciation for a person can only emerge in a clearing created by completing the experience of past appreciations and resentments.

- *Speak in the present tense.* Just because you are talking about something he did in the past, don't say, "I resented you." You still resent that person, right now, for what he did or said in the past, so state the feeling in the present tense. In the past tense, resentments are only descriptions or stories about what happened or how you were. They won't change the nature of your relationship — of how you are now. When resentments are stated in the present tense, you get the chance to feel angry again and to experience the anger. When you can experience the feeling, it disappears. As I have said over and over, when you avoid the experience of anger, it persists in the form of apparently reasonable thoughts. The thoughts are poisonous and not constructive. They are destructive, because they distance you from the other person. They allow you to avoid contact with the other person and contact with your experience in your body, and to maintain your righteousness, rather than express the anger and get off your pose.

- *Eventually, get specific.* Even though you can't always identi-fy the particulars, you probably resent the person for what he specifically did or said. For example, if you say to some-one, "I resent you for being a snob," or "I resent you for act-ing snobbish toward me," he won't be clear about what you resent—although he may imagine he understands. He'll probably just say, "I'm not a snob." You haven't told him what he actually did or said that you resented—what led you to the conclusion that he was snobbish. You are demanding that the person "buy in" to your judgment of him. You might begin by expressing a judgment, but you must eventually get specific. If you haven't gotten down to the specifics, you aren't finished. Look closer into what the person actually did that made you conclude that he was snobbish, and say that. In this example, the real resentment might be expressed by, "I resent you for turning your head and not answering me when I said 'Hi' to you at the grocery store." Or, "I resent you for saying, 'Only hicks like country music' the other day."

- *Don't stop with general descriptions of behavior or general judg-ments.* When you throw in the words "always" or "never," the person won't get what you're talking about and you won't get over the resentment. He doesn't have to get it. It isn't true. He hears only that you're trying to make him wrong. "I resent you for constantly complaining," isn't spe-cific. Report the specific incident(s) that you remember: "I resent you for saying I bought the wrong groceries last Thursday, and I resent you for saying, 'I *guess* I'll *have* to buy groceries' yesterday." Similarly, "I resent you for never appreciating me," or, "I resent you for not being romantic," are both too vague and too global to be gotten over. Remember, you are doing this to get over your grudge, rather than to provide a case against your enemy. This resentment must be expressed more specifically, such as, "I resent you for getting drunk and falling asleep on our anniversary."

If you are too mad, at first, to interrupt your own mind by being more specific, go ahead and be general, but do so as loudly as possible. What you get from intensity will compensate, in the beginning, for what you lack in specificity. Just remember to go back over the same ground in a more specific way after you blow out the vents.

- *Focus as much as you can on what did happen instead of what didn't happen.* When you resent someone for what he didn't do — that is, for violating your expectations — look back to what he said or did to create that expectation. Express your resentment to him for what he said or did. Lousy as the idea may seem, you are the only one who is responsible for all your expectations, disappointment, and anger. You can, however, get over the misery you create for yourself by expressing your anger out loud, instead of living in a little hut of poison thoughts.

- *Stay in touch with your experience as you talk.* If you just present someone with a rehearsed, carefully-worded statement about your resentment, you probably won't have much of an experience of your anger dissipating. I recommend you express your feelings as they come up during the interaction. For instance, suppose your spouse reminds you of an obligation and you get mad. You might say, "I resent you for asking me if I remembered to get Grandma a birthday present." You probably already felt guilty about forgetting Grandma's present. You resent your spouse for asking you the question. When you pursue the experience further, you may resent your spouse for telling you to get a present in the first place. You may resent Grandma for having a birthday. You may resent having a grandmother, having to buy her a present, being told to get her a present, being asked if you got it, the tone of voice of the questioner, the look on the face of the questioner, or the smell in the room when the question was asked. You may resent the clerk at the store where you went for the present, who said they were out of Grandma's brand. What you need to do to tell the truth and have the resentment disappear is this: First, notice the bodily sensations associated with what you have called guilt (feeling constricted in your breathing, cowering, feeling tense, frowning) and state your resentment clearly. Start with, "I resent you for saying, 'Did you remember to get something for Grandma for her birthday?'" Then, "I resent you for your innocent, phony tone of voice" (abstract). "I resent you for your tone of voice when you asked me that question" (more specific). "I resent you for looking at me now." "I resent you for frowning." "I resent you for mentioning Grandma at all." This may sound ridiculous and unfair. Clearly your spouse is not at fault and is being blamed.

But note this: the unfair blaming is being done out loud. It is in the public domain where it can get cleared up, not in your secretive mind. People outside of you can be depended on to fight back and take care of themselves. You can count on it. You don't need to protect your spouse from your irrationality. You will get set straight in a minute. Try it. What you want is the feeling of completion and wholeness that comes when you have told the truth about your petty, selfish mind and raised the roof out loud like a fool. What a relief! You don't have to feel guilty now. You and your spouse now live in a new space.

You may have some withheld appreciation to express as well. You can appreciate someone for the same thing you resented her for, and often do. You and Grandma can also have a more alive relationship if you tell each other the truth about your anger and guilt and sense of obligation. Go see

Grandma and tell her the truth. What you put out there relieves you. What you withhold will kill you.

- *Stay there with the person beyond the time it takes to exchange resentments.* If you are willing to state your resentments, and keep stating them as they come up, and allow the other person to resent you for resenting him, eventually you won't have anything left to resent each other for. At that point, you're still not finished. If you can't think of how to end the sentence, "I appreciate you for...," you are probably still angry and haven't finished expressing your resentments — so keep going. *Don't rush to forgive someone because you are uncomfortable about having so many resentments. Be honest about whether you really feel complete with the person. Be willing to have the process take as long as it takes. It probably won't take as long as you fear. It will probably take longer than you would like.*

- *After you both have fully expressed your specific resentments, state your appreciation the same way.* Say, "I appreciate you for...," not, "I appreciate the fact that...". Keep checking your body to see how you feel. Are your shoulders tense? Are your arms crossed? Are your lips compressed? Do you feel like you want to get away from this situation as soon as possible? If the latter is true, there is more that you are withholding. Tell the truth of your experience even if it's, "I still feel uncomfortable sitting here with you," or, "I appreciate you for staying here and listening to me." When you feel warmth in your chest and a smile on your face, express your appreciation in a clear way: "I appreciate you for the way you look right now," or, "I appreciate you for agreeing to do this experiment with me." After some appreciations are expressed, some more resentments may emerge. If that happens, express those resentments and go on. *Eventually you will just be sitting in a room looking at a person. You will see clear-*

er. You will be willing to live and let live. You will be grateful to her for having stuck with you through another fight.

- *Keep it up.* After an emotional exchange in which two people tell the truth, they often retreat into superficiality. People notice that even though they felt loving and inspired after they talked, weeks may go by before they see each other again. This is not an accident. After we release our withheld anger, we discover our appreciation. More often than not we realize that we really love this person. *Most of us are scared of feeling anger, but we are terrified of experiencing love.* It's no wonder that when an authentic exchange occurs, the next time the two people meet, they will talk about anything but their real feelings. One may say as an aside, "You know, I'm so glad we had that talk last time. It meant so much to me." Then they'll switch the subject to something trivial.

Once you have broken through to another person by telling the truth, you have an incredible opportunity to have a real, alive relationship. The two of you can support each other to continue to tell the truth. It takes practice. You will tend to withhold your feelings on later occasions because you have practiced that for years, but you can always get clear with the person as soon as you realize that you are withholding.

Exercises Again

To diminish the amount of anger you have and the degree to which that anger runs your life, you can transform your relationship to anger by agreement, and change your experience of anger through awareness. Awareness is what causes change, not a moral resolve to be better. In *Radical Honesty*, I gave you some exercises and you probably chickened out. Here is another chance. These exercises are just suggestions. You don't have to do them. They will be useful to repeat whenever you are stuck on how to get over your anger.

Make an Agreement to Experiment with Anger

Get together with some friends or your spouse and members of your family old enough to read this chapter. Read this chapter. Meet afterward and make an agreement to experiment for ten days with telling the truth about your resentments to each other, as a method of support for each other. Agree that for ten days, all resentments may legitimately be expressed. That doesn't mean they all have to be acted on. For example, if one of you says, "I resent you for parking in front of the driveway and I demand that you move your car," the offender doesn't have to move the car. All he has to do is hear the resentment. If the going gets rough, keep in mind that the exercise is to go on for ten days.

Have a Conversation in a Group About Anger

Get a group of friends together and start an ongoing group to support each other for a while in learning about how to handle anger. Start by asking them to read this chapter and talk about it in the group.

Ask for Help from Friends

If you are stuck at not being able to make the arrangements to meet someone to express and get over your anger because you are too cowardly or the person won't meet with you, or if you get stuck during the meeting, ask a third party in. Get a mutual friend to mediate. Ask both of your friends, the one you resent and the one you asked to help, to read this chapter.

Further Exercises

For further exercises, read John O. Stevens' book, *Awareness: Exploring, Experimenting, Experiencing*[18], particularly the three exercises entitled *Guilt, Resentment,* and *Demand.* (John Stevens' name is now Steve Andreas.)

Guilt

There are situations in which we experience a terrible feeling of having done something bad and being caught. Or we've make a real mistake and feel bad. These situations at first don't seem to be related to anger at all. You just feel guilty.

But when you feel your way through the experience by facing it, anger will show up. Your power to get over the guilt comes from facing every detail and every imagined catastrophe.

Anger shows up when you examine your guilt feelingly, because guilt, when it was first learned, came from instances of what Fritz Perls called "projected resentment." When you were a child, you were powerless, and you sometimes got mad at the adults who made you do some things and wouldn't let you do other things. When you were mad at them and you made a mistake you knew they would get you for, you felt very bad. If you were mad at the big person who was going to be mad at you, and you had to deny your anger or else make things even worse, you felt even guiltier. You imagined they would be very mad at you, based on denying that you were mad at them, and as an attempt to keep them from punishing you too badly, you punished yourself. If you were hard enough on yourself, you might have escaped some of their wrath, and if you learned to control your terrible self, so your anger toward them didn't show, you might likewise have avoided their wrath. Better to be punished by yourself than by them.

So when you feel guilty, *check to see if some of the anger you imagine on the part of the offended party is, in fact, your anger toward them.* Mistakes are often made out of anger in the first place. People who are perennial screwups are usually angry people.

Meditation

If you are willing to confront your anger in all the ways I have discussed, and if you are not using meditation to avoid acknowledging and expressing anger, then meditation works.

Meditation can increase your satisfaction and decrease your anger. If you want your anger to decrease noticeably in a relatively short time, and if you are willing to do all of what I have discussed so far, meditate regularly. You will gradually become noticeably less angry as who you consider yourself to be changes, due to your experience of just sitting quietly. You will become more familiar with yourself as the *noticer*. You will gradually become less attached to yourself as a personality. I recommend Transcendental Meditation (TM). TM instructors are great at teaching meditation. (But don't take any of their advice about anger, because meditation alone does not do the trick of getting over anger.)

Review and Summary

These exercises and guidelines for expressing resentment and appreciation are for your use in discovering how to let the experience of anger work itself out. These guidelines are suggested as substitutes for your usual methods of controlling anger. They are intended to assist you in experiencing your anger more intensely and publicly so you will have a better chance of getting over being angry. You may get angry at me because, after following the guidelines, you will feel like you are more angry than you used to be. When this occurs, consider the possibility that you are not angrier but are simply experiencing more. Then see for yourself if you get a result that works better than your former methods of control. If not, you don't get your money back.

Here is a quick review of the guidelines about anger:

- Whenever possible, talk face-to-face to the person with whom you are angry.
- Start your sentences as often as possible with the words, "I resent you for..." or, "I appreciate you for...".
- Speak in the present tense.
- Eventually, get specific.

- Don't stop with general descriptions of behavior or general judgments.

- Focus as much as you can on what did happen instead of what didn't happen.

- Stay in touch with your experience as you talk.

- Stay there with the person beyond the time it takes to exchange resentments.

- After you both have fully expressed your specific resentments, state your appreciations the same way.

- Keep it up.

Why Do All of This?

Being honest about anger puts you on the road back home to being alive like you were as a child instead of mind-deadened by what you have learned to lie about. Telling the truth about your anger is a way to get back to your experience of being, where you love yourself and therefore have something left over with which to love someone else. Revealing the withheld judgments and feelings you have hidden, out of politeness and your protection racket, is the difference between a life lived in hate and a life lived in love. Coming forth with your anger will give you your life back. It is a way to feel complete and not be in need of someone else to make you be whole. It is one of the ways back to the path of the "light that enlightens the light," that light of being that first clicked on in the womb and which still is humming right along now, even as we speak. That is one reason. Here is one more. The survival of humankind depends on it.

In Praise of the Old Paradigm

Now the time has come to say good-bye to the old paradigm of top-down management, the feudal system of top-down teaching, the autocracy of top-down parenting. It is time to have a funeral and to give our blessings and thanks to that human inventiveness into which we were born and which sustained us until it didn't anymore.

If we are to bury the old paradigm we must forgive all the bearers of the old ways. We must acknowledge our appreciation to all the workers, teachers, parents, politicians, and technicians for the wonderful heritage into which we were born. We must affirm all the fantastic technological gifts and benefits that have come from the intellectual pioneers who preceded us. We can, for good reason, be grateful for their creations and their sufferings and for all the modifications of the ideas and ideals they inherited, that were changed through their experimentation in how they lived and created, just as we are experimenting and creating in our own lives with what they gave us.

To all those people we say: "We appreciate you for all those solutions that worked in your lifetime. Even though they will not work for us anymore, and we have new insight about their pitfalls and side effects, we still thank you for building that last rung we climbed up on."

Thanks to the Industrial Revolution, we have the Information Age. Thank you for all the miserable wasted lives under top-down management that led to our current prosperity and comfort. Thanks to all the wage slaves and scrooges and people in between. Thanks to all the union organizers and cops and corrupt politicians. Thanks to all the religious people and the warriors who defended beliefs to the death. Thanks to all the misguided educators and parents who brought this chance into being. Thanks to all the alcoholics and factory workers and military personnel. We appreciate all of you for sacrificing your lives for us.

Thank you for all those nights of walking and rocking, when we were little, and all the hours you worked and all the care you showed, along with the abuse you propagated. Thanks for the abuse. Thanks for those hundreds of years of experimentation with altered states of consciousness when you had only alcohol to work with. Thanks for all those attempted celebrations of life, both those that worked out and those that didn't. Thanks for all the material goods and better food and better shelter and better toys. Thank you for all the shows on television, the good, the bad and the ugly. Thank you for all the moralism and the shoulds and the systems of self-torture you taught us. Thanks for that most-destructive-of-all twentieth century and all the bloodbaths from which we learned so much about malice aforethought and malice after-thought and malice via thought. Thanks for movies and television and technology. Thanks for all the images of romantic idealism and its corollary suffering. Thanks for the computer. Thanks for the cars and highways and buildings and cities and access to the countryside. Thanks for aviation and all its advances. Thanks for the exploration of outer space and the perspective and technology it brought us. Thanks for television and video games and movies and movie videos. Thanks for all the great radio shows and all the talk shows. Thanks for recorded music and CDs and for giving us access to the greatest moments of all the artists and performers of the world. Thanks for the Internet. Thanks to the framers of the

Constitution of the United States and everyone who has helped put it into play and kept it alive.

Thanks for listening to the Native Americans who taught us so much that eventually became a part of our Constitution. Thanks for the Great Books of the Western World and for passing on to us the Great Conversation. Thank you for translating and teaching all the wisdom traditions of the East and of the Middle East in the second half of the twentieth century and all the practices that came from them. Thanks for all the mythologies of the world and for the evolution of modern psychology. Thanks for all the poetry. Thanks for all the fiction. Thanks for all the drama. Thanks again for all the music. Thank you and goodbye.

Chapter Eleven

Creating Your Life

One of the ideas to be gotten from the previous chapters is that your own mind is the source of your anger. You are the one responsible for creating your anger. You are the only one who makes it happen and you are the only one who can do anything about getting beyond it. You can express it and feel your way through to forgiveness or you can remain righteous.

You and I are the source of our own anger and can be the source of forgiveness for others and ourselves. If we do choose forgiveness, the freed-up energy we have as a result of forgiving other people, is both renewing and useful. The benefits of forgiveness can be extended by taking even further responsibility for the quality of our own lives. To sustain the benefits of forgiveness, use the energy that results from it to create with — and contribute to — other people by taking on greater responsibility. Our ability to discover our true identity as creators of the world, by virtue of being perceivers, is a direct result of transcending the jail of the mind through the process of forgiveness. Hanging out with people who share these assumptions and have chosen to live in this kind of story, where getting over things is more valued than being right, *is way more fun* than living among the merely righteous.

I got the following summary outline many years ago and have been using it as a handout in my workshops. I cannot remember who wrote this so I cannot give anyone credit; I believe it was one of my clients. I have added to it and modified it and can't remember what is mine and what was theirs, but I appreciate with all my heart the person who first wrote this down.

You Are the Creator Of the World

Victims are not Creators. Creators are not Victims. People who create their lives as artists operate from a fundamental set of assumptions. We ask you to adopt these assumptions for the duration of a chosen time period, inspect the results, and then if you like what you discover, use them the rest of your life:

- All my *perceptions* are my own doing. They occur only inside of me. I influence them and in the process "do me." This is my existence. There are no other objects, no others except the "objects in me." I am the sole authority on my *feelings* and perceptions. I have complete responsibility for how I do myself; and no responsibility for how you do yourself (unless you are my young child). My existence is the process of "me doing me."

- All parts of my fantasies are my own doing. They occur solely inside of me. They exist only as manifestations of me.

- All my dreams, my writings, and my constructions are my own doing. They occur solely inside of me and they exist only as manifestations of me.

- I am not an agent acting on me. I am an expanding, changing organism. I am always in some "state." I am a unitary whole. I do not have "parts." I ache, anger, fear, love, frustrate, depress, bore, joy, pain, exhilarate, tense.

- I am my body.

- I AM.

- TO OWN THAT YOU ARE THE SOURCE IS THE KEY TO RESOURCEFULNESS.

- WE ARE ALL CITIZENS OF THE UNITED STATE.

The Mind as an Instrument of Creation

People in groups can help each other to organize their lives as acts of creation rather than a system of "survival in spite of" their early childhood training. There is a way to use your mind to keep yourself from falling back to the neurotic survival skills of the mind. You do it by living into a vision of the future, creating *in* the present *from* the future, rather than having the present be a reaction to the past.

Creation in Community

A community of support for radical honesty is a living context of support for individual creation. *Imagined projects become reality when shared in a community of committed listeners who speak and listen projects into being.* The community of support for radical honesty also supports the practices that allow for the constant renewal of enthusiasm. We don't lead a creative life because we should. We live a creative life because of constant delivery from the frozen concepts of mind, so that we are called forth by vivid imaginings of what our creations will make possible. This empowers people to create individual projects they can point to as something they brought into being, as Robert Fritz says, simply because they loved the idea of it existing, and this makes a community of mutual love and respect possible. The skill required to play at this level of the video game of life is considerable.

In our little subgroup of this larger community of wisdom and compassion, we play at this work pretty much all the time. Here at the Center for Radical Honesty, we publish a quarterly newsletter, run a lot of workshops, write books, and do tours of various kinds. We work for each other on each others' projects. The *Radical Honesty Rag,* our newsletter, and our related E-Zine come out regularly to support everyone who has a vested interest in this work. These and discussion groups on the web keeps us up on the news that folks like us all over the country generate. People are invited to continue in the creation of an ongoing community of support for themselves by participating in the Course on Honesty, and the Course on Forgiveness and Creation that is held three or four months after that. *Personal power is the result of personal growth.* After learning to practice honesty, we develop skills in forgiveness. Then we have the power to create successful projects in life with friends in a community and help them to do the same. The ongoing Radical Honesty Community is organized around living as creators. Our primary mission is to create a world community of friends who support each other.

The purpose of the whole curriculum is to apply the fundamental principles of radical honesty as taught in the workshops to each individual life, such that individuals become creators of their lives using their minds, rather than being victims of the past, used by their minds. In other words, our lives change when we change how we live, in our ongoing real life, where the rubber meets the road.

The workshops are about how each person's mind reacts and rationalizes to provide an illusion of control while remaining constrained within the confines of habit. That enemy, the mind, must be tamed, to be made into an ally. The purpose of the trainings is to empower all participants to live their lives out loud and design their futures as players, *based on the regular practices of mindfulness designed to keep you centered in the experience of being in the here and now as the only place from which you can powerfully design the future.*

Whatever freedom you gain from your mind can only be protected by putting the mind to work creating. That is why the end focus of all the training groups is to integrate the benefits of freedom from domination by the mind into your day-to-day life by using your mind to bring about the results you envision.

The Courses cost money and time (hours and hours) and each participant has to agree, in advance, to pay for and attend all sessions. There is homework between sessions that takes some time and some ongoing coaching from the trainers using the Internet and telephone system. The time spent is mostly for you to organize your life, as you actually live it, to be consistent with your vision of how you want your life to be and what you want it to be about. The commitment spreads out over a long period and is usually a lot of trouble and gets people in trouble they never predicted. As they say at Landmark Education, where they conduct The Forum, The Advanced Course, and other excellent trainings about taking responsibility for your life, "The way to generate breakthroughs is to generate breakdowns."

Whether you do this work in one of our groups, or do it on your own using this book and a group of friends, it *is* work, and you have to do most of it. On the other hand, the point of it is not to *add* to your burden of work but to *reduce* it by realigning and reorganizing the way you live, to waste less energy pretending and worrying. You can spend your energy with less strain because your whole life is doing what you want. The point is to work less, play more, be happy, accomplish a lot that you are proud of, feel productive, be healthy and in love, and have a community of friends you'll love the rest of your life, who really know you and whom you can trust to tell you the truth.

How We Teach

Workshops and tutorials are conducted by people trained by me and they are happening more and more frequently all over the country. Now, people who want to have more coaching in applying the principles and practices of radical honesty in their lives can do so. A modification of this workshop, called the Radical Parenting Workshop, will be generated next year when my next book, *Radical Parenting: How to Raise Creators*, comes out.

Every person who is able to make their life work by telling the truth rather than manipulating is a candidate to be trained to conduct these workshop groups and tutorials and make at least a part of her livelihood from doing so. Several assistants co-lead the Course in Forgiveness and Creating as well as some of the coaching sessions, directed and coached by other trainers and me. We are becoming a movement.

We are conducting all these groups to help organize an ongoing community of support for people in their local area, to found communities of support for radical honesty. We will be conducting the two-day Introduction to Radical Honesty workshops repeatedly in cities all over the world and the eight-day Course in Honesty in Virginia at the Center for Radical Honesty and occasionally at other central locations in the world. Graduates become invited participants in already existing radical honesty communities. People in these groups invite friends to take the workshop and join the community by participating in Radical Honesty Practice Groups. People who have completed a workshop once can repeat it for half price and come to Courses at a reduced rate on an ongoing basis.

Eventually, *almost* everything will be available in a curriculum that is partially tutored and coached on the Internet with face-to-face meetings for three days about every three months and then more coaching and tutoring and support by local community meetings. We will be using a combination of 800 numbers, a web page, conference call bridges, chat room meetings, and email to keep in close touch with each other as we grow together in the power to make things happen in our lives.

Here is a brief sample of a Curriculum Outline, and although you cannot tell exactly the content of the training, you can get an idea of its direction. If you can't do our trainings you can use this as a guideline for your own.

The Core Curriculum: Self-Reliance Aand Dreaming Up An Alternative Life

1. Get fed up with putting a damper on your life.

2. Read *Radical Honesty: How To Transform Your Life by Telling the Truth.*

3. *Read Practicing Radical Honesty: How To Complete the Past, Live in the Present and Build a Future with a Little Help from Your Friends*

4. Enroll in and complete the Introduction to Radical Honesty Workshop (two days).

5. Enroll in and complete the Course in Honesty (eight days).

6. Do the tutorial program and the homework assigned and agreed to at the end of the Course in Honesty.

7. Participate in the Course in Forgiveness and Creating (4 days) — the advanced course — as often as you like.

8. Remain in an ongoing Practice Group, meeting every week or every couple of weeks, in your local community, during and after participation in the rest of the curriculum and stay in it thereafter. Each of these meetings has a core set of practices that occur on an ongoing basis: group *meditation* at the beginning of every session, some yoga or "Dance Yoga for the Insane," group work, hot seat work, and work in pairs. We have a series of videos about Radical Honesty and movies as well. Tutorials, chat rooms, conference calls, and parties exist for support of practices between sessions.

9. Enroll in a Trainers' Intensive if you are interested in helping conduct the work and eventually making part or all of your living by running Radical Honesty Workshops.

10. Create your life and contribute to other people until you die.

The overall goal is that through participating in this learning series:

• Each person has brought something into being in his life which he can point to as his own creation that didn't exist four or five months before, and

• A community of supportive friends has been formed.

I am regularly leading trainings in Virginia, and we at Radical Honesty Enterprises headquarters are coaching Practice

Group leaders around the country. As we all learn together how to make a community of friends work again, and how to make a really honest community work for the first time on a large scale, we expect to create miracles in the community of the world. I am really happy to be in this work and feel lucky to have the chance to work with such great people who teach me over and over again the value of sharing information about how life really is.

We are taking on the problem of raising a generation of human beings the world over who are prepared to love and share with other human beings. I have declared that the purpose of my life is, to bring about the possibility of a lifetime of play and service for every human being on the planet. A lot of people have joined me. Come play with us and we'll serve each other and see if, out of this, the reorganization of the world will occur. Part three, which follows, shows in a step by step fashion how the reorganization of your life can contribute to the reorganization of the world so that the whole thing works better for all of us.

Part Three:
Creating Your Own Destiny

The Workbook for Life Design

This workbook section is about the real work of honesty and freedom. It also describes a method of creating a new culture to live in, one that transcends the culture in which you were raised. Honesty with others creates freedom from being embroiled in managing other people's impressions of you, which is one of the main things that keeps you trapped in your own mind. "Making it" in a culture is usually dependent upon making a good impression with others so that you are accepted. It is also something that takes a lot of energy. When you quit managing impressions, the energy you used to burn for that becomes newly available to create your life based on what you want.

Once you have the courage to live completely out loud and have escaped the jail of your mind, you can use your mind to do the work of this section. You can use your mind to keep yourself from falling back into the neurotic survival skills of that very same mind, by developing a vision and creating the present from your vision of the future, rather than from reaction to the past.

Deliverance from the suffering caused by being trapped in your mind begins by being grounded in your experience. The minimum fundamental requirements for grounding in your experience are regular solitary meditation, the interpersonal meditation known as radical honesty, and additional ongoing practices like yoga, martial arts, or physical exercise. Once you are capable of maintaining being grounded in your experience, you can transcend your mind and use it as a tool to create your life in whatever ways you want to dream up.

Freedom comes from refusing to hide. You come out from under your bushel basket and show yourself by asserting your preferences. When you create something, you assert what you want without justifying, editing, or withholding anything. In the process of creating based on clear communication about what you want to bring about in your life, you experience freedom.

The toughest part of learning radical honesty comes when you head out into the world to live it. Your mind's unique survival strategy, so perfectly formed, will immediately begin to reassert itself as the dominant control. Like a computer with a circular program, you will run that program over and over again and still be mystified as to why the same results happen. With the help that comes from communicating your intentions to others, and in the process of asserting yourself, these usually dysfunctional programs will come right to the surface. You will see them in action—then go ahead and live them. Ultimately you want to *use* your limiting rackets *rather than be used by them.*

This section guides you through the process of putting your preferences on paper and taking the first steps of asserting yourself to the world. The big picture is the umbrella projects model, a tool to organize your life in a direction you choose. This is a model to use to make your life an act of creation rather than a system of "survival in spite of" your early childhood training. As Stephen Covey says in *The Seven Habits of Highly Effective People*[19], a highly functioning human being operates from consciously chosen values and conscious design. This whole workbook section details a way to do that.

If you hit a spot that seems to be tough sledding, you're doing good work. Keep after it. Stay in conversation with other people. Find friends and co-conspirators to create with and support you. The journey of a thousand miles begins with thousands of steps, so go for it.

Chapter Twelve

A Programmatic Approach to Personal Growth

"Evolution proceeds not through adaptation but through creativity. We must create who we want to be, rather than merely imitate what we have recently been."

— *Marianne Williamson*

After we have transcended the old paradigm that limited who we consider ourselves to be, and have found practices to ground us in the reality of our present experience, and we continually practice those practices, we also need to give our mind some work to do, or else it will recapture the space we have freed up.

In the following chapters covering The Workbook for Life Design curriculum, you will learn how work can come to be play and how to create with the added power of a community of support, helping you to "source" resourcefulness. The end result is to create a life *through a way of speaking and listening that makes things happen in the direction you planned.* This is not done by controlling yourself and manipulating other people to live up to your expectations the way old-paradigm motivational speakers advocate. It is done by speaking and listening honestly and clearly as an advocate for an exciting vision you are committed to bringing into reality. There is a way of speaking that only comes from excited detachment. That speaking is obsessional. It is also detached.

You Want to Get Obsessed and You Want to Stay Obsessed

I want to remind you of the joke I told in the authors preface: *Do you know how many Buddhists it takes to change a light bulb? Three. One to change the bulb. One to not change the bulb. One to neither change the bulb nor not change the bulb.*

Belief is the enemy of consciousness. In an interview, Ken Wilbur, that bald-headed guy who's always stealing my stuff, said, "It's not the truth that will set you free, it's truthfulness." I couldn't have said it better myself. Truthfulness sets you free.

Truthfulness about beliefs sets you free from unconscious domination by beliefs you have come to think are reality. Then, once you are free of the illusion that beliefs are real, you can *choose* to be consciously dominated by beliefs you *know* are *not* real. You surrender—by choice—to addiction. We are all addicted to belief. Consciousness of addiction allows for a perspective that unconscious addiction does not. It seems very strange to me, but true, that good obsessive behavior comes from detachment. Take, for example, some of my beliefs:

- Belief is the enemy of consciousness.

- Truthfulness will set you free.

- The intimacy that comes from honesty is more lively and adventurous than the attempt to maintain security by lying.

- People who tell the truth about what they think and feel and do are able to work together more happily and more effectively than people who don't.

- Freedom is a psychological accomplishment. Freedom is detachment from unconscious domination by the reactive mind and by belief.

- The good life is a life of powerful creation with friends.

- Power to make a world that works for everyone comes from people who love each other and share common beliefs without too much attachment to those beliefs.

- People who are obsessed together with making a contribution to other people and each other, can do so in a *totally committed* and at the same time *completely nonchalant* way.

Now, how does my obsession with these beliefs exemplify detachment? The attachment to those beliefs enough to list them shows that I am committed to these beliefs. I spend a great deal of my life's energy operating according to them and propagating them in the world. *I have harnessed being obsessed with these beliefs through the surrender allowed by choosing.* I did this by choosing consciously to do what I have been condemned to do, just like Sisyphus transformed Hell by choosing to do what he had been condemned to do. Based on many experiences of liberation, I have come to believe these things and have chosen with great enthusiasm to pass them on. I am totally committed.

I am nonchalant at the same time. I know these are only beliefs I am obsessed with. They are not real or holy; they are just useful. They are not the only beliefs available or the one true set, nor are they to be worshipped. I am totally committed, but at the same time utterly nonchalant about proving them or defending them or making them real or making them come true.

Joseph Wesley Mathews was a great Christian theologian who was in charge of the Christian Faith and Life Community on the campus of the University of Texas in the late 1950's and early 1960's. He later became the head of the Ecumenical Institute of Chicago, which became the research and development wing of the World Council of Churches. He was the first man to tell me that it was possible to be totally committed and completely nonchalant at the same time. I think he learned it from Paul Tillich, another of the great minds of the 20th century.

Carlos Casteneda had Don Juan tell me, in *Journey to Ixtlan*, about the possibility of what he called *controlled abandon* – that complete and dedicated and unswerving attention to being impeccable while at the same time surrendering completely. That, he said, has something to do with power.

Werner Erhard and his associates, in all the programs they designed and that have grown out of his original impetus, have stressed both impeccability and surrender.

I have learned by standing on the shoulders of these giants that not only is it possible, it is much more powerful, to be completely given over to creating with every ounce of strength and attention I can muster, while at the same time being perfectly willing to have things turn out however fate dictates.

I remember clearly a particular moment of feeling much more capable, in the general movement to end nuclear proliferation. Back when the atomic clock that showed how close we were to the midnight of final nuclear holocaust said it was now ten minutes to twelve, a friend of mine, Charles Erickson, said, "Well, we all have to die anyway. I guess it's not so bad if we all do it together." Hearing that was a relief. Some of the desperate sense of obligation to hurry up and do something to save the world disappeared. The liberation of acknowledging that the possibility of the end of humankind was not necessarily something we had to run around trying hysterically to avoid, allowed for so much more freedom from that point forward. I spread that conversation all over the place, and so did others, and I believe the whole conversation about the possibility of *not* ending the world through nuclear ignorance grew by leaps and bounds after that. What we could communicate then was something like this: "I would rather, as a preference, live and have my offspring and my offspring's offspring and the whole human experiment continue, but that may not happen. We may wipe ourselves out. That's okay, too. But, given that we prefer the former outcome, and you probably do too, what should we do to ensure bringing it about? Let's focus obsessively about how to do that for a while and then let's be obsessed with the doing of it. But let's be obsessed with a little detachment, given that we are all going to die anyway and it wouldn't be all that bad to do it together."

At the same time that I am now giving my days and nights and energy to accomplish the deliverance of all human beings from the jail of belief, it doesn't really have to happen. In fact, I think it is exactly the same as the situation we faced with nuclear proliferation during the Cold War. We are still faced with extinction by a threat even greater than the bomb. The bomb is just a small-time instrument of destruction compared to the overall destructive power of attachment to beliefs in the old paradigm system of top-down management.

Without the nonchalance that comes from knowing the difference between our beliefs and sensate reality, we become Shiite Moslems or Baptists or fundamentalists of some kind looking for the chance to kill or die for our beliefs in an attempt to make them real. We become Serbian townspeople who don black masks and force their lifetime-neighbor Albanians out of their homes, stripping them of their legal identities and abandoning them to shelterless, cold, and unsanitary fields, or killing them without remorse.

I believe, when I confess beliefs as important but not real, that the distinction between belief and reality — the detachment from the obligation to prove my beliefs are real — allows me to choose the beliefs that use me. I believe that knowing that my beliefs are beliefs, and *not* reality, allows me to present them to other people as merely a recommended set of options that are somewhat counter to common knowledge but possibly more functional.

I am obsessed with getting these beliefs about belief passed around in the world. I am obsessed with teaching and learning through practice how to operate using these beliefs. I do not think that these beliefs are reality. I do not think these beliefs are holy. They are just beliefs, not reality. I am obsessed with the possibility of teaching the world the wisdom of *not* making beliefs holy. I am obsessed with teaching the world the possibility of choosing to have *these beliefs* be what uses them, rather than *being used by conventional beliefs in belief as reality.*

This story from the book *Tales from India* is quite a vision of controlled abandon through transcending futility.

The Bodhisattva Avalokitesvara looked down into the many hells and saw they were filled with suffering beings.

A great vow spontaneously arose in his heart. "I will liberate all beings from the sufferings of the hells," he said. And so through countless ages he labored, descending into and emptying hell after hell, until the unimaginable task was at last done.

The great Bodhisattva ceased then from his eons of heroic exertion. He wiped the glistening diamonds of beaded sweat from his brow, and, looking down into the empty hells, smiled. It was done. Here and there a curling wisp of smoke still rose up. Now and then, in some vast cavern far below, faint echoes sounded as a loose brick shifted on a pile of rubble. But the raging fires had been quenched and the great iron cauldrons were quiet. Sweet silence flowed through the dark halls. Even the demons were gone for they too, in the end, had been released, liberated to the heavens, by the mighty efforts of the Compassionate One.

But what was this? Suddenly, there came a wailing scream, then another, and another. Flames leapt, clouds of smoke whirled, blood-filled cauldrons bubbled madly. The radiant smile faded from the Bodhisattva's face. Once again the hells were entirely filled. In less than an instant all was exactly as it had been before.

The heart of the Bodhisattva filled with sorrow. Suddenly, his head split into many heads. His arms shattered into many arms. The one thousand heads looked in all directions to see the sufferings of every being. The one thousand arms were enough to reach any realm, to save those in need.

Rolling up his one thousand sleeves, the great Bodhisattva settled down once more to the unending task.

The Unending Task

Hell continually recreates itself by making experiential reality into beliefs and then substituting those beliefs for reality. Hell is being lost in the mind. We are delivered from the jail of our minds into the heaven of experiential reality and then we reconvert that reality into the hell of the belief jail again.

I am a futilitarian. It's a religion I invented. Futilitarians believe that there is no use trying to give up belief because you simply can't, and that believing in anything is futile. That is what allows for detachment from belief. The freedom that comes from the affirmation of futility is unbelievable. (Pun intended.)

What gives futilitarians so much energy is we don't need a particular result in order to be happy. We are happy for no reason at all. We know there is no reason to be happy. We were going to have annual conventions like most groups, but when we got together to plan it, we thought, "Ah, what's the use? Having meetings is completely futile." So we gave up, and now have an annual unconvention instead.

I am working on finishing this book now and I am obsessed with it. I believe this is the best book I have ever written. I like being obsessed. I think it is a good thing. I believe in being obsessed. I believe a good way to live is to get obsessed and stay obsessed. I think it is best to do this with detachment.

I am obsessed with the vision I am trying to articulate in this book and at the same time bring it into being in reality through a new corporation we have formed, called Radical Honesty Enterprises, Inc. Our main overall vision is of a University for Living based on the model of personal growth from endarkenment to enlightenment for individuals and societies. It is a vision of the growing up of the whole interconnected world of humankind. The curriculum that unifies all our programs is based on the image of personal evolution shown in Figure 2 in the following flashlight beam model. It pictures how we all grow in our life together, beginning with believing our own invented stories about our lives and progressing to living in a community of non-believers who interrupt each others' minds for the benefit of each other's beings.

You are living in a story not of your own creation	You are living in a story not of your own creation, and you know it	You are living in a story not of your own making	You are integrating both stories and programming relief	You belong to a community of non-believers
AND	AND	BUT	AND	AND
You believe you can "figure it out."	Now and then, you have experiences of being outside your beliefs. You notice and remember those experiences.	You are also inventing a new story and have more accumulated memories of experiences that transcend your story.	You experience consistent meditation and frequent, honest sharing.	As an independent and interdepedent being, you participate in a community of friends who interrupt each other.

Figure 2. From Belief to Non-belief

The New University

In the old paradigm system, an undergraduate education consisted of an attempt to give adolescents a balanced overview of the humanities, science, and liberal arts and then an area of focus or "major" to specialize in. The general direction was to be able to make a living by doing what you were interested in after a sufficient review of the possibilities. This was not a bad idea and it still works to a limited extent when teachers who have the whole vision of that system's intent are in charge.

The new paradigm university is more focused on how to live than on how to make a living. The new university is directed toward the psychological accomplishment called freedom.

Personal growth as an ongoing lifestyle does have stages that can be delineated and supported with information and processes that further the action. This model of the new university for

Table 1. From Illusion to Creation

Name of Stage	State of Mind; State of Being	Training Content	Radical Honesty Program
Stage 1: The Illusion of Control	Keeping up and judging; judging and keeping up. Belief that judgments are real.	Explicit teaching about about the illusion of control. Distinguishing between noticing and thinking.	Introduction to Radical Honesty (Two Day Workshop)
Stage 2: Completion	Meeting with people from the past to tell the truth about what was withheld.	Gestalt hot seat work, group process work, life story telling, awareness exercises. Homework in the real world.	Course in Honesty (Eight Day Workshop)
Stage 3: Paradigm of the Relativity of Paradigms	Living more out loud, focusing on ending the anxiety-based life, getting over anger, forgiveness.	Life is just sensational training; modeling detachment. Kleenex™ model for paradigms: use one and throw it away.	Course in Forgiveness
Stage 4: Mindfulness	Developing skills in meditation, noticing, and mindfulness; articulating the noticing.	Sharing what you notice with others becomes the foundation of intimacy. Shared projects and mutual coaching.	Course in Creating
Stage 5: Groundless Being and That's Okay	Responsible individuality and individual responsibility.	Change of primary identity from performer-noticer to noticer-performer. Becoming identified with being.	Cumulative Courses and Trainer's Training
Stage 6: A Life of Loving and Creating	Ongoing responding to and co-creating with others.	Project creation and project management with love and without attachment to results.	Trainers' Trainings and Coaching

living is what the Center for Radical Honesty programs support. The Omega Institute, Rowe Conference Center, Esalen Institute, The Learning Annex, and many other growth centers operate more consistently within this model than within the older model.

Table 1, on the preceding page, lays out stages of development from "The Illusion of Control" to "A Life of Loving and Creating." These stages of growth in community are a universal model having to do with all developmental work. Our programs, which are designed to help with the transitions, are identified following each stage.

This chart summarizes the stages of personal growth and the assistance offered to birth each stage. We start from the isolation we all learn in adolescence (when we have completed substituting belief for reality and are living almost exclusively in our minds), and progress toward compassionate participation in community.

The Course in Honesty

To bring alive what is outlined in Table 1, and to make it useful to you whether you ever do any of our courses or not, I will describe what happens during the Course in Honesty. Sixteen people get together on a Saturday morning and make some agreements about what they will do together for the next eight days. One of the most important agreements is that they will tell the truth to each other completely for the next eight days. If that was all that occurred, and there were no other agenda whatsoever, the course would be powerful because the power of that alone is incredible.

The agenda for each day goes something like this: we all start with yoga from 7:30 to 8:30, meditate together until 8:50, then run a couple of miles or do alternative aerobic activity for 20 minutes or so. We do this because yoga and meditation and exercise put you in touch with experiential reality. Breakfast is available from 9:00 to 10:00 and there is time for a shower. Then the entire group meets from 10:00 to 2:00 with occasional 15-minute breaks. The content of the meetings varies, but generally includes Gestalt hot seat work, lectures, directed conversations, paired exercises, small group exercises, and other training geared toward the distinction between noticing and thinking for all participants.

Lunch is at 2:00 followed by a break until 5:00, during which time participants meditate for the second time each day, as they have agreed to do. They can also take a nap, interact with others, read assigned material, write in a journal, and so on. We do our second meditation individually during that break. From 5:00 to 8:00 we meet again, often watching feature length movies like *Secrets and Lies, Little Big Man, My Dinner With Andre, Bagdad Cafe, The Karate Kid, The Englishman Who Went Up a Hill and Came Down a Mountain, Ikiru* or other films selected on the basis of representing what I call abnormal mental health. Generally they are stories of people who were able to remain sane while the society around them was crazy.

At 8:00 we break for supper. From 9:00 to 11:00 we hear two life stories. Each person spends an hour telling the whole story of their life, which is videotaped. A timekeeper prompts the storyteller every fifteen minutes and a little time is left at the end for people to ask questions to get the honest details. Before this workshop is over, every participant hears everyone else's life story, tells their own, and receives their videotape to use later to start conversations with parents, ex spouses, brothers, sisters, lovers, and friends with whom they have unfinished business in life.

Also, about the fifth day of the workshop, everyone gets naked in the hot tub room. One person at a time stands up in front of a mirror and talks about what they like and don't like about their body. This is also videotaped. Then they tell their sexual history—when they first found out that they were a sexual being; when they first masturbated; whether they like doing it with men or women or vegetables, animals, or minerals; how many people of each gender they have had sex with; their best and worst sexual experiences; and so on. Each participant stands naked in front of us, recounting these details while being video-taped, until we who are listening and watching (and also naked) feel they are no longer embarrassed. They often are embar-rassed, but with good coaching and persistence and complete sharing of the truth they get over it. Everyone always thinks this will be a sexy experience. So far, it has never been very sexy at all. Mostly it is about embarrassment and shame and suffering more than pleasure, and about how avoidance of all those aspects often controls our lives.

The next day, we review the videotapes together. Each per-son sits next to the video screen when their image appears, observes their segment of tape, and receives feedback. The process of watching themselves on television, naked, while talk-ing about their sex lives is a more confrontational process for some people than the original experience of standing naked before the group. Again, the willingness to face the experience and live through it provides a decrease in the intensity of the sensations related to shame and a change in perspective on their own life in the direction of compassion for themselves as well as others.

As you can imagine, by the fifth or sixth day, people get to know each other pretty well. What happens, and it happens over and over again with very diverse groups of people, is the same every time. *Everyone falls in love with everyone else.* The very peo-ple who were categorized as jerks the first day are the same peo-ple who, just a few days later, have you, their greatest enemy and most severe judge, put an arm around them and say some-thing like: "Bless your heart! You've come through some really hard times. You have a lot of courage. Good for you! You're just like me. I had no idea we were so much alike. Aren't we funny? Aren't we pathetic? Isn't life strange? I just love you to pieces!" *When people really get to know each other, in detail, they fall in love with each other.* Now, isn't that a hell of a thing? Imagine all that time wasted "putting on airs," in hopes that someone would love us for our act, when all we needed to do was drop the act and tell the truth!

Because everyone very much likes being in love, even though afraid of it because of the unfamiliarity and vulnerability, the question arises, "What can we do to sustain this feeling of connectedness?" Here lies a place of great danger. Here is where the mind makes its first attempt to take control and make assessments and judgments and determine how to *hold on* to something. Here is the critical point. *If we are going to remain enlightened and alive, we have to do it without holding on too tight. If we try too hard to preserve something like this, we kill it. That is what a mind is for. Making dead memories more important that the living present is one of the functions of a mind. Making obligations out of past joys is the kind of thing any mind knows how to do and will do at the drop of a hat.* That is what makes the mind such a killjoy.

The curriculum for the continuation of the work beyond this point requires a built-in method for correcting itself or it will surely go awry. That curriculum involves the continuous completion of unfinished business from the past and keeping up with honesty day to day. It also involves consciously designing and creating with friends.

Our reunion groups, which meet three months and six months after the end of the Course in Honesty, are called the Course in Forgiveness and the Course in Creation. They have a curriculum intended to support participants in continuing the practices that enabled their original authentic contact. It is designed to assure continual renewal rather than sentimentalizing precious memories.

Ongoing Community

Whether the ongoing connection between people to interrupt each others' minds and create together happens within the context of our particular training program or in someone else's program is not important. What is important is that a certain evolution of consciousness is occurring and we experience a certain joining together of people who have come to understand and connect with each other at a deeper level. As Marianne Williamson so eloquently says in *Healing the Soul of America:*

"This renaissance will come from neither the Left nor the Right. It is neither a bridge to the past nor a bridge to the future, but a bridge to who we most deeply are. The bridge to a better future is a shift in mass consciousness, to a part of ourselves we have tended to keep out of the public realm....who we are when we are hushed in church, near tears when they blow the shofar on Yom Kippur, honest and vulnerable with our therapist. It is the part of us least acknowledged, maintained, or seemingly even valued at all by the social order we have created around us."

The next several chapters go into detail about one way of using a mind to organize a life so it has better odds of staying in love and out of the jail of categories and reactions. These chapters can be used to create a life among friends whether you do workshops or trainings with us or not. Please feel free to join us or try this on your own. You may make a bunch of mistakes and learn many valuable things, and if you want some coaching, give us a call.

Confronting the Past to Get Complete and Have Energy to Create

The first step in creating your own destiny is to complete some of your major incompletions from the past. You have to talk seriously with your parents, old flames, ex-spouses, brothers and sisters, and lost friends and any other previously unresolved separations. Go wake up all the sleeping dogs and don't let them lie anymore. I suggest a systematic methodology for this and have many examples of people who have done it before. Take, for example, this email I received recently.

Brad,

I appreciate you for sharing with me ideas that have fueled a rocket-like takeoff in my life. Here's a summary of what's been happening for me since the last Reunion Group meeting.

My first project was making my business (Teaching Violin) be the way I want it to be. Students now come for three individual lessons and two group lessons per month, and it works out so I have one week per month free from work. I redesigned my group violin classes to reflect what I care about—adding body awareness (yoga,

Feldenkreis, and so on), improvisation, creative visualization, music history, and lots else. The classes are fun to plan and conduct, and I'm getting well-paid in the process. Next I took on getting divorced. My goal was to be friends with Arnold, and to provide a stable home for our kids. We succeeded big time. We are divorced as of December, are best friends, and still living together. My kids have never been as together as they are now.

We're thinking of writing a book called *1001 Platonic Dates.*

My next project was finding lover(s). The universe provided again, with a guy who is blowing me away with new sexual experiences, as well as plausible backups in case this relationship blows up. Enclosed is one of the letters I wrote him in response to him sharing fears about his history of promising more than he can deliver in relationships and hurting people as a result. I imagine you will notice your influence.

Dear Ralph,

One of my goals for 1999 is to find and discard old mental baggage. Experiencing life with my baggage detector switched on helps me find it. For example, I notice as I write to you that I'm feeling insecure about you finding my thoughts tedious. Where would such an idea come from? Probably not from anything you've done or said. I imagine it might have something to do with the fact that my mom doesn't do process very well. The only acceptable utterances in my childhood home seemed to me to be cheerful ones, so I stuffed my concerns and reflections. Being aware of that baggage, I can go ahead and write and send despite my insecurity, waiting for you to cry uncle if you choose. That's new for me; I used to keep my thoughts private, to Arnold's chagrin. This year I'm an eagle, observing the world and speaking my truth, soaring on the winds.

I invite you to speak your truth with me, to share your unfiltered feelings day-by-day, even if that means breaking my heart if your positive feelings for me ebb away. First of all, I've never been rejected by a lover, and I'm collecting varied life experiences. Second, though I felt guilty at the time I rejected Arnold as a lover, I look back on that as an act of integrity and kindness. He's grown enormously through the process of dealing with his broken heart. Third, my heart was broken by my father's rejection, and may need to be broken again in order to be reset better than ever as a healing grown-up.

To use Harville Hendrix's paradigm, I've come into my own with my mother as a result of my struggle with Arnold. They are both card-carrying members of the thought police if you let them be. Now it's time for me to come into my own with respect to my dad. As a strong match for my dad's imago, you're the lucky one to help me with this project. So again, be yourself. I chose to let you into my heart knowing full well your history with women. I am not an innocent victim. Of course, I say all this as I chart unfamiliar territory. I am not used to allowing myself feelings of deep caring for men. It may hurt so much when we separate that I choose not to do this "in-love-with" routine to myself again. But at least I'll know that much more about life. I am unlikely to try to saddle you with blame; it's not my style. My guess is that beyond the hurt feelings, we will be friends again.

Statistically speaking, I may be more likely to leave you than be left, despite my more intense feelings. I say that because I am more in transition, having no idea about who I am or what I want now that I'm free of marriage. Am I polyamorous or monogamous, or something else? What's the rhythm of my sexual desire outside of that decades-long relationship? What sort of people am I most attracted to? I'm an adolescent in an adult body running loose in the world. And this isn't even considering the baggage factor; my old tendency to withdraw when I get scared by love. All I can promise is to behave as gently as my skills allow me as I try to live a life true to myself. I'm quite through with living a life governed by "shoulds."

Love, Georgia

Brad, this kind of communication helps to create a nuclear reaction in my body. Sometimes I wonder if I'm going to get arrested fully clothed, there is so much life force coursing though me.

My next project is getting closer to my family of origin. I've got a date lined up with my dad tonight, and on Saturday I'm going out to California, to spend a week with my sister. I'm organizing a three-day reunion in April for the women in my extended family, including my cousins, aunt, and mother, to talk about how we want to handle death, money, family feuds, and other big topics.

So again, thanks. I look forward to seeing you in a few weeks.

Georgia

Completion Leads to Creation

Isn't it just wonderful how casually Georgia reports outstanding, life-changing, risk-taking, consciousness-altering, freedom making, taking-it-all-on-and-running-with-it life changes? I have heard lots of these stories from graduates of Radical Honesty workshops. In the workshops, we have developed a series of exercises that lead to more freedom. If you can't come to a Course in Honesty, give these a try in a Radical Honesty Practice Group you organize yourself:

Exercise 1

Videotape telling the whole story of your life to a group of friends. Answer all questions honestly and get it all on tape. Do this in about an hour or and hour and a half. Open up and tell it like it is for you.

Exercise 2

Show the tape to your parents, spouses, brothers, sisters, best friends, and your children over twelve years of age. In the discussions that follow, tell the truth about your resentments and appreciations of all the people who watch your tape and tell them you intend to forgive them whether they agree that they are guilty or not, and hold the intention to forgive them before you quit the conversation. Focus on how you feel in your body to be able to tell whether you are complete. When you feel relaxed with energy and you are not avoiding eye contact or dreading what might happen next, you are complete. When you are tense and paranoid you are not through yet. If it takes more than one meeting, go back.

About ninety percent of the time, beginning an honest discussion works to entirely renew the relationship. It doesn't work all the time to renew all relationships. If it doesn't renew the relationship with some of the people involved, it can still work for you personally. Not everyone in the world is up to forgiveness and completion. If they don't get over your resenting them or hurting their feelings, be as compassionate as you can without compromising your integrity. If you persist, they may come around. If not, you've lost an aquaintance who didn't have the courage to be a friend. As we say in our commercial for Radical Honesty, maybe one of the world's few honest commercials: "Radical Honesty! It works pretty good!...Most of the time!"

Completion of unfinished business from the past creates the space for a new beginning. The courage to tell the truth and live out loud and tell the truth about events and feelings and judgments from the past is critically important to becoming a creator of your life in the future. If you are willing to bring up important unfinished business with important people from your past, whether they want to or not, they will almost always end up admiring you for it. If you are unwilling to risk their possible alienation by telling what you remember doing and having had done to you, what you think, and what you feel from the past, you maintain constraints to being a creator in your future. Having the power to create your life the way you want it with the help of others and then be able to enjoy what you have done with them *depends on your courage to complete the past.* The good news is, once you have faced the unfinished business, you can begin planning and designing a new future with new power and freedom. The bad news is, until you complete unfinished issues, powerful creation is severely inhibited. Go back and tell the truth. Go back again. Go back until you are finished with your story or finished with the person or both.

Chapter Fourteen

Planning the Future
So You Remain Called Forth
From Your Mind

Breakthroughs in learning that liberate you from your mind are initially experiences that bring insights, then insights that help for a while, and finally yesterday's reconstructed memories. Once that occurs, the breakthrough is used up. For the quality of your life to be good, breakthroughs from *mind* to *being* must constantly recur. Once your mind has reconstructed its memory of a liberating insight, it is mostly no longer liberating. The mind makes things stale fairly quickly. That is why we know better than to trust nostalgic love stories. Nostalgia ain't what it used to be. Love either recurs or it ends. A memory of love is not love.

People who are more concerned about belief than experience tend to dominate and control institutions. Institutionally defensive people hold tightly to belief out of fear. Defenders of belief in the institutions of religion, government, and business are the enemies of liveliness. If creators do not constantly reclaim their own governance from the fearful controllers, the human world loses its aliveness and after that its life. The judging mind of each individual is parallel to—and representative of—the institutions of belief.

It's artists who win. It's creators who have the good life. Artists are on top of life. Creators have the courage to be.

The artfully lived life is consciously designed in an ongoing process where *discovery through sharing is as important or more important than original intent. This means you have to plan a lot and revise plans a lot, while keeping the vision of the end result of your creation continually calling you forth.*

Because the mind makes things stale fairly quickly, we need to take on the process of continual re-creation as a lifelong, permanent task. This means making plans and writing them down and systematically projecting into the future with our imaginations. Then we do some of the work of the plans and dispense with them like Kleenex™ tissues, rewrite and dispense with them, and continue. Attachment to plans can be as much of a restraint to freedom as attachment to ideals from the past. Eventually your life gets a certain rhythm to it: clear the past, plan the future, act; clear the past, plan the future, act; clear the past, plan the future, act.

Being on top of life seems to be the opposite of being overwhelmed by life. The tendency is strong in all of us to fall back into that "feeling imposed upon" way of being, which is the usual reliable source of anger, depression, and anxiety. These states of mind are very familiar to us, and therefore very precious. *We preserve them through trying to fix them.* The way to transcend your limitations is to use them rather than trying to fix them or change them. Use them to create a life you want, where you live, how you want to live, and doing what you want to do.

Many of us are caught in a kind of despair created by hoping for the best. We like to be lost in a vague hope that someone is going to rescue us from responsibility for our lives. God or the lottery or some sugar daddy or mama or a rich uncle or an inheritance or some good luck or some wise person or teaching will finally make it all okay, the way Mom or Dad never did. We'll be happy and taken care of and it won't take anything but believing and waiting on our part. Maybe if we're lucky, we think (in the back of our minds), somebody will take care of us the way we always should have been taken care of, and we won't actually have to take care of ourselves. Believers have explanations for what went wrong and hope for salvation just ahead. Creators enjoy consciously going about the work of designing and bringing into being their vision of whatever they want to create.

Unfortunately, in spite of how hard we wish for deliverance, being on top of life requires taking responsibility for how it goes. This means the work of planning and doing. It doesn't mean trying, or doing the best we can, or getting an A for effort, or whatever we learned was important about putting on a good show in school. It isn't hoping. It requires giving up hope. It is not performing for an audience. It is work. It is engaging, involving, concentrated, sometimes exciting, sometimes hard, meditative; more than anything else persistent work. But it is fun. It is more fun than worrying about being right or not being wrong, etc.

Because of what I do for a living—psychotherapy and running workshops about deliverance from the unconscious control of the reactive mind and the illusion of control by the reflective mind—I have had hundreds of opportunities to witness retreat in the face of the real work of creation. When I ask people, "Would you like to give up the suffering and the satisfactions involved in being neurotic, being trapped in the indulgence of being a victim?" almost everyone says, "Yes." When we finally get to the place where they understand how much commitment, intentionality, and work is required, some people back off and return to their old ways. Having someone or something else to blame for how life has been and how it goes is just too sweet—and it requires less work and less risk.

Conscious artistry in the creation of the good life for any individual requires *constant* centering, *constant* planning, and *constant* sharing of what you are about in the world.

Without doing the work it takes to be on top of life, one doesn't get as many of the breaks, the time off, the periods without guilt, and most especially, the *results* one wants. Lee Trevino says, "Golf is mostly a game of luck, but I find if I practice a lot I have more of it." I say, *life* is mostly a game of luck as well, but the practice of planning, and doing the plans, is absolutely necessary to increase the odds of having more luck in life.

Practices that Lead to More Luck

To stay in good form in all sports, you have to play and practice constantly, get coached continually, keep yourself well-equipped and well-informed of recent advances in technology and equipment, and play competitively to develop your skill under pressure. In life you have to play and practice constantly, keep yourself well-equipped and well-informed of recent advances, and it often helps to make a cooperative agreement to compete and develop your skills under pressure. Having a coach, and using the recently developed technology you can learn by reading this book or attending our workshops, also helps.

There are a number of other *practices* that bring more luck as well. *Planning* is one of the forms of practice that helps you have more luck in life. Another one is yoga. Another, meditation. Another, physical exercise. Another, keeping your word. Another, completing what you start. Another, creating your environment so it calls you forth. Another, laughing a lot. Another, having meaningful work. Another, telling the truth. Another, contributing to and loving children. Another, contributing to and loving other people. Another, music. All of these practices, and many more, *when they grow naturally out of the compassion that comes from paying attention,* help you have more luck in life.

Planning is the practice that allows you to practice the other practices. If you practice planning you have more luck, you win more, you increase the odds in your favor. Really good planning takes into account how you can use the skills you have to bring your plans into reality.

Planning is the beginning of making things happen according to my vision, using the equipment I have evolved in the course of defending my image when I thought that image was me. You need to know yourself well, and be honest simultaneously with yourself and others, to make things happen effectively in alignment with your vision and according to your plan. Your personality, developed from what happened to you in life and how you survived and adapted to outrageous fate, is the equipment you use to create with. Your neuroses are to be used to construct a better life for you and yours.

I have finally learned that taking responsibility for using my past neurotic survival schemes rather than trying to fix them works better than trying to fix them. The odds are we can't be fixed. Nobody and no thing is going to make up for how we got treated as children. The scars are not going to go away. We *can* use what we have learned by adapting to the past as a tool to create the future.

My Life Themes and Skills: From Stumbling Blocks to Stepping Stones

When I was a child, I developed skills for dealing with my life circumstances, which required me to take care of my younger brothers because my mother and stepfather were usually too drunk to do so. I learned to be wary, alert, and quick to respond to cues to predict mood and likely behavior changes in alcoholics, so I could keep them from killing each other or hurting one of the kids. I considered myself a smart kid and a hero and I couldn't afford to admit to being scared and sorry for myself. As a psychologically reactive, homemade, individual humanoid, I ended up wanting to help people, take care of them, teach them how to take care of themselves, and show off my perceptiveness. I resented people if they didn't appreciate me a lot, do what I said, and turn out the way I thought they should.

I had the dumb luck of my father dying when I was six years old. My brother was four. My mother remarried when I was seven to an alcoholic wife beater and child abuser. My youngest brother was born when I was nine. Because of this dumb luck, I was raised in such a way that I became sensitized to subtle cues about human behavior, and I wanted to try to help people who were hurting. I am designed by my life to be a helper who wants to keep those already hurt from being hurt more, and I purchase allegiance by helping others. I charge this allegiance to the helpee in an inexplicit way, such that a vague sense of obligation binds them to me, protects me from them, and gets me praise. I am a manipulative, co-dependent, lying survivor.

I have here a hand-built, home-built set of neurotic survival techniques, my carried-around-with-me-at-all-times way of getting along, feeling protected and surviving. By transforming my relationship to this fine system of survival, instead of being victimized by it, criticizing it, and resisting it, or trying to "fix" it, I can decide to serve people of my own free will, much like the mythical hero Sisyphus. Albert Camus wrote that Sisyphus' condition of being condemned to roll a big boulder up a mountain and have it roll back down again for all eternity was a perfect analogy for the human condition. We are all condemned to engage in completely futile tasks that require all we've got. Sisyphus, who used to be a hero like Hercules when he was on Earth, was thrown into this hell forever just as we, who were once happy as children, have been thrown into the hell of the meaningless meaning-making machine of the mind and the obligations of adult life. If we are to discover the secret to happiness as human beings, said Camus, we must be able to imagine a way Sisyphus could come to be a happy man in that hell. We catch a glimpse of him just as he turns to walk back down that mountain to find his rock and push it up again, and we see a beaming smile on his face. How could that be?

Sisyphus was condemned to the hell of rolling that rock up and having it fall back down, for all eternity, as his punishment, and he conquered hell by transforming his relationship to what he was condemned to do by *choosing* to do it. Sisyphus decided to choose to do what he was condemned to do. He said, this is *my* job, this is what I do for a living, I am good at it; it is what I do. I roll my rock up my mountain and back down again. This is what I do and I'm doin' it.

I, Brad Blanton, can choose to serve people as a design for my life simply because it is a good choice given my design, which I am condemned to live with. I can escape the oppression of the historical personality that drives me, even though I cannot escape the personality itself. The meaning made for me—by the life, times, family, and culture I was born into and formed by— was not under my control. What *is* under my control is the use of that personality. By using the equipment I now luckily have available to me, I can choose to serve people.

To summarize: I learned to survive by taking care of some people and being wary, paranoid, and defending against other people. I will always operate from that mode, and I have no choice in the matter. Still, serving people *can be a choice* for me and can be very fulfilling and fun if I go about it in a certain way.

The way I was built to go about serving people was as an oppressed but surviving secret hero, acknowledged by few, a staunch defender of the helpless—a cross between the Lone Ranger and Jesus. I can have that paradigm use me and be a victim of my psychological conditioning. Or, I can choose to use that model to create a life with. If, in this moment, I consider myself to be this being who is writing, and my history to be something my present-tense self possesses, I can use my memory to design a future. Rather than continue to function from and react to the past that designed how I should live at about age seven or eight or nine, *I can transform my life by my own design, by choosing to do what I have been condemned to do.* I can design any project, and do the work of planning and the work of the plans, using my developed skills in surviving to bring about the results I plan to bring about. I get to use my personality to bring about my dreams for the future. Instead of trying to fix myself, or change myself, I can simply use myself to create a life I want.

We are all like this. This is true of everybody. Unless we create some star to hitch our wagon to, or focus on, we will automatically fall back into being controlled again by mind-made reactions and moralism based on formative experiences. We will become merely neurotic again just like we were before we last escaped the jail of the mind and freed ourselves from the relentless taboos and controls of our unconsciously-built minds.

This choice to do what one is condemned to do is called transformation. My life is transformed by my choice to serve people because the purpose of my service is no longer to manipulate and control them to get what I want. As a being, satisfied in the present, I already have what I want. I don't have to have people pay me for serving them to compensate for what I lack. So it turns out, as a secondary effect of transformation, some healing of the wounds of the past does occur. By giving up the demand that other people make up for how I was deprived, I do get fixed, as a side effect.

So, being of unsound mind, as is herein amply demonstrated, and using that to create a future,

I DO DECLARE: MY LIFE IS TO SERVE PEOPLE.

That declaration is my declaration of independence. When I speak this as a declaration of intent for how I am choosing to live, it is a different kind of speaking than normal speaking. The usual language of evaluation and assessment is a different language than the language of declaration. I do this now because I say so. My life is to serve people because I say so. It is not caused by the conditions of my past or my adaptations to them. It is caused my speaking as a conscious, intentional being.

I invite you to try talking this way and see what happens to you. So, if you are willing, let's get to work!

The first step is to make your declaration of what your life is to be used for. This will immediately give you a number of problems you didn't have before you made the declaration. The good life is shared problems. Solving big problems together is the best game on earth. If playing with problems is substituted for whining and complaining, help is on the way from inside you and outside you. Here is the task: use the survival skills you learned by being abused in a dysfunctional family to create projects and solve problems of your own design. Live from your vision of the future rather than the conditioning of your past, but use the conditioning from your past to bring your vision into being.

Select from your own life story the major themes, both good and bad. Friends to whom you tell your life story can help. Write up your life themes and skills as I have just done using the model provided for you in the upcoming section of the book. After answering the questions there and composing your life themes choices list, then make your project vision statements. Come up with bodacious, glorious vision statements. Come up with something new that is worth doing with your life, or some way of doing what you already do that inspires you so much you can't wait to jump out of bed in the morning. Make sure the vision statements or background commitment statements for all your projects are consistent with the life purpose statement you will compose by answering the trick questions in the Life Purpose Statement chapter.

Write to inspire yourself, your friends, and to enroll other people in your project. Write to have an impact, to make an impression, to be remembered and talked about, and to have your projects talked about by other people when you are not present. If you are inspired by your own vision of the future, other people will be inspired as well. *You can proclaim what your life is about* and use all the skills and faults you've developed in the past to make it happen. The adventure of creating what you want in life from skills you already have is the best game in town.

Exercises

Pair up with someone and take a half hour each to talk about your life. Tell your partner what your main survival skills and adaptations were. Tell them how you survived the circumstances of your family. Then tell your partner what your main vision is for the rest of your life and how you intend to use the skills you learned from surviving to use as instruments for creating the future you envision. After both of you have done this, take a break and write down what you remember from the conversation under these two headings: survival skills and future vision. After about fifteen minutes, get back with your partner and compare notes and make revisions of both lists and talk a little more about the creative usefulness of what, particularly, you have considered to be your most negative characteristics. Then discuss the usefulness of your most valuable skills. These are the instruments for creating the future you envision. Keep the revised list to be used in a later assignment in this book.

On Continuously Being Centered in the Present and Using the Mind to Transcend the Mind

After you have begun to complete your past in preparation for the act of creating your future, and you envision a future you want to create, and you begin to plan, you must then engage in practices that repeatedly restore your experience of yourself as the being-in-the-body-who-simply-notices. Continual practice in noticing is as necessary as continual practice in sports or music; even when you know the basics, to stay sharp, you must practice.

This chapter brings up a dilemma that confronts every writer and teacher. If I catalog and explain many of the practices that can help to ground you in the present moment, I will give you an intellectual understanding of the practices rather than an experience of learning them in the real world and in your body. You need to learn these practices experientially from people who can teach them because they have learned them experientially and have practiced them for some time.

If you call us, you can take a Radical Honesty workshop or we will help you connect with someone in your area who can teach you yoga, meditation, body awareness practices, martial arts, or other paths to assist you in noticing and becoming present to present tense experience.

What we teach in our particular workshops includes:

- Instruction in a blend of meditation and self-hypnosis,

- A movement and stretching technique we invented to restore sanity called Dance Yoga for the Insane—a body-awareness-dictated free-form movement and stretching,

- Sometimes I Pretend—an honest sharing of pretenses done in a group context, and

- Radical Honesty exercises: I Observe and I Imagine, Noticing vs. Thinking, and Distorted Listening.

Continual practices like these help you re-identify yourself as a present tense experiencer and rescue you from being overwhelmed by your mind. They are absolutely essential to the ongoing life of a creator.

Once we gain a perspective on our own mind and have the possibility of using the mind rather than being used by it, an ongoing set of practices (including continuing to tell the truth, meditating, and planning for the future) is necessary to keep the mind from recapturing the space of freedom.

The mind takes experience and turns it into concepts. Yesterday's brilliant, liberating insight becomes tomorrow's bullshit. The mind takes formerly transcendent perspectives and turns them into ideals that life has to live up to, leaving us once again complaining about life not living up to our expectations.

We can use our minds to transcend our minds by remembering to direct our attention *to the constant practice of noticing,* and *to our vision of the future.* We can create, in the present, work that seems like play because it is based on the future we envision and want to bring into being. Rather than being used by our minds' defensive reactions to things in the present that vaguely remind us of our past, we use our minds to envision and create a future from the present.

While we do this series of activities to design the future, pay attention to paying attention. We are the beings who pay attention. What we create through planning is our plaything, called a life design. When we carry out the design we are playing with our lives. This is the alternative to the reactive life.

The Life Purpose Statement

"So the meaning of the Grail and of most myths is finding the dynamic source in your life so that its trajectory is out of your own center and not something put on you by society. Then, of course, there is the problem of coordinating your well being with the goods and needs of the society. But first you must find your trajectory, and then comes the social coordination."

— *Joseph Campbell (in conversation with Michael Toms)*

In the next several chapters you will learn to create and manage projects to achieve your vision of the future, but first you have to come up with a purpose for your life.

Don't worry, this is not serious. You can change it anytime. You are the creator of your life, so you can modify, paint over, erase, or destroy the life purpose statement whenever you choose. This chapter has some fill-in-the-blank pages. On completion, the reader/creator will have chosen a direction of focus for her life that is a self-determined measuring stick to judge the "fit" of relationships, work opportunities, recreational endeavors, career, and so on.

Now you will get a chance to make your own projects and your own umbrella project to manage them with. First you have to come up with a purpose for your life so you can measure all your vision statements for your projects and opportunities that come up in life against something you have chosen, rather than just reacting. You can change your life purpose or your vision statements for your projects anytime. We just need a life purpose statement to start with.

Pull out your pencils and put on your Being Cap. You are the creator of your universe. Let's begin with an exercise created by Phil Laut and presented in his book *Money is my Friend,* modified slightly to fit our purposes. Do these steps one at a time. Do not skip ahead. Just complete one exercise and then go on. It is important to do things in this sequence so your mind doesn't get in your way.

Exercise 1: Characteristics

1. List below fifteen characteristics of your Self. You may have previously considered some of them to be negative, but you can transform them in developing your life purpose. You may be intelligent, humorous, joyful, driven, slovenly, weird, whatever. Make sure you have fifteen. If you don't know fifteen, make them up. Have some fun.

1_____	6_____	11_____
2_____	7_____	12_____
3_____	8_____	13_____
4_____	9_____	14_____
5_____	10_____	15_____

If you didn't put fifteen down, get back up there and finish!

2. Now circle your five favorite personality characteristics. Do it quickly — don't think too much, and move on to Exercise 2.

Exercise 2: How You Enjoy Expressing Your Characteristics in Concrete Action in the Real World

1. Referring loosely to the five favorite personality characteristics you just circled, make a list of fifteen actual behaviors
   that are ways you enjoy expressing these characteristics.
   For example, if one of your characteristics was generosity,
   a behavior you actually perform in the real world that
   exemplifies generosity could be "feeding the homeless by
   working in a soup kitchen on Sunday mornings." Other
   specific behavior examples could be writing, researching,
   cooking, pottery making, walking, or taking the children on
   an outing.

1 _____

2 _____

3 _____

4 _____

5 _____

6 _____

7 _____

8 _____

9 _____

10 _____

11 _____

12 _____

13 _____

14 _____

15 _____

2. After you have completed a list of at least fifteen activities, and not before, pick your *five favorite* activities and circle them.

Continue with Exercise 3.

Exercise 3: The World You Want

Write a brief statement (twenty-five words or so) of your vision of an ideal world. Write this vision in the present tense and in terms of how you want it to be rather than how you want it not to be. Begin your statement this way:

"An ideal world is one in which...

_____

_____

When you finish the statement, move on to Exercise 4.

Exercise 4: Your Life Purpose

Now you are going to cut and paste your life purpose together. It's easy and fun. Here you go.

The purpose of my life is to use my (list the five general characteristics you circled) _____ ,

_____ , _____ ,

, _____ , and _____

by (list the five specific behaviors) _____ ,

_____ , _____ ,

_____ , and _____ to bring

about a world in which (write in your ideal world statement)

_____

_____

_____

Congratulations! You have a good draft of a life purpose statement of your own. Now edit it a bit. After you edit and/or revise it (if you want), type and print it, or copy it neatly. You can put it in your billfold or purse and carry it around with you. If you're on a bus or in a singles bar or at a party and you strike up a conversation with somebody and they ask you what you do for a living, whip that puppy out and hand it to them. In fact, carry a few extras so they can keep one if they like. This is the beginning of the conversation you generate that has you creating the kind of world you want to live in with the help of a whole bunch of other people.

Because I don't know exactly what you wrote, I'll review a sample life purpose statement in case you want an example to follow while you are revising yours. You can work on a life purpose statement like you would work on a poem or a song. Polish it and make it sing, make it move people, make people cry when they hear it. Write a song from it. Make a poster from it. Do a photo essay on it. Make a display of it. Write it on the wall next to the telephone. Put it on the refrigerator.

Here's one that someone just wrote in a workshop, and it's ready to cook with:

> The purpose of my life is to use my listening skills, communicating ability, courage, charisma, and joyfulness by giving speeches, telling stories, writing, teaching, being in my body, and embracing loved ones to bring about a world in which every person lives in a family and in a community in which they are listened to and spoken to with honor, and supported to live a life of honesty and constant creating.

You can see that in this individual's statement there are six characteristics and six specific behaviors. In your own statement, add or subtract whatever makes this more powerful for you. Play with this to make it as clear and inspiring for you as possible. Make it inspiring to other people as well.

Phil Laut, who created this exercise, says: "It is possible that several iterations will be required before you have a statement of purpose that you will like well enough to write on a slip of paper and carry around with you. Some of the benefits that you can expect are that thinking and behavior that do not support your purpose will be more evident to you and goal setting and decision making will both be easier. The statement and expression of your purpose is derived from your values. For this reason, clear definition of your purpose may require some careful thought to resolve conflicting values. Without a clear sense of your purpose all of the education you receive and all of the improvements that you make in yourself serve only to make you a more productive slave to someone else's purpose."

Congratulations again on your creation! There is your life purpose in bold print. Write it on slips of paper and drop it from the Goodyear blimp at the Super Bowl. Write it on a flag and fly it from the back of a 4x4 driving down Main Street on the Fourth of July. Put it in a bottle and throw it in the ocean for Robertson Crewsole to pick off the beach in a year or so. Print a tee-shirt that says: "Grandma went to Florida and all I got was this lousy Life Purpose."

You now have something to use to consider how you spend the moments of your life. You now have something with which to compare your vision statements in your projects. If what you envision for your projects doesn't match what you envision for your life, change one or the other. If what you spend your time on in your life is consistent with the purpose of your life, go ahead and create away and have a hell of a good time doing it. If not, then it's time to change your life projects or your life purpose again. Hang loose and celebrate. This is not serious. This is only your life purpose, which you created, and you can change it when you like. Be nonchalant. Be totally committed without attachment. Go meditate now and release yourself from any sense of obligation. Regain your freedom as a being, and then go play some more life.

Domains and Projects

To take some actual control over your life, first determine what the domains of your life are. You use domains to identify the multiple dimensions of your life in a way that seems intuitively correct to you (for example, family, career, recreation, money, and so on). Later, when you write up your projects, you will have at least one project (and usually several projects) for each domain.

When you name your domains, you want to include *everything you are currently doing in your life and everything new that you want to do.* You will probably create between five and nine domains.

Remember that this work of planning and sharing is really for fun. You don't just do it to make hell bearable. You do it to make hell fun. You are beginning the process of transforming the hell of having a mind into the blessing of a useful mind. You are beginning this sequence of activities:

1. Get clear about the purpose of your life and articulate that in a comprehensive sentence. If you followed the directions in the life purpose chapter one step at a time, you were tricked into coming up with a life purpose statement. If you didn't do that yet, go back and do it now.

2. Determine the *domains* of your life and write them down.

3. Determine the *projects* for each domain. Just come up with the titles to the projects to begin with.

4. Plan and write up the projects in great detail using the model presented in the next chapter.

5. Continue the practices of meditation and telling the truth to stay in touch with your essential self, the being who lives each moment. This is so you don't get too attached to your projects or get to believing that who you are depends on their success. *Share your projects with your friends and get them to help. Continuing these practices of noticing what is so in the moment and noticing the noticer* is absolutely critical to bringing the projects you envision into being. As you do so, the work will become play.

Use names that make sense to you for your life domains. Let's say you have determined them as work, family, recreation, health and well being, entertainment, and money and travel. If those headings cover everything you are now doing as well as everything you plan to do, then you are finished with this part and are ready to move on to identify the projects for each domain.

What Is a Project Outline?

A project outline is a learning tool like the foot outlines on a dance floor, a chess diagram in the newspaper, or training wheels on a child's bike. Creating in the social world — the creating done through speaking and listening — requires some discipline so you improve through experience and practice. The project outline guides the creator in the first slow steps toward creating a powerful life. Like a novice guitar player, the creator carefully plucks the strings of a project precisely as the book instructs until, with time and experience, the melody of creating is the expression of the creator.

The mind is a tricky devil and will work hard to make this process stale very quickly, categorizing the goal, creating shoulds, and questioning the logic of the creation. The mind gets attached to anything envisioned and written down. To avoid the distress caused by attachment to models of the mind, creators must continually practice distinguishing between noticing and thinking. The practices that develop noticing sensations in the body, noticing the world with the senses, noticing thinking, and being aware of noticing itself, allow the being you are to be grounded in sensate experience in the here and now. These practices keep the creator one step ahead of the mind, so that recreating projects and achieving breakthroughs continue.

As life changes and moves around us, a project outline gets revised and moves with us. It's a fine line between continually recreating a project and being trapped by it. Remaining grounded in experience and noticing what is happening NOW by meditating, telling the truth, and being present to a community of friends who are co-creators is all you need to do to stay free.

The format of a project encourages its constant recreation and modification. A project outline, once written and acted upon, is immediately stale and obsolete. The project outline format that follows helps keep the project simple and focused. Project outlines are to be treated like tissues. Life moves too fast to have a single writeup remain the same. Many of us have had project writeups get obsolete within hours of pulling them from the printer. Action creates change. Changes in available information, perspective, or goals are a natural part of the creating process. Eventually, the fun of "writing history in advance" becomes a looked-forward-to enterprise. Constantly fiddling with and updating a project encourages you to tap into fresh passion and adopt a wider perspective with each new success or defeat. The commitment, action, and focus of attention on the overall vision of the project remain intact even though new information that shows up may have you doing many things you didn't originally anticipate. This ongoing pleasure in new learning is like "that seriousness of a child at play" that Nietzsche spoke about.

Embracing changes by dreaming them up, rather than dreading changes, allows you the flexibility to take advantage of emerging opportunities. We suggest that you, as creator of the world and a good life, format your projects as outlined below.

Domain: Name of domain here.

Project Name: Name of project here.

Brief History: This is the story of what you have done on the project previously if you have any history with it. If it is a brand new project, skip this step when you write it up. As the project continues and you hit major milestones, a short addition to this section keeps a running account of the ups and downs.

Background Commitment: This is a statement of the values that make this project is important to the creator. It states what you value and how you intend to act on these values; it is a picture of the future of which this project is an expression.

Vision: What the finished project will look like, in detailed pictures. For instance:

Picture 1: A sensory rich description of the experience of this project when it has been brought into being.

Picture 2: Another sensory rich description of the experience of this project when it has been brought into being.

Picture 3: Another sensory rich description of the experience of this project when it has been brought into being.

Now synthesize these three pictures into one. We want you to make a compelling vision you can almost taste, touch, feel, hear, and see. This is what you will communicate to others and picture for yourself *to maintain the conversation you continue to create* because that is how visions become reality. This vision is also to keep you going through the harder parts of creating — the work that is not as much fun as you thought it would be. A clear vision of where you are going with what you are doing helps a lot. You picture something and keep on talking about it and it shows up.

Committed Listener: A fellow creator who will listen, support, and coach you in the process.

Network of Support: People whose experience and interests provide information and resources for accomplishment of the project. This usually includes friends who want you to be happy and successful, or people whom you are helping with their projects.

State: Choices are:

FORMULATION

CONCENTRATION

MOMENTUM

STABILITY

BREAKTHROUGH

These states determine how you will manage your project. (They are explained in more detail in chapter twenty-two.) In the beginning, when you are writing up a project for the first time, you are in the state called FORMULATION.

Measures: Where the creator wants to go. These are milestones that mark the stages of accomplishment of the project. This section keeps focus on the "creative tension" described in Robert Fritz's book *Creating*. (Buy that book.) The tension is between where you are and where you want to be. In that gap there are degrees of attainment. Much of the updating of your project occurs here.

Description of Overall Plan: This is a description of how the creator will organize his actions to bring the future and ongoing measures into reality. It is the way you come to speak to others about your projects. It later becomes the heart of the "laser statement" you will eventually create to describe each project so you can have a powerful impact on others when you speak about your project.

Action (What to Do and by When): A simplified example follows. Get logo, 9/20/99. Send logo to printer, 10/5/99. Get business cards, 10/15/99.

Date Printed: Frequent updates can get confusing. This line keeps you current.

Now if you will put those bold headings on a page, you have a skeleton on which to put the flesh of your own creations. If you want more powerful coaching in greater detail, enroll in the Course in Honesty and then the creators' reunion groups. If you feel inspired to, go ahead and write up at least one project to completion and then continue reading this book. If not, read on and come back later.

Now you know what you do with your domains. You come up with project titles for every project in each domain. Then you formulate a vision statement for the project and proceed to fill in the blanks for the other elements.

Let's say you have six domains. Two of the domains may have just one project, which has the same title as the domain. Two domains may have three projects each. One may have five projects. I suggest you proceed with making project titles and vision statements first, and cover all your domains. You will probably come up with somewhere between 6 and 20 projects. Don't worry about whether you have too many or too few. Just cover everything you are doing currently in your life and attempting to manage, and everything you want to do in the near future. After you look over the project titles and vision statements, you can make plans to change some aspects of your current life, or invent new elements of your envisioned future by planning changes in how you spend your time right now. For now, complete just the project titles and vision statements, then read on.

Sample Domains And Projects — A System Of Organization

Now that you have seen one project writeup and its results, you may be ready to get a picture of the overall use of a project design system to focus energy in your life. What follows is the model of the overall system or organization I used in a recent writeup of my projects.

My Domains

The domains of my life in 1999 are listed in the following outline. These domains cover every activity of my waking life. They include everything *I do now* and everything *I plan to do.* I have at least one project (usually a number of projects) for each domain. I work simultaneously on those projects, and manage them with what is called an "umbrella project," which is written and used *after all the other projects are written up.* You will get more coaching from this book about doing that once you have written up all your projects. For the time being I want to just mention one goal that came from my umbrella project because it fits in nicely here. This also gives you an example of the value of organizing your visions for the future. One of my overall objectives is: BALANCE.

I manage my projects with an eye to keeping a balance of time spent on these activities.

- Physical exercise and attention (including golf, physical work around the farm, running, yoga, meditation, skiing, working out with weights and machines, running, kayaking, and swimming).

- Social interaction (including running workshops, seeing clients, traveling, spending time with family, spending time with friends, and partying).

- Intellectual recreation (including writing books and articles, reading, teaching, planning and organizing projects, engaging in the Great Conversation).

That is, while participating with people in these domains of my life, I aim to maintain a balance of physical activity, social activity, and intellectual recreational activity, serving people all the while. That said, I will now use the format you are learning for writing up projects.

A World that Works for Me and Everyone I Know

1999, Brad Blanton

Domains

- Radical Honesty Enterprises — (A Career Gone Wrong)
- Family, Friends and Love Life
- Sparrowhawk Homestead
- Health, Well-Being and Recreation
- Money

Projects Listed by Domain:

First Domain: Radical Honesty Enterprises — A Career Gone Wrong

Title: WORKSHOP LEADING (This is a full project writeup that you can use as a model for your own projects.)

Vision One: I lead one two-day (Introduction to Radical Honesty) workshop each month and one eight-day (Course in Honesty) workshop every six weeks. These workshops are organized and filled by everyone else who works for Radical Honesty Enterprises, and I have an intern and a co-leader in each workshop. I have an intermediately detailed workshop manual that is revised every eighteen months. Other trainers are running Introduction to Radical Honesty and Course in Honesty workshops together without my participation. Twice a year, I co-lead a trainers training. Six weeks to one month in advance of two-day workshops, I lead three-hour introductions to Radical Honesty in six selected cities. There are usually between 100 and 150 people in these presentations. Fifty-person enrollments in the two-day become standard and Ed and Taber also learn to lead these introductions this year. We have a digital video of each one of these for use by people being trained to give these presentations. We generate applause, enthusiasm, communications afterward, enrollments in workshops, and lots of media coverage to help the cause of honest permission to share how life is among human beings so that the redesign of culture itself becomes possible.

Vision Two: I see a group of people sitting in a circle being led by someone who is really good and trained by me, and it goes on without me being there. I see a meeting of the United Nations that begins with a twenty-minute meditation and proceeds with reports of projects using a version of this model I now teach.

Background Commitment: I am committed to helping people live happier, more productive lives and to empowering them to help other people do the same. I am committed to enjoying the process of growing for other people and myself. I am committed to creating communities of people capable of intimacy; that is, relating to each other based on telling the truth rather than pretending. I am committed to:

- delivering people from domination by their own minds;
- freeing people enough from their minds that they can use them rather than be used by them;
- inspiring people and making them happy;
- exemplifying and encouraging a life of play and service;
- building therapeutic communities of lifelong friends;
- seeding the culture of the world with therapeutic communities and making the world into a therapeutic community.

I want to create the future human culture as a place of love and nurturance instead of moralism for young humans. I want to continue to affiliate with the work of Landmark Education and support that work and be supported by it without us duplicating or substituting for each other; working alongside each other toward the same end. I also want to continue to affiliate with Marilyn Ferguson, Gay and Kathlyn Hendricks, Stan Dale, Deepak Chopra, Neale Donald Walsch, David Korten, Tom Peters, Robert Fritz, and other authors, workshop leaders, management consultants, and people with wisdom from all walks of life to support their work and have their work support our whole community.

I am committed to generating successful communities of support in the world for telling the truth, so that participants can pass on the benefits of living out loud to their families and people they are related to outside the community of support. I am committed to every member of every workshop group being trained and disciplined in skills of grounding in their own experience of being in their bodies and noticing what is going on in the world and listening powerfully and creatively to other people and designing and conducting their lives according to their own plans. I am committed to the continued existence of these communities of support. I am committed to the success of everyone in these communities in designing and bringing into being the results they plan for. For every participant who completes the Course in Honesty and consequent groups, one or more Trainer's workshops, and an internship, I am committed to supporting them in becoming capable of running the workshops.

Brief History: I have designed and conducted a Workshop called Telling the Truth since 1989. I have now created the Course in Honesty so that

- it can be replicated and conducted by others,

- people can get great results in life from doing the workshop, and

- workshop participation, along with some additional training, prepares selected people to conduct the Introduction to Radical Honesty and the Course in Honesty.

I have now conducted what was formerly the Nine Day Workshop over a dozen times, and the Eight Day about fifteen times. These workshops have become the Course in Honesty. The manual is written and gets revised and added to regularly.

Committed Listeners: Ed Greville, Tina Oehser.

State: FORMULATION...CONCENTRATION...MOMENTUM...STABILITY...BREAKTHROUGH.

Measures: Full enrollment in six Course in Honesty workshops for the year 1999. At least twenty trainees participating in the Train the Trainers workshop in May. Accomplishment of the goals set by people for the Reunion, by their own report and that of their friends. One-fifth of new participants coming from enrollment by former participants because of those participants' enthusiasm and success.

Network of Support People: The Gang of Graduates

Description of Overall Plan: For the year, conduct six Course in Honesty Workshops and one Trainers' Training Workshop for twenty/thirty participants who have all done the Course in Honesty workshop. I will conduct twelve two-day Introduction to Radical Honesty workshops and have at least four led by other trainers by themselves. The Course in Forgiveness and the Course in Creating will integrate more powerfully the results of the workshops in people's lives. These workshops will be the way people can learn from my trainees and me after reading *Radical Honesty*, doing a two-day Introduction to Radical Honesty workshop, and continuing on for more intensive work. Out of these I will found The Point of Light, a religious organization dedicated to the memory of George Bush (not really).

What To Do and By When: (Transferred to Daytimer and weekly to do list.)

Using the Project Writeup Model

You can use the models and forms from this chapter as a template for your projects and you can refer back to my sample projects if you have questions that are not answered by the instructions in these upcoming chapters.

I generally have twelve to twenty project writeups each six months, in January and July of each year. I recommend you write up all of yours completely, at least once in this fashion, however many you have. You will need a minimum of three to continue on as designer of your life through the assignments in the next section of this book. So go ahead and give it a shot right now and do three project writeups. Make your life a work of art. Good luck.

Summary of the Project Writeup Format

Domain:
Project Title:
Brief History:
Background Commitment:
Vision:
Committed Listener:
Network of Support:
State:
Measures:
Description of Overall Plan:
Action:
Date Printed:

Reformulation of Current Work Using the Project Write-Up

This is a true story told by Paul LaFontaine, a graduate of the Course In Honesty. It is an example of how, by reformulating what he was doing at work—through writing up his project according to his vision—Paul changed his life at work. A review of Paul's project proves that the future is not destined to be a replication of the past, and actually makes us excited about the possibilities of our own lives. His reformulation of what he was about at work, through writing up his projects according to his vision, changed a disgruntled employee (with a recent moderately poor performance review) to a recognized significant player in the design for the future growth of his company. He also got a $2,000 raise. Here is Paul's story in his own words:

How Work Becomes Play by Paul LaFontaine

The chair was uncomfortable as I sat down. My boss had called me into his office for my annual performance review. When the company had hired me a year before, they said they needed me to examine process efficiency in the facility. Instead, they wanted me to sit and write memos. Whenever a piece of furniture was purchased or moved, they had me doing the paperwork, after which they bitched at me for not completing the forms to their satisfaction. It was boring work and it had me trapped because I needed the paycheck.

"Really, I wrote a better review," my boss said. "They changed it. There's nothing I can do."

"They're always doing things like this," I replied. "Can I write a rebuttal?"

"Yeah, but be careful," he said, handing me the review.

They deserved a rebuttal. They wrote that I had failed to document purchases satisfactorily. Of the many purchases I had made that year, only once had they caught me short of paperwork. My rebuttal would hammer this point and embarrass them with their lack of information. From my small chair in a cubicle amidst a sea of cubicles, a clever rebuttal took shape. Once it was completed and in the mail I prepared for a vacation.

My vacation was the Radical Honesty Eight Day Workshop. Brad Blanton spoke about stories, language, and personal power. He spoke of a life of play. He showed us how to meditate. He showed us movies. He talked about how we are the creators of our own experience. He put me in a chair and listened to me talk, coaching me to notice what I was experiencing. After several days, I noticed that in my mind I was blaming other people, "them," for my dissatisfactions. I learned. I learned about fear, responsibility, and telling the truth. I learned how to notice what came up for me emotionally. Most importantly, I learned about myself. As the workshop neared completion, I listened to Brad describe a technique useful in being a powerful creator. I heard him describe the writing of projects.

I was excited by his description. I organized furniture orders for the company into projects, but a project of my own was different. I could create my own life in my projects. After some instruction, I wrote my projects. In one, I recreated my work by writing a clear vision and measures of success with timelines. I would transform my work into play. I was going to expand on my furniture purchasing and become *a creator of work environments* that would transform the company from a sea of cubicles to an open space where teams would flourish. I called this project "Work Environment Creator." I would be unstoppable.

Project in hand, I returned to the company and began talking about work environments. I got out of my small chair, left my cubicle, and began walking around the building asking people what they needed to improve their workspace. I drew diagrams and talked about creating an open space where teams would flourish. I was excited by my vision and couldn't stop talking about it.

Prior to leaving for the workshop, I had been given the task to "coordinate and document company departmental involvement" on a $5 million office refurbishment. I didn't know what this meant, so I checked my Work Environment Creator project and decided that I had a better plan. I took charge.

I gathered the architect, consultants, and contractors together around a table and looked at each of them as I leaned forward in a large, comfortable chair. After a moment of complete silence, I spoke.

"This project is the first step in recreating this building as an open environment that supports teams," I said. "We will complete it and have our people move in on July 8th."

"OK," said the architect.

"Let's get to work," said a consultant.

I then said this to the management of the company and the people who would move into the space. I said it to my friends, strangers, and anyone who would listen. When quick decisions were needed, I was consulted and I said it again. When people rolled their eyes in meetings and expressed doubts as to whether a project this size could be finished on time, I said it yet again. I said it in the cafeteria. I said it in the restroom. I said it in my sleep.

On July 8th, our people moved in.

I listened as people told me what a good job I had done. I reviewed my project and was ready for more. I had a vision of the entire building being an open space that supported teams, so I set to work. Using learning from another project I had created and my experience at the Radical Honesty Workshop, I created a workshop where departmental managers for the company could develop a team-based work environment for their people. I visited the vice president of the facility.

"I am going to work with each department and develop a plan to create for them an open, team-based work environment," I said. "I'll have these plans ready for future growth."

"OK," he replied.

I started giving the workshop. I was excited as I told the department managers about the advantages of an open environment. I had fun. I drew pictures for them from which they began modifying their workspace on their own. I applauded them. I talked about a team-based facility. I drew more pictures. I was slowly and steadily bringing my vision into being.

The executives decided they were going to build a new office building. I was assigned the project. I reviewed my project and prepared to create a work environment for the executive group. I met with them and talked about an open space in which teams could flourish. I talked about how I was creating this in each department. The group who had been "they" to me months before sat and nodded their heads. "You are the example for the rest of the facility."

I concluded, "Your new space will be a team-based space."

"OK," said a vice president.

"Good idea," said a director.

"Can't disagree with that," said another vice president.

I was making my project with its vision a reality. I was creating work environments. I was having fun. I walked past an abandoned row of cubicles that I was having disassembled and went on to my new office. I was comfortable as I sat in my large chair. I felt free. I smiled as I spoke to myself. I was playing.

How To Make Hell Fun

Paul transformed his relationship to work at his company by making a paradigm shift, a change in perspective that allowed him to recreate everything at work from a different perspective.

He did what Robert Fritz, the brilliant author of the books *The Path of Least Resistance, Creating,* and *Corporate Tides,* calls a shift from the reacting orientation to the creating orientation. As a result of doing the workshop, Paul began to come from some place other than reacting to circumstances imposed upon him by his job.

An Individual Project that Changed the World

In 1993, a man named Sam, who had years of experience as a hotel and resort manager, decided, with the help of The Advanced Course conducted by Landmark Education, to become a conscious creator of his life rather than a set of reactions. He decided that he wanted to use his skills as a hotelier to increase the possibility of communication between the Eastern Bloc countries and the West to bring about peace in the world. He wanted to create a meeting place in Moscow. His vision was to create a meeting place for the Iron Curtain countries and the West to maximize the possibility of communication among the leaders and businesspeople of those nations. He wrote up his project and got funding on a joint venture with people he knew involving two major hotel chains in America, went to Moscow, bought a hotel, gutted it, and rebuilt it with meeting rooms and all the most modern electronic equipment and communications support available at the time. He put audio visual equipment, satellite communications, computerized media presentation devices, and facilities into a very modern and comfortable setting.

Sam was in Moscow in his renovated hotel in 1995 when the military coup was attempted. President Gorbachev was under house arrest and confined to his quarters at a vacation resort in the South. Boris Yeltsin was in the main legislative building which was surrounded by tanks. All television, radio, and switchboards were turned off, blocked out, or in the control of the army. The generals announced that they were in charge and that the government was under military command. The coup was accomplished.

Sam, the hotel man, put on a trench coat, stepped out into the rain, walked two blocks to the ring of tanks, walked between the tanks, and into the parliament building. He walked right up to Boris Yeltsin. He said, "I thought you might find this useful," and handed him a cellular telephone, which operated by satellite through a dish mounted atop his hotel two blocks away. Boris Yeltsin took the phone, thanked him, and stayed on the telephone all that night. The next day the coup failed. No one knows how many or which people Boris Yeltsin talked to that night; just that he was on the phone for six hours straight and the coup collapsed the next day.

Sam spoke and listened a project into being, intending to have an impact on the Cold War, and he did. He helped create a new and different world for all of us. He was at the right place at the right time and with the right listening for the opportunity to make a difference in a direction he had chosen consciously in advance. He used the skills he developed before he became a conscious creator to aid in bringing about a future he envisioned and he brought it about.

Creating: Using the Medium of Project Design and Communication

I have been formulating my life into projects, consciously designed, for fifteen years now. For fifteen years I have designed my life a year at a time, and revised it every six months, using the reactive equipment for service commonly known as Brad Blanton. Absolutely everything I do in my life now was once only a figment of my imagination, which became a project design. There is not a waking minute I spend on whatever work or play I do that is not intimately related to a conscious act of creation of my own. My daughter who is fourteen years old now was written up as a project before we got pregnant. So was my six year old son. So was our marriage. So was the house I built we now live in, the book, *Radical Honesty*, this book you are reading, the workshops, and the business called Radical Honesty Enterprises. It is not that all occurrences are anticipated, just that they show up in a context of opportunity that was created before they happened. When unexpected events occur in the world, they are in relation to projects of my design. Lots of unforeseen things occur as they do in anyone's life, but they occur within the contexts I have consciously created and it makes a big difference.

This kind of living never looks like you thought it would. As Werner Erhard once said, "You can have anything you want as long as it doesn't have to look like you thought it would." A life of conscious design is, however, a lot more in the direction you intended than the normal chances of life would take you. I will share with you the outline for my current writeup of my recent projected life in the following chapter on the Umbrella Project. This way you can see how I do it. You can do this for your life if you want to.

I hope this will inspire you to create your own life projects consciously as an artist and by design as an individual and that you will join me in teaching others by example. This is the secret to the good life. Your grandmother could have told you. It's so simple it's hardly worth mentioning. Maybe that's why she forgot to tell you.

The Umbrella Project

Once your projects are written up, you design your umbrella project to manage all your projects in all the domains of your life. This is the overview of all other projects, the perspective from which they are managed. The umbrella project ensures consistent attention to all your projects, and allows you to add the further goal of maintaining a balance of physical, social, and intellectual activity. (For example, "I want to spend at least twenty percent of my days doing physical work or play and have social and intellectual activities be about evenly split for the rest of the time.") Conscious management of your life so you can get in enough party time, golf time, reading and writing time, staying in shape time, and so forth really happens at this highest level of management.

Write up all your projects, for all the domains of your life, and then write up your umbrella project to manage them. This makes possible balance and persistent attention to all your projects. It may be modified frequently, as you steer your life's projects, with more time put in on some than others, but the consistency of your commitment to all your projects is kept in balance this way in accordance with your life purpose statement. *Your life purpose statement becomes the background commitment statement and vision statement for your umbrella project itself.* At the end of this chapter, we walk through an umbrella project from beginning to end.

Once your projects are written up, you can compare the vision statements for all the projects with your life purpose statement and make some revisions in both. Then you can design the rest of your umbrella project. Remember, it's your life you are creating and you can modify the design as frequently as you like. You will notice that you will have a tendency, as you steer your life's projects, to put more time in on some projects at some times than others, but the consistency of your commitment to all your projects is kept in balance through the umbrella project, in accord with your life purpose statement — the background commitment statement and vision statement for your umbrella project itself. The umbrella project is organized in the following format.

Umbrella Project Title: The title and your name go here.

What My Life Is Committed to and What It Will Be Like Because I Say So Is... This is your life purpose, written in the format of "The purpose of my life is to use my_____ _____ by _____ _____to bring about a world in which _____." You already wrote this when you worked through the exercises in the Life Purpose Statement chapter. You can modify it if you like.

The Story of My Personality: This is your theory about the elements of personality that have been discovered in the course of the earlier assignment in the chapter on Planning the Future. Here you define the defenses and records of the mind that formerly have been reactions and barriers to real control in life, which you will now reuse as assets.

If you are doing this after taking the Course in Honesty and before the first reunion group meeting (the Course in Forgiveness), you have a videotape made during the workshop in which you told the entire story of your life to the group and answered all questions that arose from the telling. You received feedback from the group on what appeared to be themes in your life or themes in the way you told your story. Reunion Group participants, when they write up their umbrella project, are asked to watch their tape again with significant others and discuss it. They sit before their own story like an artist in front of a canvas that is not complete yet, or a composer attempting to modify a theme already begun, or someone designing a sitting place on a promenade, waiting for the lay of the land and the view to tell him how to place the benches and the flowers and shrubs. Your life is already started. Get what it is, and modify it until it feels like a masterpiece.

You are panning for gold in your life story. It is there. Look for the themes and repeated patterns in the story of your life. Choose the skills you have developed for defense to use in the act of creation. It is worth the trouble of making a videotape of yourself telling your life story to a group of people and then watching the tape while taking notes to be used in the design of your future. You are going to explore your assessments of who you are in search of the most stuck parts, so that you can flip them around and use them in your creating.

You could use your unacceptably loud voice to become a champion hog caller, your unremitting body odor to become a wealthy bloodhound trainer, or your hangnail to become a professional hang glider. Your perceived weaknesses, as well as your known strengths, are actually your potential strengths.

These exercises may help.

Exercise 1

Write the survival strategy you employed as a child to avoid punishment, be accepted, or get more chocolate chip cookies.

Exercise 2

Write your day-to-day expression of that strategy. What carries over now from that early strategy in your family life and your work life? If you threw tantrums as a child to get cookies, do you rant and rave at work to get things done?

Exercise 3

Flip your strategy on its head. Write how your day-to-day expression of your strategy can be useful. Maybe your tantrums can launch you as a world leader of the International Order of Histrionics.

Exercise 4

Write the story of your personality. Lead with the theory developed in Exercise 1, then the day-to-day expressions in Exercise 2, then the way you'll flip this strategy on its head as written in Exercise 3.

Domains and Projects: Here is where you, the creator, list all your domains and projects, and expand them one at a time. In this context, projects will grow consistent with your life vision.

Beneath the umbrella project, individual projects are the expression of a being who is an artist creating his own life. The life purpose statement you formulated in a non-linear fashion is now used for the background commitment and vision statement for the umbrella project, and the vision statements for each project are aligned with your overall vision for your life as expressed in this statement. You have compared the vision for your life with each project vision. If they didn't go together well, you either changed your project or changed the vision for your life. Finally, you have a sense of unity concerning what you are about and a basis for clearer and cleared communication in conversation with others about what you are bringing into being with your life. You will be pleasantly surprised at how many allies show up to work with you.

Now, here is the beginning of my umbrella project.

Umbrella Project Title: A World That Works for Me and Everyone I Know in 1999.

Vision: The purpose of my life is to use my perceptiveness, intelligence, love of children, love of people, and love of life by writing books, designing and conducting workshops, giving talks and making media appearances, sharing honestly with friends, and raising children and grandchildren in such as way as to create the possibility of a lifetime of play and service for every human being on planet earth. Out of my life and the lives of friends, I help everyone born get raised by being played with, loved, fed, sheltered, and interacted with in a family and community of functional happy human beings. This new world comes about because of how my friends and I have lived, raised our children, and loved them and each other.

Vision Statement Two: I am in demand constantly to do workshops, make public appearances, write books, and do television shows. A large staff of twenty to 400 people manages our mutual empire. My books are read by business and political and intellectual leaders of the world. Many of my colleagues and I are constantly asked to deliver commencement addresses at universities and receive honorary degrees. At the end of my life, most of my work is in coordinating the work of major institutions, associations, and corporations toward a system of world organization in which the distribution of opportunity and the distribution of wealth are coordinated to bring about the elevation of all human beings, in poverty of goods or mind, to a luxurious minimum standard. Before and after I die, my name will appear in stone, in print, on street signs, in history books, on television, and become a household word when people mean to say "plenty good enough." I will become known as the George Washington of the first world government based on truly sharing the real wealth of the world—the freedom and creativity of its people.

Background Commitment: I am committed to training people and trainers in radical honesty to bring about a world in which all human beings have the opportunity to constantly be delivered from the limitations of belief and be reborn into the possibility of a lifetime of play and service to each other.

Umbrella Project Writeups

After the vision and background committment are completed for the Umbrella Project the domains and projects follow. My domains and a few of my projects that fit in here are what you read in the chapter on sample domains and projects.

Remember, as you steer your life's projects, you will put more time in on some projects at some times than at others, but the consistency of your commitment to all your projects is kept in balance this way, in accordance with your life purpose statement. Now, let's go through this process one step at a time.

Exercise

Write your life purpose statement as your first vision statement. Then come up with a further vision. Then do a background commitment statement and proceed through the Umbrella Project model for your own future life. After completing that work, proceed to the next chapter for a little more detail about project writeups and managing them from a perspective that views them all as consistently contributing to your life purpose.

Project Development Stages

The stages of development of our projects are important to know because they determine the management style we want to use to be the most effective in each stage. At the point in the project writeup where State is listed, this does not stand for where in the U.S. you were born or what nation you live in. It means the state of evolution of your project. Your choices are Formulation, Concentration, Momentum, Stability, and Breakthrough.

These phase definitions are from *Results Management* by Kaplan, and from the Mastery of Empowerment course that used to be taught by Werner Erhard and Associates, and from me, based on my experience of using their model. A brief description of each phase follows.

- The *Formulation* stage of a project is when you are first writing it up. You collect information from other sources and write up your project on your own.

- The *Concentration* phase is when you start making the project happen. You give the writeup to your committed listener. You make phone calls, write letters, send emails, contact people, buy supplies, and take initial actions. The rule of thumb for this phase is ten out, one back. That is, for every ten calls you expect one return, for every ten letters one response, and so on.

- *Momentum* is the phase where responses start coming in. You receive some that you didn't expect, showing that the conversation you started is living out there without you pushing it all the time. By this phase, you may have hired some help or found some helpers to assist you with the project.

- *Stability* is when you are humming along in a constant dependable fashion. Calls and letters come in and are handled in a clear and efficient fashion. People know what their jobs are.

- *Breakthrough* happens when you have been operating at stability and all of a sudden wonderful things you never could have predicted happen that blow your mind. It is so much fun it will test your tolerance for joy. You may not be able to stand it.

The stage you identify demarcates the current status of the project and reminds you to reexamine your management style. For example, when we are in the Concentration stage we are working to create momentum by talking to people, writing, and doing all the activities articulated in the project writeup. However, when we move into momentum we need to hand off and systematize ways of responding to the responses. Our management style changes to doing less ourselves and handing more off and developing systems and people we can depend on to keep building the project.

Management Style for Each Stage of Project Development

- During Formulation, you can work alone and get your project in some readable and understandable form.

- During the Concentration phase, you will be contacting other people. Get someone to start helping you here. Pay them or make an exchange of services. Have frequent short meetings with your helper or helpers, with short-range commitments and short range accountability.

- When you hit Momentum and things start coming back at you in larger quantities, hand off some of the authority for many of the details. Have less frequent meetings, of a little longer duration, with people you make responsible for whole areas, in which they report to you and everyone else. You need to have time for planning to anticipate further momentum.

- When you hit Stability, some meetings should be happening without you present. When you do participate, people report results to you and to each other and get your newest vision and plans for the future. You spend *half* your time planning.

- Managing for Breakthrough is done by maintaining stability. A request for information comes in and the pre-arranged packet is sent out followed by a phone call. When the President of the U.S. calls when you didn't expect it, that is a breakthrough. You have on hand the information he wants.

Part Four:
How To Speak and Listen Your Projects Into Being

A Conversation With
A Life of Its Own

All the work of writing a project outline is only preparation for the act of creation itself. Ultimately, your projects depend mostly on how you contact other people and how you talk and listen to them. You want to contact other people in such a way that you get their attention and enroll them in helping you bring your vision into being. Believe it or not, most of the people you know want just about the same thing you want.

Clarity of formulation changes your listening. The whole writeup system was for one purpose, which is *to have an effect on how you speak and listen in the real world of human interaction.*

What it takes to live the life of an artist is ongoing honest communication and completion and action consistent with your vision. The whole process of creating projects consistent with your life purpose is also for one reason, which is to *have an effect on how you speak and listen.* Projects are brought into being by speaking and listening. Of the two, listening is more important. What you hear, once you have completed the design of a project, is different from what you heard before you designed the project. In your daily life, *what you notice* when you read, watch television, overhear on the subway, and generally pay attention *changes* once you have completed your project writeups. A variety of people show up to help you, teach you, work with you, work for you, have you work for them—all in ways consistent with your project objectives. They would not show up for you had you not clearly conceptualized your projects and your life purpose and your wisdom about the patterns of survival in your own life.

When you speak about what you have noticed and what you have heard, your speaking is in the context of the projects you have created and contributes to the accomplishment of those projects by getting a conversation started that has a life of its own. People keep talking about your vision and your work when you aren't there. You become more and more articulate as the conversation goes on because you get more and more information and more and more practice articulating your goals. Your vision gets built up and elaborated on by the conversation. Eventually, you have a series of laser statements about what you are about in life. These are clear and articulate sound bytes that people get immediately, remember, and repeat to other people and back to you. These come naturally from practice in speaking while you are focused on your intentions and creations. You learn through practice how to speak so people will listen and listen so people will speak. I recommend a number of books, including *The Artist's Way*[20] by Julia Cameron and *Creating* and *The Path of Least Resistance*[21] by Robert Fritz. You can find a list of books, websites, and workshops at the end of this book.

Creating a Context

In 1977, Werner Erhard started a project to end starvation on the planet by the year 2000, and he wrote a brochure. In 1978 the brochure was publicized, clearly defining the objectives of what the founders had named the Hunger Project. This is possibly the best brochure written during the twentieth century. In this unlikely place — the middle pages of a brochure — there occurred what seems to me one of the most brilliant syntheses of the twentieth century's evolution of thought in linguistics, philosophy, and the study of the mind. A segment of that brochure follows:

"What causes an idea's time to come?" When you know the answer to that, you are no longer a mere speck of protoplasm on a dustball hurtling through space. You know how to make an impact on the world. You know what can make your life matter. The answer to "What causes an idea's time to come?" is what the Hunger Project is all about.

The Hunger Project is not about doing something more to end hunger. It is not about doing something better to end hunger. It is not a different set of solutions to the problem of hunger. It is simply about causing the end of hunger and starvation on this planet to be an idea whose time has come. The people who enroll themselves in the project commit themselves to that. What they do will be derived from that commitment.

The question, "What causes an idea's time to come?" belongs to a particular class of question. Its answer is not the normal and conventional, reasonable type of descriptive or explanatory statement that a mind likes, that we are used to handling. It is not an exposition, concept or theory. The answer to this class of question is, instead, a principle more powerful than all the forces in the world.

To answer this class of question, you have to give up your normal way of arriving at answers. Rather than knowing more and then more as you go along, you will need instead to be willing to know less and less—that is to say, to become somewhat more confused as you go along. Finally you will have struggled enough to be clear that you don't know. In the state of knowing that you don't know, you get, as a flash of insight, the principle (i.e., the abstraction) out of which the answer comes.

While this is work that transcends ordinary intellect, all it requires is an unusually high degree of openness, commitment and intention. You will need these qualities to get you past the impatience, frustration and confusion that almost certainly will result from the feeling that what you are reading doesn't make any sense. In fact, the statement we are seeking isn't sensible; it transcends the senses. One doesn't test the validity of such a statement by seeing if it fits into one's system of beliefs. The test is whether there is a resulting shift from controversy, frustration and gesturing to mastery, movement and completion.

Answers in this class are fundamental principles; they are the source of parts, rather than the product of parts. They come as a whole, which whole can then be divided into pieces. You cannot reach the whole by adding up pieces; obviously the pieces don't even exist as pieces until there is a whole of which to be a piece. Answers in this class—fundamental principles—can be known only by creating them.

Causing An Idea's Time To Come

What causes an idea's time to come? An idea's time comes when the state of its existence is transformed from *content* to *context*.

As a *content,* an idea expresses itself as, or takes the form of, a position. A position is dependent for its very existence on other positions; positions exist only in relation to other positions. The relationship is one of agreement or disagreement with other positions. This agreement or disagreement manifests itself in various forms. For example, your position is similar to, cooperates with, or supports other positions; it is independent from or ignores other positions; it protests, conflicts with, or opposes other positions. Positions exist by virtue of contrast, such as being different from, or more than, or unrelated to, or better than other positions. A position cannot stand by itself; it is not self-sufficient.

To come at this from another direction, we can look at content as a thing, because an idea as a position is a thing. That which is without limits is either everything or nothing, and therefore not something, not a thing. It follows then that a thing requires limits to exist. These limits are expressed as the boundary of that thing. Since the existence of a thing is dependent on its boundary, and a boundary, by definition, is that place between a thing and not-that-thing, (*i.e.,* something else), the existence of a thing is dependent on something else. Therefore a thing, a content, is dependent on something outside itself for existence. Content is not self-sufficient.

Context is not dependent on something outside itself for existence; it is whole and complete in itself and, as a function of being whole, it allows for, it generates parts—that is to say, it generates content. *Content* is a piece, a part of the whole; its very nature is partial. *Context* is the whole; its nature is complete.

When an idea exists as a position—when it is a content—then it is an idea whose time has not come. When an idea's time has not come, whatever you do to materialize or realize that idea does not work. When an idea's time has not come, you have a condition of unworkability in which what you do doesn't work, and you don't do what works.

When an idea is transformed from content to context, then it is an idea whose time has come.

When an idea is transformed from existence as a position to existence as a space, then it is an idea whose time has come. Now an idea as a position literally requires other positions for its existence, while an idea as space is both self-sufficient, requiring nothing else in order to exist, and allows for—is the space of—the existence of other ideas. When an idea is transformed from existing as a function of other ideas to being the space that allows all other ideas, then it is an idea whose time has come.

When an idea is transformed from content to context, then it is an idea whose time has come.

Creating a Context; Putting a Man on the Moon

Contexts are created by the Self, out of nothing. When you stop identifying yourself as a thing, as a position, and start experiencing your Self as the context, as the space, for your life—when you start experiencing that you are the context in which the content of your life occurs—you will automatically and necessarily experience responsibility for all the content in your space. You will experience that you are whole and complete and that you are aligned with other Selves, with the Self.

When you experience your Self as space, you create contexts from which you can come into the world. One such context is the end of hunger and starvation on our planet within two decades.

You are probably not yet clear about what context is—at least not how it works—so we'll use an example. On May 25, 1961, President John F. Kennedy initiated a context when he told Congress: "This nation should commit itself to achieving the goal, before this decade is out, of landing a man on the moon and returning him safely to the earth."

By creating the context, "A man on the moon in 10 years," Kennedy transformed space travel from merely a good idea—which had not succeeded despite considerable attempts, the feasibility of which had been questioned, argued, and discussed—into an idea whose time had come.

The result of what Kennedy did can be understood by analogy. It is as if he created a building named, "A man on the moon in ten years," and inside that building he put offices for all the various ideas, positions, notions and people that had to do with space flight. The first office inside the front door of the building in 1961 would have been called, "It can't be done." This office would have been inhabited by the skeptics and cynics.

A content or position can be threatened by any opposite position. Given two opposing positions only one can survive. On the other hand, a context gives space to, it literally allows, it even encourages, positions that are apparently opposite. *In fact, the most important position in a newly created context is the position which appears to oppose the context.*

It is important to get that opposing positions actually contribute to establishing a context. In the case of the civil rights movement during the 1960's, for example, all those people who opposed civil rights for blacks actually contributed to creating a national dialogue that demonstrated to the country that the issue could no longer be ignored. Every government official in the South who stood in the doorway of a school and prevented black children from entering had been a cause, a part of the persistence, of the problem, of the oppression. After the creation of a context—"equal rights and dignity for blacks"—the *very same action* that had been a part of the problem's persistence became an action contributing to the end of legal discrimination against minority races. Then, every such action contributed to an increased awareness of the issue, to the passage of civil rights legislation, and to the gradual change in attitude that ultimately evidenced itself in the recognition that civil rights was an idea whose time had come…

In a newly-created context the most important position is the position, "It can't be done." That is the first and most important content to be processed, to be realigned. Anyone who has created a context knows that context generates process; process in turn grinds up content, it changes content so that it becomes aligned with the context.

In the building of "A man on the moon in 10 years," the skeptics and cynics were working on "it can't be done" in the context of doing it, so that instead of being a threat or a stop to the goal, suddenly their skepticism and cynicism started contributing to the achievement of the goal.

All the forces of the world are not so powerful as an idea whose time has come. Context generates process. A contextually-generated process transcends the existing forces; it transforms those forces. A contextually-generated process aligns the existing forces within the context. Then the aligned forces provide a condition of workability. Every action taken in a context is a fulfillment of, an expression of, and a manifestation of that context. The pessimism, the cynicism, the position, "It can't be done," are ground up by the process generated by the context, and are transformed into the material out of which the result is achieved. When an idea is transformed so that the apparently opposing idea actually validates and gives expression to the idea, then it is an idea whose time has come. *(The Hunger Project brochure, 1978)*

The Flow From Context

I have been a member of the Hunger Project for twenty-three years. Hunger and starvation are still ongoing. The number of children dying from starvation has decreased but not been eliminated. An incredible number of events have resulted from millions of us holding the context: the banding together of artists and musicians and athletes and politicians, the creation of Band Aid and Live Aid, the coordination of all the relief agencies of the world and all their efforts, the growth of UNICEF, the creation of Results (the political lobbying group that grew out of the Hunger Project), the writing of books and articles, the production of television specials, and many, many other events. These results have brought us closer to our goal but we have not succeeded in the time we originally allotted ourselves. At this writing there are seven months left.

Kennedy's context resulted in a man on the moon in eight years. The civil rights movement, which I was active in from 1959 to 1964, had by that time resulted in the passage of legislation that outlawed desegregation. But the overall context of equality of races is still not accomplished. The anti-Vietnam War movement, which I participated in from 1963 to 1972, did eventually help bring about an end to that war. Now, thirty years later, there has been general acknowledgment that it was a terrible mistake just as we said it was then. But the ongoing use of the military so-called solutions like the Gulf War and NATO's war on Serbia of recent times reflects that the context of secrecy and force has not been effectively brought to an end. (There are still thirty-six separate secret services in the military and the government and almost a quarter of the entire national budget for the United States is still being completely squandered on the military industrial complex.) As Marianne Williamson says in *The Healing of America*[22], "We shouldn't be over impressed by terms like 'foreign policy', huge secretive counterintelligence agencies, and government departments that play the world like a giant chessboard and view it as no more than a game we're trying to win. *Our* consciousness should drive *them*; their consciousness shouldn't drive *us*." The completion of the results for any context is hard to achieve on a specific timetable, but in the minds of many hundreds of thousands of us, the time for an end to forcible solutions is long past due.

Life Purpose and Projects as Context

The life lived, as a context within which the events of life occur, consciously created by declaration and continuing in conversation with with others, is the most wonderful life possible. A life spent creating new possibilities for people that allow them freedom and power they have never known before is a vision we all share. The context for a nation that was envisioned in the

Declaration of Independence generated the United States as an idea whose time had come. The vision can be, and has been, twisted all to hell by politicians and military folks who call us forth to our mutually shared vision and then rip us off by playing adolescent war games. It is time we recaptured from those more limited folks the methodology and responsibility for bringing that vision into being.

So when you design your life and write your projects, think big. Think of your own sweet self, the *being* you are, as *the context in which the whole world occurs.* Then, based on your memories from the past and your mind's assessment, come up with a vision for our future that pleases you and also contributes to other people. Have whatever you come up with eventually lead to transformation of the world. Join with others of us who are transforming the world to help us and those we are helping. It makes all the difference.

Contact and Context

When we contact other people honestly — in such a way that we get their attention and learn about what they are engaged in and committed to — we enroll them in helping us bring our vision into being. We also become enrolled in helping them bring their projects into being. This can be learned through planning and practice. Clarity of formulation changes our listening. The whole project writeup system is for one purpose, which is *to have an effect on how the project author speaks and listens out there in the real world of human interaction.* All the work of writing a project is only preparation for the act of creation itself. A project creates a context so that creation through speaking and listening can occur.

The act of creation requires that you operate in alignment with others, and that you understand the difference between taking a position about what "should" be in the world and creating a context within which what you want to create becomes *possible,* then *likely,* and then *a reality.*

Chapter   Twenty - Two

It's a Lot of Work to Make a New Story, Isn't It? Now What?

Now that you've got your new story straight, now that you are organized, now that you have done all that work and made a good big crazy plan, now that you have thought hard and know how to speak and listen about your life projects so that you get a lot of help from other people...now what?

Now you have to commit a kind of suicide. I don't mean kill yourself literally. I just mean, let's kill the outline of your dream. Do this. Make copies of your project writeups and give them to your committed listeners. *Then burn all the copies you have of your project writeups.* Erase all the content parts on your computer. Keep no written records of your work. Burn your plans. Lose your seriousness. Celebrate the futility of all your efforts. Get in touch with the meaninglessness of life. Laugh at the futility of creating meanings in life. Look at what a fool you are. Look at what fools we all are. Become a village idiot. Talk with your compatriots about the futility of human life. As W. H. Auden said of William Yeats in his ode to him upon the occasion of his death, "Sing of human unsuccess, in a rapture of distress." Make a big party out of the despair. Become a futilitarian.

What have you done? The morning after, let it hit you. The only written copies of the elements of your dream are in the hands of your committed listeners. The only record of your hard work is in your mind and the minds of your best friends. The only possibility of anyone else ever knowing what you are up to is your speaking and your listening and theirs. The only path left to follow is the only path there is to follow — the path of your own creation...if you could just remember what it was.

One of the things we know about us human beings is *we live in a story*. We seldom come out of our stories. We act according to whatever big story (called a culture) we are born into, according to methods of image survival we developed from the dysfunctional families made up of unhappy people trying to live up to the cultural story they were born into. They were unhappy because the big story didn't fit reality, when they were led to believe it *was* reality by their parents and teachers and other intimate cult brainwashers.

The big story turned out to be an illusion. When the cult in our minds is transcended with enough awareness and enough work, the transcendence is temporary because we fall back into the waiting arms and contexts of the cult of which we are members. The only possible way of modifying the direction of the cultural flow that constantly sweeps us toward its own ends is to make a new cult of friends who know better than to believe the lies of the current overcult. That is a lot of work, but happier work, because we know that our beliefs are not reality *and we are not trying to make them reality anymore*. But watch out. They *will* become our reality.

We not only have to overcome the culture into which we were born and in which our personal stories of survival developed, but we also have to overcome the tool all cults get built with — a thing called the mind. The mind is a stone cold cultmaker. It must be frequently deposed, fired, retired, suspended, put on probation, abandoned, overthrown, interrupted, inhibited. The mind is just a tool to tool around with. Nothing any mind has ever produced is sacred. Don't ever forget that. Never mind, forget it. I'll remind you again later if you'll do the same for me.

I invite you to live among the outlaws. Come on into our cult of cults. Our revolutions come at least once every six months. If you write up all your projects thoroughly in January and then destroy them, do it all over again in June. Overthrow the government each time it forms. Legislators who are attached to tradition are ignoramuses. It doesn't take much in this day and age to know that. Don't ever forget it. Well, go ahead and forget it, but somebody keep track and remind the rest of us in six months or so.

This is how we change the world: by staying grounded in our experience in the here and now through practices focused on noticing, telling the truth and listening to our friends and helping them, and designing our lives consciously together using paradigms we build, act on, and throw away — or build, throw away, and act on. We take advantage of the shoulders we have been allowed to stand upon to see into the future with and we keep our species going and defining itself as homo creatus.

We are a cult and we plan to take over the world. We like to call this the cult of cults or the new overcult. An overcult is what you put on to go out into the cold weather out there amongst the true believers.

Orthodoxy is the enemy. Our minds are inclined to become attached to the jail of belief out of cowardice and fatigue. New energy only comes from getting over beliefs. Once you have a big backlog of beliefs, you are in danger of going dead forever. Most people die from not emptying the trash.

A cult is a baby culture. So, if you want to be a card-carrying member of our cult, here is what you do. Burn your card every six months. Write up your projects and your umbrella project every six months. Do a good thorough job. Send off sub-parts to your committed listeners. Send the umbrella project to your committed listener or listeners. Read it over carefully one last time and make the final corrections that make it almost perfect.

Then burn it. Erase the contents from your computer. Keep the structured headings. Keep this book. We will burn that later.

Have a good life playing with this now.

Part Five:

Paradigms and Contexts:

The Revolution of Consciousness

The New Heroic Story

This section is a summary about transcendence. What we are transcending is the normal life of being lost in the mind. When we do that we have to change the world. Joseph Campbell, in his book, *The Hero with a Thousand Faces,* refined from reading all the holy books, myths, dreams and stories of all the cultures of mankind, a concept he called the Monomyth, the universal theme that is to be found in human literature. Our human stories tell us what it is to be a human being. The heroes journey goes roughly like this: A very unlikely being (like a hobbit, or a carpenter, or a carpenter's son, etc.) has laid upon him the task of saving his kind. In order to accomplish this task the hero must venture into the unknown. The entrance to the unknown is always guarded by terrifying beings (gargoyles, dragons, the prince of evil, etc.). The hero must answer the call by facing the demons at the gate, win his way through, and venture into the unknown. There he must attain something (throw the ring in the fire, get the silver chalice, golden fleece, holy of holies, etc.) and bring it back into the world of the known. After that, the world is saved, but nothing is like it used to be. The past is dead and the world will never be the same, but life can go on.

Now the time has come for us to have a new kind of hero. The hero we now need is a *group.* There is now the need for a kind of heroic union of human beings, unlikely though they may be, to save the world of human beings. The demons at the gate are fearsome, multi-national corporations and a world economic order with immense power to destroy lives at the blink of an eye. Facing them is the first step to winning through to the unknown.

We unlikely heroes must bring back to the world of the known the wisdom needed to make a new world. We begin by facing reality. We end by creating a new world order together.

Normal

The following paragraphs are excerpts from *Genetic Psychology Monographs*[23]. This was the first significant social psychological study of normalcy for grownup people.

This study of personal adjustment was part of the Kansas City Study of Adult Life, conducted by members of the University of Chicago Committee on Human Development in collaboration with Community Studies, Inc., of Kansas City during the years 1952-55. The Study of Adult Life was aimed at developing methods of studying middle-aged people that would give knowledge of that part of the life-cycle comparable with our knowledge of childhood and adolescence. Four parallel studies were made, dealing respectively with social role performance, personality structure and change, social status and social mobility, and attitudes toward the process of growing older during the adult years. Each of the four studies was made with a separate, paralleled sample of people aged 40 to 65 or 70...Middle age is at once the fruit of earlier life and the foreshadower of the later years. So much has been studied of childhood and youth, it is surprising how little scientific research has been devoted to the consequences of earlier development on the adjustments people make in the middle years. Moreover, while it has frequently been observed that adjustment to old age is adumbrated by one's way of life in middle age, the observation has not been systematic. Finally, life during the middle years is of no little interest in itself, to all of us who live through these years.

For such reasons, this study was undertaken: to find out what life is like, psychologically, for Americans between 50 and 65; how personal adjustment—mental health—is related to age, sex, and socioeconomic status; and what qualities of personality distinguish the "successful adjuster" and the "unsuccessful adjusters." In the process, a test was planned of the validity and utility of certain projective analyses, as a method of measuring personality and adjustment...

The study was made by interviewing 118 people, 60 men and 58 women, who lived in greater Kansas City, an area of four counties in Missouri and Kansas, which included the cities of Kansas City (Missouri) and Kansas City (Kansas), as well as a number of smaller places and some open farming country. The selection of people was done on a stratified random pattern, using census data to locate, geographically, probably-appropriate people to interview. While recognizing the limitations of representational sampling, in one metropolitan area, it was hoped that some reasonably stable generalizations might be drawn concerning the mental health and happiness of middle aged Americans...

What is a Normal Person?

It is at once a sobering and a thought-stirring experience to become intimately acquainted with any group of people. To know for the first time, despite thousands of individual case studies in past years, that this is at last a completely representative sample of our people — this is a unique experience...

What is the "normal" person like? There are times, in studying case after case, when one sadly muses that perhaps Thoreau was literally right. Perhaps most men — and women — do lead lives of quiet desperation. Certainly, the chaos of bewilderment, the tempest of unreasoning passion, the whine of years-long unhappiness, the tremendous sorrow of engulfing tragedy — these are not strange to the typical American. He, or she, has lived with them and is living with their echoes...

The joy of utter mastery of life? This is a rare experience, encountered by few people. More typical is a quiet, slightly puzzled sense of some things lacking, some spots of grey where colors ought to be; and all beyond one's comprehension to identify, or one's skill to remedy...

For more than half of us, life is a matter of settling for a good deal less than we want. We know it; we've known it for years; and we are decidedly not happy at the many moments when we think about our losses, our disappointments, and our never-will be's. For such of us, life is never brilliantly happy. Unalloyed joy is an unknown or forgotten sensation. Too many hurts, big and little, have chipped the bright colors away...

Yet for this "almost average" American, life is not really a matter for despair. On the contrary, he and she pride themselves on "making out," and "getting along"; and what is more, they do get along, and make their way. If they don't have nearly the love, or stature, or pleasure, or security their hearts hunger for, they don't sink into self-pity. If bright happiness is out of reach, a more shaded kind is still attainable. Above all, there is the self-respect, dimly but proudly felt, of the person who makes his own place in life...

Are there completely happy people? No. We find no one whose life is, and has been, without some hard-hitting frustration or some profound sorrow. When a beloved parent dies, or a just-grown child—what door of escape is there? There is no way out of the grief except to live through it. Depression and devastating flood once swept away the economic roots and the psychological roots of many of these people in Kansas City, for example; and many more have needed years to heal the scars...

Sometimes it seems as if we ask too much of life and of ourselves. We want "perfect" happiness, "perfect" peace of mind, "perfect" mental health. As far as all experience indicates, along with all the present data, the best one can reasonably ask for is good health, mental and physical, with which to meet each day...

Our respondents have covered every gamut. Indeed, a roster of them sounds like the cast of an overcrowded "Our Town": the burned-out shell of a man, an ex-convict; the "social butterfly" of Society Hill, still flapping seductively after 20 years; the long-widowed relic of a Continental nobleman, living in restricted circumstances; the jolly blacksmith and his wife; the poor but honest serving woman who is putting her four children through high school; the man of affairs, who "glitters when he walks;" the winsome, wholesome, happy housewife (even she has known prostrating sorrow for her first husband committed suicide after military service); the "world's best cook" and sternest housekeeper; a raffish, slatternly wife with a loud guffaw, a dirt filled house, and a craze for baseball; an aging but agile Don Juan; a profoundly religious deacon of the church...

What is it to be "normal"? It is to be unreasonable with one's spouse, or children, several times a week, yet try in a fumbling, half inept, but sincere way to make it up. It is to spend money foolishly, then work hard to stretch what's left till payday. It is to work all your life as a railroad man, all your life wishing you'd finished school and gone into law, yet proud of your 25 years of service. It is to get drunk every week for years, then "get religion" and stop drinking, start doing church work. It is to marry in haste, divorce in haste, and marry five years later to a person you love all the rest of your life.

This may not be a very "scientific" way to end a scientific report; but on the other hand, it is a direct translation of the evidence on what it means to be a typical, normal American...

The Norm of Suffering

I have always loved that beautiful piece of writing by Robert Peck. That study, conducted with some care and expense over forty years ago in the very middle of the twentieth century, is a believable report on normalcy at that time. It is that picture of mental health upon which we have to improve if the lives of *even the average economically better-off people in the world are to have less suffering.*

What stands out for me in the lives described in the study, based on the perspective given me by my teachers and clients over the forty years since it was written, is the courage and persistence human beings can manifest in the face of loss. What also stands out is the possibility we all have of getting through and getting over things by facing into them completely and fully experiencing what life brings even when it hurts real bad, and then going on, having worked our way through without avoidance. The wisdom of feeling one's way through to resolution of life's unavoidable hurts is hinted at but not quite fully acknowledged in the report. The most powerful benefit of that report is the perspective of the study itself, because I think that perspective is the most critical element of the ability to transcend suffering.

A Transcendent Perspective and Community

The final part of this book is a focus on perspective. We have lots of different names for transcendent perspectives — models, paradigms, contexts, prototypes, archetypes — and we have developed a kind of hierarchy for how some contexts subsume or are subsumed by other ones. Something happens when any individual wakes up from mindsleep and meets other individuals who have awakened. Our life together in community is one of constantly giving each other transcendent perspectives. Contexts are transcendent perspectives created by taking an honest look at the way our lives *are* and envisioning new ways to live and be together.

We can get systematic about this. We probably cannot *conquer* suffering, but we can surely use it to create less of it. We can surely get through suffering and over it more efficiently by being willing to face and feel our way through what comes to us. Then we have a transcendent perspective and a community of support that allows us to love on. We can then go on to screw up again.

Our goal, as an end result of the wisdom we have discovered through sharing and thinking together, is a transcendent vision for a new political and economic order based on a greater wisdom than just one culture's limited view.

Creating a New Paradigm by Creating a New Context in an Old Paradigm

Paradigms are models of the mind. Models for the interpretation of experience that are agreed upon by a large group of people are called cultures. Cultures are the context in which children are raised. Attachment to cultural beliefs is a primary source of suffering. *It is time to create a new paradigm in any human culture when the value of fulfilling cultural expectations is generally held to be more important than the quality of life of the individuals themselves.* As Denise Breton and Christopher Largent say in their brilliant book *The Paradigm Conspiracy: How Our Systems of Government, Church, School and Culture Violate Our Human Potential*[24], whenever "roles come before souls," it is time for a new look at what we are doing.

Children are taught to interpret their experience of being, using cultural paradigms, thereby maintaining the culture and supporting the paradigms of their forefathers *as though they are what is real.* This works okay only briefly and when it doesn't work anymore, it causes suffering because models of reality are not to be mistaken for reality — they are just a way of dealing with reality. When paradigms become ill-fitting enough, the suffering they cause exceeds their usefulness.

Currently, in the information age, we are capable of suffering more quickly, more intensely, and more frequently from outdated paradigms than ever before in history. When enough human beings suffer intensely as a result of the bad fit of the paradigms they use to interpret the experience of being alive, they will change the paradigm. Unless there is enough opium for the masses, a revolution occurs. We are living in the most speeded-up time of paradigm breakdowns in the history of humankind because we are communicating more about our suffering. We are also being provided more opium than ever before by the guardians of the old paradigm.

The Paradigm Conspiracy comes from, and is written for, the "recovery movement." Read that book to catch up on the current state of paradigm crashes and to learn about the paradigm called "paradigms." The authors clearly describe how people who have suffered from addictions of all kinds have learned to overcome them by telling the truth and joining together in a new culture of support. Not only do they end their victimization by addictions through a transcendent perspective, they also lead our whole culture of sufferers to see that the paradigms we live in don't work and that's why we are all suffering.

People become addicted to drugs and habit patterns as a way to avoid suffering, and the number of addicted people reflects the degree to which the paradigms they are living in don't fit. The need for painkillers and the need to dissociate through ritual avoidances of commonplace experience can be taken as evidence of ill-fitting paradigms.

Suffering and stress is caused by the minds of the individuals who are suffering and under stress. *Cultures live in the minds of individuals.* Cultures are collectively reinforced through the common conversation people live in. I will refer to *The Paradigm Conspiracy* frequently and paraphrase some of its contents, but do not substitute my use of their wisdom for their full brilliance. Go buy that book and read it.

The leaders of what has been called the recovery movement and their interpreters are on the leading edge of the revolution of consciousness. Breton and Largent say,

"Applied to addictions, systems thinking shows that a global explosion of addictions doesn't happen because of a few bad apples, neither are people in pain defective oddities. Global substance addiction into the trillions of dollars is not an anomalous event. There are system causes and, behind them, paradigm causes. Addiction sounds the alarm. We're acting out in our own lives and on each other what it's like to be in systems that are soul-abusive by nature."

The recovery movement, some of the psychotherapy and self-help movement, practitioners of holistic medicine, the followers of various spiritual teachers, public speakers, authors of books like this one, corporate trainers and many others are now synthesizing and broadcasting the wisdom that will create the new, and bring down the old paradigm. Some of the best American spokespeople like M. Scott Peck, Marilyn Ferguson, John Bradshaw, Deepak Chopra, Werner Erhard, Sam Keen, Tom Robbins, Cormac McCarthy, Chris Kristofferson, Dolly Parton, Denise Breton and Christopher Largent, Marianne Williamson, Neale Donald Walsch and many other artists, songwriters, scriptwriters, teachers, authors, journalists and people at large, didn't really start out seeing themselves as revolutionaries trying to overthrow the government. They are good people who have lived and learned and shared what they have learned. They have shown us that dysfunctional family systems, belief systems that people in families live by that don't work and cause suffering and alienation for most of the members, apply not only to little nuclear families and fragmented families but to towns and states and nations and the big world family. As e. e. cummings tried to tell us, we all live "in one enormous room."

Family Therapy

When clients in my therapy practice and people in my work-shops catch on to how their families have conspired to control and manage them, a revelation dawns on them that is usually expressed this way. "Hey! I don't have to put up with this crap!" And then, "Hey! I'm not putting up with this crap anymore!" Then they mostly like hanging out with people who have made the same discovery. They all join together, shouting "Hey! We don't have to put up with this crap! We're not putting up with this crap anymore!" These people then become a new family, usually dysfunctional in some new way, and so it goes.

The most obvious paradigm, the top-down or power-over model of control from the top, is reflected in the world econom-ic structure. It is based on making more and more money for fewer and fewer people and doesn't fit to serve anyone well in the system generated by that paradigm. As Largent and Breton point out, there are a lot of miserable junkies at the top as well. The best chance that those on top of the world economic struc-ture have to survive is the illegal drug trade and the pharma-ceutical industry—the masses need a lot of opium these days. We have already developed the world economic system to a point of ridiculous, unbelievable unwieldiness. The rich are get-ting richer and proportionately fewer every day.

The small number of individual people who are billionaires control more resources than the poorer half of all the nations of the world. Giant corporations now control enough of the world's resources to determine the direction of the use of *all* resources. Of the one hundred largest economies in the world, fifty-one of them are not nations, but corporations. The top two hundred corporations have combined sales of over seven trillion dollars—greater than the combined Gross National Product of all but nine of the largest nations and more than the combined economies of one hundred eighty-two nations![25]

As pointed out earlier, the average workweek is seventeen hours longer than it used to be in 1954. *In the past forty years the average workweek has not only extended by seventeen hours a week, but two people are working it while strangers raise their kids.* The parents think earning money is the way to take care of their kids. Witness the growth of such child-care chains as Creme de la Creme, charging $900 or more per month. Every 30 minutes, toddlers are shuffled off to another classroom and a different caregiver[26]. The kids suffer from not being with their parents and the parents suffer by missing out on one of the primary joys of life: sharing being with their children. Everyone suffers because the paradigm they are living in doesn't work. Hey! We don't have to put up with this crap! Whatayasay we stop putting up with this crap?

Community From the Bottom Up

We are going to have to start over again on a new economy right away. We have to locally come up with a transitional economy of new paradigm people on the local level—something like communal visa cards and communal bank accounts or communal money. Local groups of people governing themselves on the fringe and doing okay in caring for each others' needs—like the government of Denmark—can be largely their own economy and more separate from the world economy. Michael Linton (of Landsman Community Services, Ltd. In Canada) says that *local* currency systems will someday replace international money for about forty percent of the total accounted economy.

We need to come up with a new, soon-to-become-dysfunctional family of our own. The whole world—made up of little local new dysfunctional families—is going to have to change its economy so we don't have to suffer in the old ways and can come up with new ways to suffer instead. We may even learn how to decrease suffering by decreasing our attachment to whatever models we come up with.

All of us want just about the same thing. We all want an ecologically stable, economically secure world for everybody and an opportunity for a good life for everyone in the world. Let's build a model for it and see what happens. Let's make this a project. Let's get clear about where we are and then about where we want to be. First let's take a look at the world as it is. Marianne Williamson has showed the world to us in clear terms:

"If we could, at this time, shrink the earth's population to a village of precisely 100 people, with all existing human ratios remaining the same, it would look like this:

- There would be 57 Asians, 21 Europeans, 14 from the Western Hemisphere (North and South), and 8 Africans.
- 70 would be nonwhite; 30 white.
- 70 would be non-Christian; 30 Christian.
- Fifty percent of the entire world wealth would be in the hands of only 6 people. All 6 would be citizens of the United States.
- 70 would be unable to read.
- 50 would suffer from malnutrition.
- 80 would live in substandard housing.
- Only 1 would have a college education."

We, the privileged classes in the wealthy part of the world, have had the luxury of ignorance about the non-privileged world out there, even though many of us have compassion for those we know about but who are not among our group. Just to drive this difference between the haves and the have-nots home, of that 100 people, as yet, *not one would own a computer.*

We have an opportunity to act, based on knowledge and compassion, that many of our kinfolk in poorer circumstances do not have. Our lives can be a contribution to our fellow human beings by sharing what we know and what we have. Not only can we contribute, we can do so in such a way that it allows others who want to contribute to their fellow human beings a chance to do so. Let's do it. First, let's go back to the context of being—the context of the self. It is out of that context of the self that the new paradigm for how we live together can be created.

Chapter Twenty - Five

A Sufficient Fundamental Identity—

The Living Being in the Body from Moment to Moment

Happiness and freedom depend upon not losing touch with the sensate being-in-the-body-in-contact-with-the-world, even as we grow up and develop minds. From childhood to adulthood, in schools and families in western culture, we are so preoccupied with the development and performance of our minds that we not only separate our minds from our bodies, we identify with our minds and their accomplishments as who we are, to the exclusion of our bodies. Because our bodies are the only source of our aliveness, they are the only instruments we have with which to experience being. Therefore, when we are identified with our minds to the exclusion of our bodies, we are essentially trained to be out of touch with life. This sets us up for a curious duality of living and *it is the single most responsible cause for psychological illness and susceptibility to physical disease.* Out of our culturally-biased identification of ourselves as our minds comes most lying, pretense, critical-mindedness toward ourselves and others, and most of our stress.

Continuous Body Centering Practices

By getting back in touch with our physical experiences, and assigning them primary importance, we can reconnect with the source of our true passions, curiosity, and willingness to try anything. Even clarity of thinking itself depends on grounding in experience. Once we have broken free of our own minds' control, we need practices that keep us grounded in the present moment. We can do this through yoga, meditation, participation in sports, exercise, conscious sex, massage, altered states of consciousness induced by practices and by certain drugs, and by sharing these experiences with others. We learn to stay grounded in the experience of being-in-the-body-in-the-world-in-the-moment by noticing, moving, touching, playing, and manifesting energy in all the other ways that are not primarily thinking. This is important.

Why is this important? What is the real value of being centered in the experience of being in the body in the here and now? The real value is that we have a place to stand from which to view our own mind and our own cultural insanity — the being we are who notices; the true self, not the self image. This being we are is the *context* within which all the world occurs. The Indian philosopher Krishnamurti wrote a book entitled, *You Are the World.* I think he was trying to do the same thing with that title that I am doing with the title of this book — try to get all the important information on the cover. You are the context in which the world occurs — the being you are includes the whole world.

The Self as Context

If the being you are is the context in which the whole world of existence and of time occur, you yourself are the largest context of all. If you think of yourself as the context within which everything occurs, your identity is as a witness. Even though this is a useful perspective, few of us seem to hold it. More often, we think of ourselves as our case history or our values, principles, and beliefs or sensations and images, and so on. You have those things but they are not the essence of who you are. You are essentially, as your most comprehensive self, the context in which the world occurs. You are the witness to the world that creates the world by being in it as a perceiver. You are both the witness and the world created by witnessing.

The practices of Hatha Yoga can be seen as a number of exercises for regrounding ourselves in the experience of being in the body for the sake of being present to the world. Presence to the world creates the world. We are the context within which the world occurs.

There is also an apparently even larger context than yourself, which is time. *Even though you are the context within which time occurs, time is also the context in which you occur.* It's a paradox. We will take this line of thought up again, after we become more familiar with the idea of the big picture of time as explained by Michael Dowd in the next chapter.

The Big Picture—The Larger Context for All Human Activities

by Michael Dowd

Stories Within Stories

"All professions, all work, all activity in the human world finds its essential meaning in the context of a people's cosmic story."

— Brian Swimme

Each of us is a story within stories. My daughter's life story is part of both my story and her mother's story. The story of our family is likewise part of other stories larger than our own: the story of our town, our state, our nation, Western civilization, humanity, planet Earth, and the story of the Universe itself. Each of us is a story within stories within stories.

There is a dynamic relationship between every story, the larger stories it is part of, and the smaller stories that are a part of it. Larger stories influence and add meaning to the stories that are nestled within them. For example, if my wife and I were to move across the country, my daughter's story would be affected. Similarly, if my nation goes through a severe economic depression, experiences prolonged drought, or undergoes a major spiritual awakening, my community's story, my story, and my daughter's story will each be affected.

The destiny of every story is affected by the larger stories of which it is a part. Importance or significance, of course, is relative. An important event in one story will be an important event in all the stories that are nestled within it, but may be relatively insignificant for the larger stories in which it itself is nestled. For example, if the major employer in my town, a factory where I have worked for the past twenty-five years, closes permanently, this would be a significant event in the story of my community, as well as in my story, and in my daughter's story. But it would not be particularly significant within the story of Western civilization. Something significant in the story of Western civilization, however, like an economic and ecological collapse, or a nuclear war, would also be significant for each of the smaller stories nestled within the story of Western civilization, such as the story of my community, my story and my daughter's story.

When we ask the question, "Why?", we ask about the meaning or context of something. We can understand personal meaning by using the metaphor that I just described; we are each a story within stories. The meaning of some thing or event is apparent in its larger context. A tragedy has meaning in terms of the bigger picture, or larger story. An elderly woman who dies while saving a young child's life can be said to have died a tragic, yet meaningful, death. The question, "Why did she have to die?" may be answered meaningfully by looking at the larger perspective. When we want to know the meaning of something we are asking, "How does this fit into the bigger picture? How does this make sense in terms of the larger story?" The larger the context, generally the deeper the meaning.

Cosmology: The Largest Context

> *"Every transformation of humanity has rested upon deep stirrings of the intuition, whose rationalized expression amounts to a new vision of the cosmos and the nature of the human."*
>
> — *Lewis Mumford*

"Science without religion is lame. Religion without science is blind."
— Albert Einstein

In every human society, the largest of all contexts is the story of how everything began, how things came to be as they are, and where everything is going. This story, a people's cosmology, as the "big picture," gives meaning to our existence in every area of experience. It helps us understand the mysteries of life and death. It is the soil out of which all of our beliefs, customs, behavior, traditions and institutions grow. A people's cosmology crystallizes into a set of unquestioned assumptions and beliefs about life in that culture. Like sunglasses with colored lenses, our cosmology colors everything we see. It determines the way we perceive things, what we perceive, what we can and can't see as possible, and what we can't see at all. Its rules and boundaries are generally transparent. It is our reality.

Anthropologist Margaret Mead remarked that every culture she ever encountered had an account of how things came to be in the beginning. Every human society developed a story or set of stories that revealed "the truth"; as revealed by observation and intuition, of the origin and nature of the world, why things are as they are, and our role in the destiny of things. Such an account helped people in each culture decide what was good and bad, what was to be avoided, and what was to be pursued. Written down, it often became scripture. A people's cosmology is their Sacred Story.

The cosmology of the Bible has had a great effect on the thinking and institutions of the West, and on our understanding of our relationship to the rest of nature. Our law, medicine, religion, politics, economics and education have each been shaped extensively by biblical cosmology. For centuries we imagined that God was a Supreme Landlord who resided off the planet, separate from and superior to nature. We thought of ourselves as separate from and superior to nature also because we believed we were created in the image of God. Nature, in our view, was corrupt, due to "the fall" of Adam and Eve. Thus, "progress" became equated with exercising increasing control over nature for the benefit of humans. Until recently these beliefs were taken for granted and rarely discussed. They were inherited and unconscious assumptions and beliefs about reality.

While these beliefs may be directly or indirectly responsible for much of the ecological devastation taking place on the planet today, they have also made possible enormous scientific and technological breakthroughs. Ironically, some of these scientific breakthroughs are now the foundation of an eco-spiritual awakening that may usher us into the only viable future for humans; an age characterized by a mutually enhancing relationship between humanity and the rest of the community of life.

Recent discoveries in biology, geology, chemistry, physics and astronomy indicate that the Universe is nothing at all like the Great Machine mechanistic science assumed it was for the past three hundred years. A growing number of scientists now suggest that the Universe is more like an evolving, maturing, organism—a living system—which has been developing for 15 billion years. It has become increasingly complex and diversified, beginning with hydrogen, then forming galaxies, stars and planets, and evolving more complex life-forms over time. The Universe, in us, can now consciously reflect on itself, its meaning, what it is, and how it developed. "The human person is the sum total of 15 billion years of unbroken evolution now thinking about itself" Teilhard de Chardin noted a half century ago.

"The Universe shivers with wonder in the depths of the human."
— Brian Swimme

"Heaven is my father and Earth is my mother and even such a small creature as I finds an intimate place in their midst. That which extends throughout the Universe, I regard as my body, and that which directs the Universe, I regard as my nature. All people are my brothers and sisters and all things are my companions."
- Chang Tsai

The astronomer or hobbyist looking through a telescope is literally the Universe looking at itself. The child entranced by the immensity of the ocean is Earth enraptured by itself. The student learning biology is the planet learning in consciousness, with awareness, how it functioned instinctively and unconsciously for billions of years. The worshipper singing praises is the Universe celebrating the wonder of the divine Mystery from whence it came, and in which it exists. We humans are a means by which the Universe can perceive its beauty and feel its depths with conscious awareness. We are not separate beings in the Universe, who live on Earth, we are a mode of being of the Universe, an expression of Earth. We did not come into this world, we grew out from it, in the same way that an apple grows out from an apple tree. Every cell of my body is part of the larger living system that is me. Similarily, each of us, with all life, is part of a larger living planetary system. Earth is our larger self, our larger body. As physicist Brian Swimme is fond of saying, "The planet Earth, once molten rock, now sings opera."

"Our planet and its creatures constitute a single self-regulating system that is in fact a great living being, or organism."
- Elisabet Sahtouris

"On the return trip home, gazing toward the stars and the planet from which I had come, I suddenly experienced the universe as intelligent, loving, harmonious."
— Edgar D. Mitchell, astronaut

"It is a peculiar fact that all the great astronomers of the 15th and 16th centuries were deeply convinced that the whole universe was a huge living being. Even during the height of western culture, the Greeks thought of the Living Planet organism as a fact of life."
— Eugene Kolisco

"Viewed from the moon, the most astonishing thing about the Earth is that it is alive...Beneath the moist, gleaming membrane

of bright blue sky, it has the self-contained look of a live creature
full of information, marvelously skilled in handling the sun."

— *Lewis Thomas*

Earth is not a planet with life on it; rather it is a living planet. The physical structure of the planet — its core, mantle, and mountain ranges — acts as the skeleton or frame of its existence. The soil that covers its grasslands and forests is like a mammoth digestive system. In it all things are broken down, absorbed, and recycled into new growth. The oceans, waterways, and rain function as a circulatory system that moves life-giving "blood", purifying and revitalizing the body. The bacteria, algae, plants and trees provide the planet's lungs, constantly regenerating the entire atmosphere. The animal kingdom provides the functions of a nervous system, a finely tuned and diversified series of organisms sensitized to environmental change. Each species is a unique expression of planetary consciousness, with its own unique gifts to the body. Humanity allows the planet to exercise self-conscious awareness, or reflexive thought. That is, the human enables Earth to reflect on itself and on the divine Mystery out of which it has come and in which it exists. We are a means by which nature can appreciate its own beauty and feel its own splendor; or destroy itself.

This shift, from seeing ourselves as separate beings placed on Earth ("the world was made for us") to seeing ourselves as a self-reflexive expression of Earth ("we were made for the world"), is a major shift in our understanding of who and what we are. It is a shift at the deepest possible level: our identity, or sense of self.

"The Earth belongs not to us, we belong to the Earth."

— *Black Elk*

"Indeed, this shift (to seeing ourselves a part of a living planet which is our larger self) is essential to our survival because it can serve in lieu of morality. Moralizing is ineffective. Sermons don't hinder us from pursuing our self-interest. Therefore, we

*need to be a little more enlightened about what our self-interest is.
It would not occur to me, for example, to exhort you to refrain
from cutting off your leg. That wouldn't occur to me or to you
because your leg is part of you. Well, so are the trees in the
Amazon Basin; they are our external lungs. We are just beginning to wake up to that. We are gradually discovering that we are
our world."*

— Joanna Macy

The Great Sacred Story of Life

"Everything begins with a story."

— Joseph Campbell

*"The universe is the primary revelation of the divine, the pri-
mary scripture, the primary locus of divine-human communion."*

— Thomas Berry

*"Our most powerful story, equivalent in its way to a univer-
sal myth, is evolution."*

— Lewis Thomas

It's tough to get a handle on concepts like millions and billions of years. They are too large to conceptualize so they tend to
remain abstractions. To help us see our story as a whole, from
the "big bang" to the present, imagine our 15 billion year history compressed into one hundred years. At this timescale, each
decade equals 1 billion, 500 million years. Each year equals 150
million years. Each month is 12 million, 500 thousand years.
Each day is approximately 425,000 years. Each hour is 18,000
years; each minute, 300 years; and each second, 5 years.

If we put the fireball, or "big bang," at one second after midnight on January 1st, Year 1, with today being one second before
midnight on December 31st of the 99th year, then the first atomic elements, hydrogen and helium, formed two days after the
beginning of the Universe. The galaxies formed by the hundred
billions when the Universe was about 7 or 8 years old. The Milky
Way galaxy, of which we are a part, is a spiral galaxy. It is

100,000 light-years side-to-side and 16,000 light-years thick at the central bulge. (A light year is how long it takes light, which travels at 12 million miles per minute, to travel in one year.) The Milky Way spirals and makes one complete rotation every 200 million years. As it turns, stars are born from clouds of gas and elements formed by previous stars. Stars live anywhere from a quarter of a billion years to ten billion years or more depending upon their size and composition, and then they die.

Our solar system formed from the elemental stardust of a previously exploded supernova when the Universe was 70. The third planet out from the Sun, Earth, was at the right distance to allow liquid water to exist, and had the right amount of gravity to allow atoms to form communities of molecules. As Earth cooled, it formed a crust around its molten core, like a film on cooling pudding. The vapor from its boiling interior rose upward, cooled, and formed clouds. When the surface temperature dropped below the boiling point of water, it rained for aeons, and formed a planetary womb, the oceans. The Universe was 72. The planet came alive in the seas, in the spring of 73, with bacteria. Bacteria are the most important expression of planetary life. All other forms of life are totally dependent upon them. Bacteria would do just fine without us; we would not last a day without them.

Planet Earth learned to consume the Sun, by way of photosynthesis, by the Universe's 74th birthday. Things went smoothly until the great pollution crisis of 88, when oxygen, a gas deadly to anaerobic bacteria, poisoned the atmosphere and threatened the continued existence of life. This first environmental crisis was solved by way of a process of cooperation and mutual benefit, or symbiosis. The first plants achieved multicellularity in March of 91. As cells gathered together and committed themselves to one another, they found, in community, that their own survival and development was enhanced. The innovation of sexual reproduction two years later, in March of 93, made possible an enormous leap in planetary creativity. With sexuality, however, death also came into existence. For the early bacterium, death was not an inevitability. Some of the earliest bacteria may still be with us today. For life forms that are sexual, however, death is an integral part of their existence. Sexuality and death are intertwined. Death eliminates biological forms and cleans the slate for new genetic forms.

In September of 94, some creatures began consuming other creatures instead of feeding directly off the Sun. This practice made it possible to have an ecosystem, a biological community. The development of the nervous system and brain, in worms, happened in July of 95. Backbones appeared a year later. Living beings came ashore, for the first time, in February, 97. The plants were first, followed soon by the insects. The first amphibians emerged four months later. Reptiles and coniferous trees both came into existence in December of 97. The dinosaurs appeared in May of 98. They became extinct a year later when planet Earth was hit by a comet off the coast of what is today Mexico. Mammals began to nurse their young in August of 98. The first birds diverged from the dinosaurs four months later, a year ago, on the last day of December in the Universe's 98th year.

During the first week of April, 99, eight months ago, the planet exploded with color due to the ecstatic celebration of flowering plants. Our ancestors, the primates, began monkeying around only a few months ago. The earliest ape/humans, walking upright, appeared less than two weeks ago, on December 20th. The first species to get classified as fully human, Homo habilis, appeared in Africa on December 26th. Human beings domesticated fire during the early morning hours of December 29th. Our species, Homo sapiens, is a very recent expression of the Milky Way galaxy—emerging from the life of the planet only twenty-four hours ago, at the beginning of the 365th day of the Universe's 99th year of existence.

It is important to note here that at no point in time during the past four and a half billion years, the age of our solar system, did anyone come from the outside and put anything on the planet.

"God" is the inner Love, or incomprehensible Life, at the heart of the process; the Great Mystery revealed in and through the Universe. When Genesis 2:7 speaks anthropomorphically of God forming us from the dust of the ground and breathing into us the breath of life, this is a poetic or mythological way of describing the evolutionary process I am outlining here.

The process of evolution continues. The story is far from over. Polar bears originated only three hours ago. What is important to remember is that this is the Universe story, "The Great Sacred Story of Life." Humans are an expression of Life, but are by no means its crowning achievement. Indeed, from the planet's perspective, as evidenced by our industrial plundering of the air, water and soil, and our wholesale slaughter of millions of other species, reflexive consciousness may be more of a planetary liability than an asset. Only time will tell. It may be true that humanity has gifts and abilities that other species lack. But it is equally true that other species have gifts and abilities that we lack. It is a good spiritual practice to remind ourselves that we are totally dependent upon bacteria for our very lives and sustenance. Also, the fact that dolphins and many whales have a larger neo-cortex brain than our own suggests that they may be more intelligent than we can possibly know. In any event, humility is certainly preferable to ignorant arrogance.

How will those living ten thousand years in the future, a half hour from now on our timescale, tell the story of our times? Will there even be a human expression of Earth in ten thousand years? The answer depends in large part on how humans deal with each other and the natural world over the next fifty years or so. Assuming that we do not suffer the same fate as the dinosaurs (i.e., something colliding with the planet), if we survive it will be because we made large and creative strides in cooperation, community and love.

"A human being is part of the whole, called by us 'universe',
a part limited in time and space. He experiences himself, his
thoughts and feelings, as something separated from the rest – a

kind of delusion of his consciousness. This delusion is a prison for us, restricting us to our personal desires and to affection for a few persons nearest to us. Our task must be to free ourselves from this prison by widening our circle of compassion to embrace all living creatures and the whole of nature in its beauty."

— Albert Einstein

"The new cosmic story emerging into human awareness overwhelms all previous conceptions of the universe for the simple reason that it draws them all into its comprehensive fullness.... Who can learn what this means and remain calm?"

— Brian Swimme

Deep Ecology

"From the point of view of deep ecology, what is wrong with our culture is that it offers us an inaccurate description of the self. It depicts the personal self in competition with and in opposition to nature... But if we destroy our environment, we are destroying what is in fact our larger self."

— Freya Matthews

Deep Ecology is a worldview and associated way of life grounded in the new cosmology. It branches out of the awareness that the environment is not "out there" separate from us, but that we are part of vast cosmological, geological and biological cycles which are concentric and interrelated. My own body, for example, is constantly exchanging matter, energy, and information with the "environment." The atoms and molecules of my body now, what I collectively call "me," are not the same ones that made up my body a year ago. Every five days I get a new stomach lining. I get a new liver every two months. My skin is replaced every six weeks. Every year, 98% of my body is replaced. The molecules that are continually becoming "me" come from the air I breathe and the food I eat. Before that they were part of fish and snakes, lizards and trees, birds and humans, and all that we eat. I give out as I get. It makes little sense, then, to overly identify with my "ego" self, for that is only a very small part of "me." My larger body is the body of Life itself. Earth is my larger self. This is the essence of Deep Ecology.

"If the Rhine, the Yellow, the Mississippi rivers are changed to poison, so too are the rivers in the trees, in the birds, and in the humans changed to poison, almost simultaneously. There is only one river on the planet Earth and it has multiple tributaries, many of which flow through the veins of sentient creatures."

— Thomas Berry

"A living body is not a fixed thing but a flowing event, like a flame or a whirlpool: the shape alone is stable. The substance is a stream of energy going in at one end and out at the other. We are temporarily identifiable wiggles in a stream that enters us in the form of light, heat, air, water, milk... It goes out as gas and excrement — and also as semen, babies, talk, politics, war, poetry and music."

— Alan Watts

Through the lenses of deep ecology we can begin to see clearly the nature and serious magnitude of our global ecological crisis. Consider the following parable. Once upon a time, a group of brain cells debated the relative importance of the rest of the body. Some suggested that the body was dispensable. "After all," said one, "we are the only cells in the body that know that we know things." "Only we can reflect on our dreams," said another, "so we must be the only part of the body that is spiritual, right?" "Why just think of the awesome accomplishments we are capable of!" And they all thought... thinking that they were separate from and superior to the rest of body. Occasionally a brain cell would realize that it was one with the entire body; but it was usually martyred trying to tell the others about this good news. You see, the brain cells had convinced themselves that the Great Life lived outside the body and could be known only through their dreams. They believed that they were destined to leave the body and dwell in a place called heaven. They also assumed that the rest of the body was not really alive at all, that it was an inexhaustible supply of "resources" for the benefit of the brain. Needless to say, the health of the body worsened by the day and was soon on the verge of dying.

> *"A cancer cell is a normal cell disconnected from its genetic memory, cut off from the wisdom of millions of years of evolutionary development. It doesn't cooperate in harmony with the rest of the body. It experiences itself as separate from the body, overpopulates, and consumes the organism which supports it. Cancer eventually kills itself by consuming its own environment."*
>
> *– Brian Patrick*

The message of deep ecology is timely news for humanity, and for the planet as a whole. It offers reconnection to our genetic memory and billions of years of evolutionary wisdom. Its application can empower us to live in synergistic cooperation and harmony with the rest of the body of Life. We can begin to experience a harmonious connection alien to us when we thought of ourselves as separate from and superior to our larger body. We can begin to experience a consciousness of heavenly rapport with all of life.

Timely as it may be, the message of deep ecology must be taught and integrated into our society on a massive scale if our grandchildren and theirs are to be saved from a toxic and literal hell on Earth. It must be put into fervent daily practice in every area of our lives. The planet is calling us to create communities that live and love ecologically. This is essential for the salvation of millions of species, especially our own.

> *"To be a philosopher is not merely to have subtle thoughts, nor even to found a school, but to so love wisdom as to live according to its dictates, a life of simplicity, magnanimity and trust. It is to solve some of the problems of life, not only theoretically, but practically."*
>
> *– Henry David Thoreau*

"The main task of the immediate future is to assist in activating the inter-communion of all living and non-living beings in the emerging Ecozoic era of Earth development. What is most needed in order to accomplish this task is the great art of intimacy and distance: the capacity of beings to be totally present to each other while further affirming and enhancing the differences and identities of each."

— Thomas Berry, Human Destiny

"Our present situation, I think, can be summarized by the following three sentences: 1. The glory of the human has become the desolation of the Earth. 2. The desolation of the Earth is becoming the destiny of the human. 3. Therefore, all human activities, professions, programs and institutions must henceforth be judged primarily by the extent to which they inhibit, ignore or foster a mutually enhancing human/Earth relationship."

— Thomas Berry

"A thing is right when it tends to preserve the diversity, stability, and beauty of the life community. It is wrong when it tends to do otherwise."

— Aldo Leopold

In this last day that the Universe has reflected on itself in and through Homo Sapiens, for nearly 23 and a half of the past 24 hours we were in the tribal-shamanic period of Earth's cultural development; as hunter-gatherers. This is also known as the paleolithic era or Stone Age. From 11:20 p.m. to 11:40 p.m., we went through the neolithic village era. Writing developed at the end of this period and, with it, the beginnings of "recorded history." The next nineteen minutes, to 11:59 p.m., is the period of the classical civilizations, or the age of the classical religious cultures. For the last 60 seconds we have been in the scientific-technological-industrial period. During this last minute we have toxified the air, water and soil upon which all life depends to such a degree that we are now faced with the possibility of a collapse of the planetary life-support systems, or ecocide.

The human is an expression of Earth. We are totally dependent upon the health of the community of Life for our own health. Our own healing and destiny, as individuals or as a species, depend entirely upon our relationship to the land, air, water and life of Earth. What we do to the planet, we do to our self.

It is, of course, possible that the destiny of Life may not include a human expression much longer. This will certainly be so if the destiny of the human becomes the desolation of the Earth. But whether or not our species survives, Earth will continue to evolve, eventually healing the damage done by us. The Milky Way galaxy will continue to spiral, with countless new solar systems being born, living and dying. And the Universe will continue to expand and grow more complex for billions of years after our solar system is but a distant cosmic memory. We are part of an awesome and divine Universe. We are also only a very small part of it. We must keep this perspective in mind when discussing "human destiny." Humility may be the single most important attitude of the heart we will need if we are to continue into the future. Humility and survival go hand in hand. Pride goes before a fall.

We are now at what may be the most significant turning point in the Sacred Story of Life since the 185-million-year Mesozoic era, the age of the dinosaurs, came crashing to a close some 65 million years ago. That was when the dinosaurs all died out. The last 65 million years have been called the Cenozoic era, the age of the mammals and the flowering plants. As a direct result of human activity over the past 200 years, we are now bringing to an end this 65-million-year age! It is important to see things from this larger perspective.

Today, species are being eliminated at a rate faster than perhaps any other time in history. Biologist Norman Myers, a specialist in the rain forests and vegetation of the world, says that we are bringing about an "extinction spasm" that is likely to produce "the greatest setback to life's abundance and diversity since the first flickerings of life almost four billion years ago". Thanks to our addictive industrial culture, we are altering the geological structure, the chemistry, and the biological systems of the planet on a scale that would normally have taken millions of years. Yet we are accomplishing this feat in a few short decades.

As the Cenozoic era collapses around us, the logical question becomes, "What's next?" Geologian Thomas Berry suggests two possibilities. The first possibility he calls the Technozoic era. In the Technozoic, humanity would continue to understand "progress" in terms of increasing mechanistic control over the forces of nature for its own superficial, short-term benefit. Through continued scientific innovation and technological cunning, we could create delimited artificial environments to "protect" us in isolation from our despoiled and dying world. The Technozoic would be an isolated hell of existence. Humanity would become ever more alienated from the rest of Life. In the long run, of course, it could not even hope to last. Without spirit, matter decays. The Technozoic could never be sustainable.

Another possibility, perhaps the only viable option for humans, is what Berry calls the Ecozoic era. The primary aspect of the Ecozoic would be the deep somatic awareness of the natural world as our larger body, as our larger self. All species would be granted their habitat, their freedom, and their range of life expression. The Ecozoic would further be characterized by our harmonious alignment with, rather than domination over, the biological processes of the planet. This would require abandoning many of our destructive mechanistic technologies. The natural world itself would be taken as the primary referent for all that we do, and the primary model for all our technologies. In the Ecozoic, all of our activities, professions, programs, and institutions will be judged primarily by the extent to which they inhibit, ignore or foster a mutually enhancing human/Earth relationship. This is the way of human destiny!

When we see things from a larger perspective, it becomes clear that something more is needed to "save the Earth" than recycling our paper and glass, not using styrofoam, and driving our cars less. Specifically, two things are absolutely necessary if the human expression of Earth is to continue into the future.

As a species, we must make a profound shift in consciousness in the direction of deep ecology if we are to survive. We must grow from seeing ourselves as discrete, separate beings that walk around on Earth, to feeling and knowing ourselves as an expression of Earth. Our thinking and behavior must align with, and flow out of, the reality of our situation: the planet is our larger body, our larger self. We are dependent upon the community of life, air, water and soil in every conceivable way. Unless we make this shift in consciousness, we will continue to be a "cancer," a parasite, consuming its own host environment. We will survive only with the spiritual guidance and awareness of the body of Life as a whole with its billions of years of evolutionary wisdom.

The second thing necessary for the human expression of Earth to survive is for human beings to live in ecologically sustainable communities. We must live our lives in deep communion with each other and with our bioregion: sharing possessions and dwelling space, growing food together in a way that enhances our lives and the soil; laughing, working, playing and celebrating together; and, in short, living in love with each other and with all of Life. We must create ecological communities where we can be most truly ourselves, where we can experience loving physical touch, where we can share our finitude and brokenness and feel loved unconditionally, and where we are both supported and challenged to be all that we can be, especially for future generations.

None of us asked to be alive at this moment in Earth's history. We did not choose to be born at this juncture in the Story. We were chosen. Each of us has been chosen by Life to be alive and to participate in the most significant geological and biological transformation in 65 million years. This is a fact! Can you feel the sense of personal destiny, or a sense of mission or purpose, that such an awareness awakens within you? (If you want to, take a few moments and allow yourself to feel your connectedness to the larger body of Life, and your place in the Sacred Story of Life.) Thomas Berry calls this awareness "the grace of the present moment." The degree that we live the values of the Ecozoic era now will be the degree to which we participate in its inauguration. Love and Truth must be our guiding realities. As we love Life with all our heart, mind, soul and strength, we will quite naturally love our human and non-human neighbor, and our planet, as our self. That is the true state of affairs. Living the values of the Ecozoic requires being lovingly truthful and gently honest with ourselves and with each other. It means being real and open with the Life that is our Source, Body, and Destiny.

We are all stories within stories within stories, as we discussed at the start. The Great Sacred Story of Life is the biggest story. This story, the Universe story, provides the context for, adds meaning to, and affects the destiny of every other story in existence. That is why everything in human affairs must now be seen in light of this "big picture" in order to have any lasting meaning for present and future generations.

"For peoples, generally, their story of the universe and the human role within the universe is their primary source of intelligibility and value. Only through this story of how the universe came to be in the beginning and how it came to be as it is does a person come to appreciate the meaning of life or to derive the psychic energy needed to deal effectively with those crisis moments that occur in the life of the individual and in the life of the society. Such a story... communicates the most sacred of mysteries... and not only interprets the past, it also guides and inspires our shaping of the future."

— Thomas Berry

Intimacy and Community

We are the context for a story within a story: That is my true identity. That is your true identity. We are also each contexts within which time occurs. Time is a context in which all that is, occurs, including us. That context is made possible by the Self, which is the context within which that context called time resides. The body that houses the context for time to occur resides in the context of time. Let's take those two contexts that contextualize each other seriously. Listen up now.

The greatest possible context arising from the integration of the wisdom of East and West in the twentieth century is this: Beings who relate as *beings*, one to another, can work out the problems that come from having minds and personalities. We can change how we live together by acknowledging the being we are as the context in which the mind occurs. Time is a mental construct within the context of being.

Membership in an on-going bonded community of support—what we occasionally find in families—seems to be the best fundamental source for creating the world, by using our minds, from within the primary context of the self (the witness to, and therefore creator of, the world). The process of owning oneself as a context within which the world occurs is called transformation. The transformation is from victim to creator. You are the creator of the world.

We can create intimate families among people who are not blood relatives through radical honesty—which is essentially sharing real data rather than phony data, so we can get on with the task of re-creating the world. (We do this for recreation.) Our work is *to live the good life that comes from being centered in the body and consciously creating with a bunch of friends who love each other and continue to tell each other the truth, to continually overthrow the structures of the mind and bring about a world that works for everyone.*

The Context Called Death

I am walking down a path through an archway. The sign on the left side of the path says, "Make a joyful noise unto the Lord." The sign on the right side says, "Abandon all hope, ye who enter here." This pathway leads into nowhere. Oblivion seems appealing. R. D. Laing once said, "There are some suicides that can only be explained as the result of an intolerance for joy." John Prine in one of his folk songs says, "To believe in this livin' is just a hard way to go." God bless him. He is a great poet. He's got little kids now and cancer. He reminds me of this ongoing lifedeath of being out here—playing with the other kids at the funeral.

Life, lived into and out loud, is itself a big event full of little events. Life is what kills you. People always want to know, "What did he die of?" What I want on my tombstone is, "Here lie the remains of Brad Blanton. Life just killed him."

Someday soon we will each be all used up. The worms will get us. Then the worms themselves will die and the universe will reclaim our basic elements and we will be long gone.

This is how I want to be used up. This is the legacy I want to leave behind. This is the life I recommend. I want to have died all along the way. And when we get to the end, it's just another day. This is the good life. It is still hard at times but hard in a wonderful way. Our task as humans in the great conversation now about what it is to be a human being, is to build up our tolerance for joy—the joy that comes from sharing the truth of our existence with each other. Unless we do this, in our whole human family our time on earth is over. Our individual time will be over soon enough, anyway.

Consciousness of Self and of Context = Revolution

People simply cannot go through all the work of learning to transcend their own minds and learn to love each other, and still put up with institutions that oppress them and their loved ones merely to make more money. Therefore, it is likely that the world will be significantly changed quite soon. Radically honest communities help individuals to change not by *trying* to change, but by transcending their own minds. When enough people transcend their own minds, the culture in which these people live has to shift. As Swami Beyondananda says, "Shift happens!"

Cultures are dysfunctional families made up of habitual mind-sets with a lot of emotional attachment. In an honest community of support, the speed with which antiquated mind-sets can be shucked is increased. Giving up traditional values becomes less painful with a little practice. Many of us share a vision of a world reorganized based on principles of intimacy, sharing and honoring the *being* of human beings within the context of all of being, rather than any traditions of the mind or of institutionalized minds. We are becoming a movement. We are creating the following declaration as a context.

> We declare that the possibility exists because we say so, that at any given moment, human beings can change frameworks to operate from and it won't kill them or cause the permanent breakdown of social order.

Temporary breakdowns of social order are to be cherished greatly, for they allow corrections to occur. Just as the true self remains when the mind goes, the spirit of a union of friends remains when the organization they belong to breaks down. Uncertainty now and then won't kill us. We can live without certainty periodically. In fact, we must do just that to thrive as well as survive.

The United States of Being, A New Nation

"So we pretend we don't care, or that someone else is going to fix things. Which fits perfectly into their plans, whoever 'they' are. Every once in a while we get our hopes up again, but what we long for is one of the hardest things for most of today's politicians to give us: an honest conversation. Just put the facts on the table, guys. Democracy cannot survive in an environment where the electorate is treated like children who are not quite mature enough to be told the truth. Especially when the ones withholding the truth are the ones going around acting like children."

— Marianne Williamson

For several years now, I have been talking to hundreds of people every month in cities all over the United States. I do seminars at Learning Annexes in cities, growth centers in the country and workshops organized by my company, Radical Honesty Enterprises, all over the place. I do book signings and public talks and radio and television shows about my book, *Radical Honesty* and my Radical Honesty workshops. I also do talks and visits to churches, corporations, and associations. I meet a lot of people I like and who like me. Many of us stay in touch after we meet this way.

I tell people how it has been for me in my own life of creating and they tell me how it has been for them. Something happens to us as we talk. My friends and cohorts and I are changing the world by how we share and be and create together. I believe we can create together more consciously now for the benefit of the whole world and that we all have lots of friends out there who want to create with us.

For some of us, everything in our lives now, everything that we work and play with from daybreak to bedtime, was once only an idea that we, as individuals, took upon ourselves to create. Then we all helped each other with our projects. What helped a lot was honest conversations along the way. As we have grown, our community has grown and the re-invention of the meaning of the word "political" is happening right before our ears. We must now face squarely the political implications of our knowledge.

An Alliance of Creators: Building a Parallel System of Government

Let me name a few of my friends and tell, very briefly, about what they are doing with some of their special projects. Ronnie Dugger and I have known each other since 1959. At that time, he was the editor of *The Texas Observer*, the only honest newspaper in Texas. Ronnie Dugger's *Texas Observer* and I. F. Stone's *Weekly* were the only consistently whistle-blowing paradigm-kicking believable media in existence as far as I was concerned. Ronnie has been at Harvard at the Kennedy School for the past several years. In 1995, he wrote an article in *The Nation* entitled, *Will the Real Populists Please Stand Up* and so many people responded, it became a movement called *The Alliance for Democracy*. I am proud to be a member of that group. The mission of the alliance is to bring about an end to corporate rule of the world. Our third annual convention met in Boulder in May of 1999, where I told them of my idea to start a new country in cyberspace and in the imaginations of human beings everywhere. In a few moments I will tell you more about that idea.

Marianne Williamson speaks for herself. I do not know her personally but I consider her my friend. Her wonderful book *The Healing of America*[27] keeps me awake at nights and has inspired me for months. She wrote also *Return to Love*[28] and was greatly responsible for the popularization of *The Course in Miracles.* You can tell quite clearly what she is about by reading *The Healing of America.* (Read particularly pages 304-306, subtitled "What Should I Do?", because those words have inspired a lot of what you are reading now.) Since that book came out, she has become the minister of a large Unity Church in Michigan. My friends Denise Breton and Christopher Largent (authors of *The Paradigm Conspiracy*) have gone there and visited with her and the conversations those people have started are at this very moment changing the world's consciousness.

Mike Foudy, recovering lawyer, author, and radio talk show host is a friend of mine and he introduced me to Mike Gravel, the former Senator from Alaska when I introduced both of them to Ronnie Dugger. Mike and Mike have been calling for a new Constitutional Convention in Philadelphia, to reorganize the way we are governing ourselves. Mike Gravel says that the evolution of government in recent centuries has gone like this: the Divine Right of Kings where the Sovereign had total power eventually evolved to representative governments. But then the representatives still retained the authority kings used to have, so elected representatives became sovereign. Mike Gravel says it is now time to depose sovereign representatives and make the individual citizen sovereign.

I couldn't agree more. Technological advances have made true democracy available on a large scale for perhaps the first time in history. We could have government created by sovereign individuals voting on referenda via 800 numbers and email. We could still elect representatives, but their power would be limited to funding and doing the work we assigned to them by referendum. Gravel's proposal is that the Secretaries of State in each of the fifty states form a committee that solicits ideas for referenda, writes them up, submits them to the public and has them voted up or down by the citizenry in thirty to sixty days, using voiceprints on 800 numbers or security-protected email or whatever other electronic secure system we could set up. This way the politicians would *really* work for the people. The sovereignty of the individual would be established.

Many of you may have participated in the online moveon.org movement that grew to over 40,000 people in a matter of weeks during the Clinton impeachment hearings debacle in 1998-1999. The movement was a gathering of citizens disgusted with the self-righteous and out-of-touch Republicans in the House of Representatives (as well as the lying politicos among the Democrats and the media.) We wanted the House to censure the president and move on, rather than waste another forty million dollars and three or four months on whether the president lied about some sexual activity. Well, eventually the impeachment failed as it was destined to do from the beginning. We have moved on, but it took four whole months longer than was needed, plus the dollars required. Meanwhile, every real problem in America and the rest of the world was ignored as usual. It was a part of the usual bread and circuses to keep us distracted from the truth rather than any kind of search for the truth as they were pretending. Now, many of us in moveon.org have pledged millions of dollars in campaign funds against the representatives and senators who kept the pretense up. More than anything else, we have already pointed out how out of touch with reality the media and the representatives in our government are.

David Korten, also a member of the Alliance for Democracy and author of *When Corporations Rule the World*[29] and *The Post Corporate World*[30] is a brilliant synthesizer of known information and an articulate teacher in revealing the truth about banks and international corporations. He points out how through campaign contributions, lobbyists and bribery, they simply overrule nations and democratic processes as need be if that helps the bottom line. His vision of a new economic order based on spiritual/experiential principles in the post corporate world is entirely consistent with and in alliance with many of the rest of us who are mostly outside the loop of big business, economics and international development.

Neale Donald Walsch, author of *Conversations With God*[31] Books One, Two and Three and *Friendship With God*[32] and other books, is another friend with a political and economic view of the future out of which this new, more fair and equitable world order we are all envisioning together will be born. He is becoming world famous and he wants to help. His web site www.conversationswithgod.com is the source of the same kind of world community we are all working toward.

On book tours I meet many friends of old, most of whom I had never met in person before. I meet many people who were in the same struggles I was engaged in — the civil rights movement from 1959 on, the anti-Vietnam war movement from 1964 on, Haight-Ashbury in the summers of '66 to '68, and in school buses all over America in the early 70's, smoking pot and experimenting with psychedelic and other drugs for many years. I meet people involved in the personal growth and human potential movement during the 80's and 90's (est, LifeSpring, The Forum, Arica Training, Pathwork, family systems work, growth centers, couples therapy, group therapy, Organizational Development work, Outward Bound, and many more ongoing adult education and development events), as well as those supporting the furtherance of freedom for women and gay people and all second class citizenry based on cultural prejudice. We have been like a widening stream over all those years, and we have discovered ourselves to be the ones who knew and transcended the cultural limitations that all those movements for liberation represented.

I meet people who joined the movements early and people who joined late. I meet many who knew about but didn't know the import of all of these enterprises until after many of them were over, but now see the value of what was done. Many of us who are older now and more in charge of the world now, and who were often right, as it turned out, in advance of the majority, are still aware of how the world goes wrong. We would like to do something about it on a larger scale and in a more potent way than we currently have the structures for.

I could go on and on about many more of my friends, most of whom are less famous than the ones I've mentioned. But one thing has struck me over years of working with people in individual and group psychotherapy and workshop groups. Whenever anyone talks about what they really want in life, or writes or tells me their description of an ideal world or writes up their life purpose statements in my workshops—I am amazed at how similar they all are. WE ALL WANT THE SAME THING!! Everyone's life purpose statements are almost all the same. We all want everyone in the world to be fed, and have shelter and the opportunity to live and love and learn. We all want to have everyone taken care of and happy and provided for. We all want to contribute a context of love and security to everyone else in the world.

As T. S. Eliot foretold in the 50's, this community is that "...strange beast, its hour come round at last, stumbling toward Bethlehem to be born." John Lennon envisioned in the 60's this conclusion we are coming to in these days. I'm sure you can remember the tune to "Imagine."

"Imagine there's no heaven
It's easy if you try
No hell below us
Above us only sky.
Imagine all the people
Living for today."

"Imagine there's no country
It isn't hard to do.
Nothing to kill or die for
And no religion too
Imagine all the people
Living life in peace..."

"Imagine no possessions
I wonder if you can
No need for greed or hunger
A brotherhood of man
Imagine all the people
Sharing all the world..."

"You may say I'm a dreamer
But I'm not the only one
I hope someday you'll join us
And the world will live as one."

If that is what we all want, why can't we do it? There is nothing in our way except outdated paradigms and habit and ignorance. So, if we all want the same thing, let's do it! I have an idea about how to start.

Creating a New Nation

My friend, Tom James, along with some friends of his, including me, and some other friends of mine, have the bright idea to create a new nation. We are starting, through the Internet, this book, and by talking to everyone we know, to invite people to become citizens of a new nation. We envision this new nation to be based on honesty and freedom. We envision a nation where an honest conversation is the *main* ongoing method of sustenance and management of the nation itself. *We envision this new nation as a context within which the existing structures of control are transformed.*

We hope to build a parallel system to the current world government and economic order and run it alongside the old one until it has been well tested—just like you build and operate simultaneously two parallel programs for a while when you are switching to a new computer system. Once we complete the structure of our nation, test out the new system and grow a little bit, we will then use our new government to replace the old one.

It is, of course, a naïve and ridiculous idea, and if we were not creating it as a context big enough to include all of the reasons that it is ridiculous, we could just quit after we were amused by the possibility for a while. But noooo! We have to create it as a context! And, as you may remember from chapter twenty-three, creating a context is different from taking a position about what should be. By creating a context we are empowered by opposition, criticism, and resistance that cause the furtherance of our success rather than stopping us.

When we grow bigger in influence than the highly paid lobbyists for the international corporations, we will take over more and more of the old government based on the bottom line of business and the military, and then just replace it with ours. Join us. If anyone asks you what we are about, tell them that we are a cult and we plan to take over the world. (We want to start out by telling the truth and do it all the way through.) In fact, the way you actually vote in this form of government is by speaking about and listening to the truth about what is going on in the world and how you feel about it and what you think first, and then saying what you are in favor of as policy second, and then giving all the rest of us a chance to choose among alternative ways of dealing with what has been brought to our attention in the whole conversation.

Here is the plan: Our new nation is called The United States of Being. Everyone who lives on planet earth belongs to this country. Signing up to vote makes one a voting member rather than just a plain citizen. To become a *voting citizen* of the United

States of Being, all you have to do is sign up and vote on referenda you help create.

You do not have to secede from your current country. You can have joint citizenship with us and with any other world state at the same time as far as we are concerned. Give us your email address and home address and we will continue to notify you of our growth and development and ask you to keep participating with us to make ourselves a viable alternative to the current world order. At our website; www.radicalhonesty.com, you can sign up as a citizen of our new country and then send an email to all your friends and ask them to sign up.

I propose that we build this thing together from scratch through referenda and simulation of government in parallel to the other world order and economic setup. We'll run this parallel system until we are ready to take over the world. It may take a while and be a little bit of work, but what the hell? What else are you going to waste your life doing, anyway?

If you don't have email or if you have friends who don't have email, call 1-800-EL-TRUTH and we will sign you up. We only need about a couple million enrollments before we make our first big move. Pass this around and let's get started.

The initial geographical center for organizing the new United States of Being is at my house, on Sparrowhawk Farm, a 92-acre piece of land in the Shenandoah Valley of Virginia in the United States on the continent of North America. We plan, by the time we reach 10,000 members, to come up with a way of creating basic documents, such as a constitution for our new country, by voting on referenda. Our first vote will be on a few beginning referenda concerning the primary values of the new U.S. of Being.

Every referendum will be available for people to vote for or against for 30 days and they can vote by email or by calling our 800 number. Minimum voting age is 12. As we get bigger, we will need some money for setting up voiceprint identities and securing the email way of voting so we can prevent cheating on the vote. We will eventually develop systems for creating a new world economic order. Please join now and help us create a new world order for everyone in the world by everyone in the world who is willing to help. All we have to do is let people know what is possible here. The less than one percent of us who own computers can get this started, and then spread this as the availability and use of computers worldwide spreads at the same time. We are developing software for governing.

Free Radicals

This book was going to be called *Free Radicals,* but we changed the title because we thought we could sell more books if everyone who read *Radical Honesty* recognized this book as a sequel. We have come to call ourselves "free radicals" because of our destructive and creative function and intention. In the biological world, free radicals are a bad thing. Too many of them destroy the body by causing cancer. To avoid cancer we are supposed to eat right (for example, lots of carrots for beta carotene) and do what we can to put a damper on free radicals. But free radicals are also important in causing mutations and elaborations in genetic structure so evolution can occur. We call ourselves free radicals to own, by analogy, our destructive function and our re-creative function.

We are here to destroy the current body politic of the world. Cheerfully and without violence, we want to end corporate rule, top-down management, borders, the world economic order and all the established religious institutions of the current world. They are all the organism within which we live and which we intend to destroy and replace by our growth. We are mutants. We are as certain as death and evolution. (Taxes are no longer certain; we haven't voted on that yet).

Here is how you sign up: You declare yourself a citizen of the United States of Being, a new nation in cyberspace and in the imagination of people everywhere. We will work to build, in actuality, in the real world, a substitute government that will be both more compassionate and efficient than the poor ignorant way we had world order set up at the end of the twentieth century.

After passing a series of referenda, including our new constitution, we will form the parallel government we imagine while at the same time becoming a political force in the governing of the United States of America and of other nation states. When we have strong alternatives to what management systems currently exist, we will substitute them for the antiquated structures.

If you are willing to help, please read, endorse, and pass on this new declaration of independence. You can go to our web site and download this and email it to all your friends.

A Campaign To Form A New Nation

If you want to help, write a personal letter or e-mail to your friends, something like this:

Dear Joe, I have joined a cult. It is gigantic and growing larger every day. It is a community of friends who focus on being honest about what we think and what we feel and what we do. We have helped each other grow up a lot and we contribute what we have learned to other people by helping them to undo and then reorganize dysfunctional families — starting from nuclear families, but now expanding to governments, corporations and international corporate interest groups that influence governments.

Our work is based mostly on the personal growth of people in groups who have been healing themselves from cultural damage in the context of therapeutic communities (like AA, Al-Anon, the Forum, LifeSpring, and many others). One of our cult leaders, Brad Blanton, has written a book and started a web site to further the conversation among all these communities. We have come up with a big idea, which is this: What if we formed a new nation?

A lot of us are fed up with the current state of government and politics and out of frustration with current affairs, we would like to build on the wisdom of the past but start over again with the new paradigm we all are already operating from based on what we have learned in our lives that makes the old top-down managed paradigm obsolete. It will be a lot like designing new software and then running it parallel to the old software until it has been tested, and then put it into place replacing the old software.

We have formed this new nation to include everyone in the world, based on the principles articulated in the Declaration of Independence of the United States. But now, instead of organizing against the King of England, we organize against the outdated paradigms maintained by the current world economic order. And instead of a bloody revolution we can just have a revolution of consciousness—a redesign revolution—a change of models from one that is not working so well to one that works better. How hard could that be? (Ha!)

So we have written a new Declaration of Independence, modeled very closely after the first one, and we are founding a new nation. We invite you to join us. Here it is:

Declaration of Independence for a New Millennium

When in the course of human events it becomes necessary for one people to dissolve the political bands which have connected them with another, and to assume among the powers of the earth the separate and equal station to which the Laws of Nature entitle them, a decent respect for the opinions of humankind requires that they should declare the causes that impel them to the separation.

We hold these truths to be self-evident, that all human beings are equal, that we all have certain unalienable rights; that among these are life, liberty and the pursuit of happiness. That to secure these rights, governments are instituted among human beings, deriving their just powers from the consent of the governed. That whenever any form of government becomes destructive of these ends, it is the right of the people to alter or abolish it, and to institute new government, laying its foundation on such principles and organizing its power in such form, as to them shall seem most likely to effect their safety and happiness.

Prudence, indeed, will dictate that governments long established should not be changed for light and transient causes; and accordingly all experience has shown that humankind is more disposed to suffer, while evils are sufferable, than to right themselves by abolishing the forms to which they are accustomed. But when a long train of abuses and usurpations, pursuing invariably the same object, evinces a design to reduce them under absolute despotism, it is their right, it is their duty, to throw off such government, and to provide new guards for their future security. Such has been the patient sufferance of all human beings colonialized by the currently existing world economy and government at the end of the twentieth century, and such is now the necessity that constrains them to alter their former systems of government.

The history of the growth of international corporations and national governments and their interactions in the twentieth century is a history of repeated injuries and usurpations, all having, in direct object, the establishment of an absolute tyranny over human beings belonging to this planet. To prove this, let the facts be submitted to a candid world.

The governance of the United States of America, economically the strongest nation currently in the world, is unduly influenced and, in practical fact, controlled, by international corporations in alliance with military interests and quasi-military secret agencies and pro-military governmental bodies. The Congress of the United States, the judiciary branch, and the presidency do not operate independently from this influence. Through hired lobbyists and campaign contributions to both parties in an illusory two-party system, corporate money controls legislation to such a degree as to virtually eliminate serious opposition. The Congress, the courts, and the presidency have failed to pass or effectively advocate any campaign legislation that limits the way they, themselves, have come into power in the first place, based on limited and non-democratic corporate interests.

The budget for defense at the end of the twentieth century, when we are not at war, takes up too large a proportion of the Gross National Product. They keep among us, in times of peace, standing armies without our consent, and with secret agencies hidden from the citizenry, render the military independent of, and superior to, the civil power. There are at least thirty-six separate secret agencies whose funding, operations, and activities are kept secret from the populace in the name of national security. When egregious activities on the part of these military and para-military organizations are brought to light, the revelations are decades after the occurrence of the offending activity, rendering it impossible to have their activities curtailed by the people of this country until those responsible are no longer in power.

Health care is a privilege rather than a right. This privilege depends on how much money an individual has. Insurance companies of such size and wealth as to challenge the power of whole nations are in alliance with pharmaceutical companies of the same proportionate financial power who are also, themselves, in alliance with a medical establishment structurally dependent upon the largesse of corporate giants and vested in the status quo. These alliances can, and do, defeat all attempts at creating a fair and equitable health care system for people in the United States, while robbing even more of the remaining peoples of the world of that same opportunity. The combination of these forces in the United States of America has made it difficult to bring into being a more fair and equitable health care system worldwide.

The rule of law in the strongest nation on earth is a myth. The entire court system is corrupt, unwieldy, and uncorrectable. The criminal justice system is correct in only one way, its name: the criminal justice system. We are building new prisons at an unprecedented rate and populating them with persons whose lives were damned to be underprivileged at birth, and who have been educated and parented in such a way as to render them, for all practical purposes, immune to further learning for the rest of their lives. When the rule of law is mentioned it is in the context of trivial arguments in defense of righteousness, where valuing belief in the rightness of principles themselves for principle's sake is held higher than compassion for living human beings. Such reification of belief, in any values whatsoever, such that they are holy and untouchable, keeps all that is felt in response to the needs of living persons from being acted upon and mitigates against the flexible creation of systems and structures that re-create those things needed for humanity as needs occur.

The largest economic enterprise on earth is illegal drugs, most of them pain killers. This is kept in place in the world by the United States of America through the decades-long so-called "war on drugs" in which the alliance of the righteously religious, the health care establishment, the para-military secret agencies and the legal system supports the sustenance of the whole corrupt enterprise of "illegal drugs" by outlawing selected drugs and bringing pressure to bear on other countries to do the same. In this way the illegal market can be maintained, the racist criminal justice system remains in place, and the jobs of the hard working but incompetent police and military personnel can be sustained. People who are missed by the illegal drug trade are even more expensively supplemented by the legal pharmaceutical industry, which gets to advertise its biochemical solutions to physical symptoms sourced by the social malaise of which they are such an important part.

The separation of parties in the United States of America is also a myth. The one party with two names is owned and operated by international and national corporate financiers, and keeps the populace under control through secret agreements, lobbying, and ownership of the public media. The ongoing news media show is controlled continuously by the selfsame corporations. For example, in the argument between the "two" parties about setting the minimum wage, Republicans advocate a smaller figure and Democrats advocate a somewhat larger figure for an hourly wage. The entire discussion is limited to the "conservative" advocates of the smaller figure and the "liberal" advocates of the larger figure. Those amounts are all that get discussed in the media. This circus continues and is reported and interpreted by a media controlled by corporate interests so there is no meaningful discussion of what a minimum wage means. The possibility of creating a new minimum wage based on some standard other than the well-established tradition of control of the marketplace by a very small minority of established financiers and institutions is never raised. The media only reframes what they are given in an attempt to sensationalize the information provided for them. This is the circus that is set out for the entertainment and substitute for thought for the public at large, and for their continual drugged state, in case the illegal drugs provided and the legal pharmaceutical industry's efforts have not sufficed.

In every stage, these oppressions are maintained and reinforced by a government of representatives, whose elections were bought through advertising in multi-million dollar campaigns financed by established interests.

Those of us who have petitioned for redress have been ignored or answered by repeated injury. We have warned them from time to time of the danger of their attempts to extend an unwarrantable jurisdiction over us. We have reminded them of our rights under the Constitution of the United States and the government and regulations set up under that constitution to no avail. We have appealed to their native justice and magnanimity and we have conjured them by the ties of our common kindred here in our native land and in locations throughout the world, to disavow these usurpations of power that would inevitably interrupt our connections and correspondence with each other. We have repeatedly demanded campaign finance reform and had everyone in both parties in favor of it and "trying" to do so for the last thirty years of this century and that reform has not occurred.

The Congress, the judiciary and the presidency of the United States of America have been bought. They are deaf to the voice of justice and consanguinity. Their allegiances are all to the same interests and controlled by the same alliance of corporations working in skillful accord with each other. They owe their elections and their appointments to the people with the money.

We must, therefore, acquiesce in the necessity that denounces our separation, and hold these current elected representatives of industry, as we hold the rest of mankind, enemies in war; in peace, friends. This is a war of minds and hearts of persons whose primary value is compassion, against persons whose minds and hearts are committed to conquest, control, and domination of other people. This is a war to be fought not on the battlefield, but in the family, the local community, the marketplace, the Internet, the personal conversation with friends, intimate conversations between couples, conversations with strangers and every other avenue of communication and aspect of life on earth, from now on out, until the conclusion is assented to by all people, that we are of one cloth and do honor each others' humanity above the pleasures and sufferings of conquest and control.

If we could represent the whole world's population in current times as a village of one hundred people, with all existing human ratios remaining the same, it would look like this;

- 70 would be unable to read.
- 50 would suffer from malnutrition.
- 80 would live in substandard housing.
- 1 would have a college education.
- Fifty percent of the entire world wealth would be in the hands of 6 people. All 6 would be citizens of the United States of America.
- Not one would own a computer.
  (from Marianne Williamson, The Healing of America)

We, the founders of a new order, intend to change the fundamental structures that maintain this obscene balance of wealth and power. This limitation of possibility for most of humankind can only be changed by changing the economic order upon which it is dependent, holding our voices and sheer numbers in alliance with each other as more important and more powerful than the numbers of dollars held by the limited few. We assert that people are more important than money and we intend to build a new world order that reflects that, even if it means proclaiming a new form of money.

We, therefore, as representatives of the United States of Being, do, in the name of, and by the authority of, the good people of this world, solemnly publish and declare, that these United States of Being are, and of right ought to be, a Free and Independent Nation; that we place as secondary all allegiance to any government whatsoever that requires of us, directly or indirectly, a participation in the violation of basic human rights to food, shelter, health care, a decent education, and the restoration of ecological balance of the earth for all of the people of the earth, now and in the future. We proclaim ourselves to be the creators of a new context and a new country called the United States of Being, within which reside all governments, enterprises, corporate entities and affiliations of humankind and under whom all allegiances to other persons or collective bodies are subsumed, toward the goal of making a world where physical warfare exists no more, starvation ends, adequate shelter is provided for all people, ecological balance is restored, health and well being are assured and the fundamental education of all peoples is provided for. And for the support of this declaration, we mutually pledge to each other our lives, our fortunes, and our sacred honor.

—Brad Blanton

If you want to sign up, go to our web site and do so. Our web address is: http://www.radicalhonesty.com. If you don't have a computer call us at 1-800-EL-TRUTH and we'll send you a copy to sign.

Chapter Twenty - Nine

The Real Bottom Line

Here is where all of this personal work on yourself counts. If, out of your personal transformation you are willing to join others who are likewise transformed in a community of people who interrupt each other's minds for ongoing mutual re-enlightenment, you then get to play in a much bigger game than the one you played when you were just trying to fit in as a personality. The new game is big enough to take everything you and all your friends combined can give — the game of creating a paradigm for a world that works for everyone. Then, as Werner Erhard has said, you can have a life that has a meaning beyond being a fly speck on a dirt ball hurling through space.

There are a number of what my friend, Nirvana Cable, calls "Gateway Projects" that involve all the humans on earth. What we are talking about here is how these gateway projects can, and must, in fact, all happen at once.

Gateway Projects

Ending world hunger is a gateway project, because it is a gateway for using our good life energy we are now in control of as a result of transforming ourselves from a whiney little mass of complaints to being an active participant in collaborating with other people as co-creators of new opportunities for life. It means creating a context for recreating the world for the sake of hungry people, most of whom are children. In ending hunger, the new opportunity for many human beings, created by many other human beings, is to simply have food to eat. Our new opportunity by joining a gateway project is to reassert our transformation from neurotics, who never can get or take enough, to contributors, who have more than they need and are giving — because we choose to out of the compassion that comes from noticing. Working on gateway projects helps you live a life more about contributing than bitching and moaning. Gateway projects help people get out of the box of the mind — their personalities and "case history" life — into a life of contribution and participation in the bigger family of human beings.

Sam Daley-Harris's project to fund micro-enterprise for the poorest hundred million families on the planet is another gateway project. (Through giving loans to poor women to start income producing micro-enterprises, profit is made to purchase and produce food and shelter and a better life.) The United States of Being to create an alternative world government is yet another gateway project. The Search for Common Ground started by John Marks and friends to resolve conflict in the hot spots of the world through finding common ground is one. The Alliance for Democracy to bring about an end to corporate rule and corporate control of nation states including the United States of America, is a gateway project. The Renaissance Alliance of Marianne Williamson and Neale Donald Walsch is another. The Nature Conservancy — buying up land to make nature preserves — is another. The list goes on: The Ecology movement. Businessmen and Military Leaders for Sensible Priorities. The Green Party. Nader's Raiders....

All these and many more I don't mention here, and many more I don't know about, reflect the magnificence of liberated human compassion, and can, in fact, operate together toward a common cause — heaven on earth. Gateway projects and those who work for them can work together all at the same time to create heaven on earth. They can all fit under what my friend, Nirvana Cable, and her partner, call "The Paradise Project," to create heaven on earth as an idea whose time has come. This is the most comprehensive of all because it includes all of the others.

The power of transformed human beings is unbelievable. We can do all of these separate gateway projects, and we can do them all at once, and quite quickly, within the next two years.

Now listen to me. Do not leave me here. I am not a damned dreamy-eyed new-age loony tune, I am talking about a real possibility. I am talking about real human potential. The context within which hunger ends, adequate housing is achieved, war comes to an end, sanitation and nutrition and medical care is learned, literacy is accomplished, a methodology for conflict resolution short of war is put in place, democracy triumphs over moneyocracy, the unjust so-called legal system is dismantled and created completely anew, the prison populations are reduced by 9/10ths, the defense industry is dismantled, nuclear "preparedness" ends, the "drug war" disappears, and many other absolutely bullshit outdated relics of the old paradigm are deep sixed forever and new, more functional models are created in their place—can all happen at once. Soon. Within the next two years.

All we have to do is realize our common humanity and our common interests, and work with, instead of against, each other. This changes the way we look at the world. We can then set it up differently—set the agreements and rules and communications up differently. We can make a new model and put it in place. All we have to do is unite and pull together and use our heads in service to our beings like transformed, intentional people can do.

Of course, it's a hell of a big job! But what else are you going to do? As I said earlier, we have found after years and years of people picturing the kind of world they want in workshops that everyone's picture of an ideal world is about the same. Everyone basically want's a good life for everyone else as well as themselves, once their screwed up parenting and cultural belief system conditioning is uncovered, noticed and transcended, and their natural human compassion emerges from the new contact with other human beings. *We all want the same thing so let's do what we need to do to get it.*

We have to let each other know that it can be done, and then design it and do it. We have to let each other know that consciously rearranging how the world works can be done, and then, with a lot of help from others and conscious communication design it, and then do it. We can make a parallel system based on the new paradigm, and then take over the job of handling the world's resources based on the new model and relieve the suffering of the slaves of the old way.

The methodology for accomplishing this is Radical Honesty. Radical Honesty is merely the methodology, the equipment, the process controller, the way-of-going-about-things, the technique to assist in deliverance from the mind and the ongoing and repeated rediscovery of being. It involves not denying or avoiding anything, particularly anger that comes from attachment to the one true way we all seem to come up with every fifteen seconds. It involves clearing our way back to contact with each other through honesty about what we think and feel and do–and to do that over and over again.

Mao Tse Tung accomplished the largest organizational task so far in human history for the largest number of people, when, between 1949 and 1952 he brought about an end to starvation in China. This is a gross oversimplification (so sue me) but here is my version of what happened: At the end of the war, he sent the Red Army into every village and town and community in the countryside and told the people to gather into cells or groups of about 30 families each, and gave them an agenda to use for meetings to run their communes with. They had cell meetings several times a week. The chairperson for each meeting was a different person each time (women were included) and responsibility for being in charge of the meeting rotated until every adult had a shot at chairperson and then they started all over again. Each meeting agenda had the same pro forma sequence for discussions to handle items on the agenda. The chairperson would stand and take off their cap and put it over their heart and say, to open the meeting, "Now speak bitterness." The people were then to complain, resent each other, blame each other, ask questions like "Why didn't we get the goddamned field mowed last Saturday?" and answers like, "Because you didn't get us the goddamned tractor part on time!" After about 10 minutes of this, the chair then stood again, put her cap over her heart and said, "Now, cease speaking bitterness." Then they proceeded to solve the problems. They did this over and over again, meeting after meeting. In less than three years starvation ended in China.

I say some form of Radical Honesty existed here, even if the liberties of interpretation I have taken are too large. Of course the Red Army also killed a lot of objectors to the process and a lot of terrible things happened as well, but the whole nation ended starvation in three years.

Here is what is required to make a world that works for everyone: People have to agree and commit to a common endeavor and then stay with their anger until they get over their attachments to "their" particular belief systems. They have to get to know each other by sharing with each other and tell the truth about their attachments and their irrational triggers and a plethora of little reactions from their past that jump up and bite them in the ass every day—and clear themselves again. They have to hold each other accountable for doing that.

Leaders of all of these movements toward sub-group unification for a common cause have to agree to a process of forgiveness and commit to do it until the cows come home.

Here is where we have to start—with consciousness leaders: Us egotists and Lone Rangers who are authors and workshop leaders and big time talkers and all of our friends around us have to duke it out until we are unified. We have to tell the truth better than anyone ever has before, about our "turf," our feelings, our bodies, our activities, our perversions, our delusions of grandeur, our savior complexes, our pettiness, our unfinished bullshit from the past, cigars, blow jobs, hand jobs, lies, human gymnastics and other things... We have to have mediators who have a sense of humor but are no-bullshit kind of people like me and my trainers. We have to learn to be funny and to become no bullshit kind of trainers for each other and work constantly with each other. We have to agree to an initial training in the very tough process called forgiveness. We have to set up structures for ongoing confrontation and completion within the context of an agreed upon greater goal – the healing of the world – Heaven on Earth – Paradise – The possibility of a lifetime of play and service for every human being on the planet.

We have to use the creative bursts that come from liberation from the jail of our own minds to make and remake the new paradigms required on an ongoing basis forever. We have to give up on believing and begin creating and take it on as a lifetime task and an unending human task. It revolves. As in revolution.

O.K., so there is a little work involved to revolve instead of devolve. Contact me. Take me to your leader. I am a revolutionary. I'll get things started. I'll make sure they don't stop. I'll keep doing it and teaching others how to do it until we empower enough leaders to change the way the world works. Then I will train others about how to do this until I die. I take responsibility for creating a world that works for all the human beings in the world, whose interests clearly include all of the other beings within whose context we reside.

Here is how we do it. Transcend the self. Transcend the Culture. Become attached to the particular transcend dance and go crazy again as humans inevitably do. Interrupt the mind's attachment. Start over again. La de da de da de da! La de da de da! A revolution every three or four years.

Thus we engage in the game, and re-attain that "seriousness of a child at play" Nietzche talked about, so this won't be the epitaph on humanity's tombstone: "Damn! We almost made it!"

A new world order is at hand, and it is a form of order that provides for conscious human participation in continuous creation and recreation without end, and we are at the forefront of the cult that controls the rudder: the telling the truth cult. We stand with clear eyes gazing into the labyrinth of lies most of us call home, talking about what we see, bringing about its downfall. At the same time, we are creating in its place, out of a more honest conversation, a new way of being together and taking care of each other. Come on in, we're doing fine; you'll love it. Thank you for reading this book. Thank you for listening.

About the Author

I'm a psychotherapist and writer and workshop leader and consultant to groups of people who live together and work together. I started out as poor white trash in Southern Virginia in a family of alcoholics. I left home when I was 13. I got a Ph.D. when I was 25 years old. I needed a lot of psychological help and getting degrees in psychology was one place I could get some. I was a borderline Ph.D.

I am 59 years old. I don't believe in God. I am in the process of becoming a modern day spiritual leader. I think that is because I can tell the difference between an experience and a thought and I can teach other people how to do that too. I got most of my real training in psychotherapy after I got my doctorate. I did that by going and finding people whose writings I had read or heard about or read about and getting them to teach me.

Joseph Wesley Mathews, existentialist theologian extraordinaire, and first head of the Ecumenical Institute of the World Council of Churches, was one of those people. Fritz Perls, the father of Gestalt Therapy, was another. Milton Erikson, the master hypnotist, was another. Abraham Maslow, the father of modern humanistic psychology, was another. I learned a lot from these people. I learned even more from other people who were learning from them at the same time I was.

All in all, though, I have learned the most about people from my friends and my life of intimate relationships to people and my clients. I was in the civil rights movement from 1959-1964. I was in the anti-Vietnam war movement from 1964 until it was over. I was a hippie and traveled all over North America in a school bus. I was in Haight Ashbury during the summer of love. I took a lot of acid and smoked a lot of pot and tried every drug extant at the time. I learned a lot from all the altered states of consciousness and drug experiences I have had. I've been smoking pot for 38 years and still do. I've been bombed with a lead pipe bomb, shot at, arrested, jailed, beat up, fined, fired and sued.

I've been married 4 times and divorced 3 times, and am currently separated from my most recent wife. We were together for 21 years. We are on somewhat amicable terms and do not know yet whether we will divorce. I am currently sexually and emotionally involved with several women and they all know about each other, and some of them know each other. I have 5 kids ranging in age from 7 years old to 31 years old. I love them with all of my heart. They are the teachers to whom I am most grateful and from whom I have learned the very most. They continue to teach me.

I've been in the human potential movement for 40 years. I went into the private practice of psychotherapy because I couldn't keep a job working for other people. I tried working in academia, the government and private enterprise. I ended up working for myself and often by myself. I've been a psychotherapist for over 25 years in Washington D.C. I have done individual psychotherapy, couples therapy, and group therapy. I have designed and run workshops on telling the truth for people who work on Capital Hill, people who work for industry related to the government, people who work for the government, and for private enterprise, and for the media. In my 25 years of practice I've seen more lawyers in psychotherapy than any other single profession. (By the way, everything they say about lawyers is pretty much true.) I went into psychotherapy to help other people and to get some more help for myself. It worked. I have done that. I have helped a lot of people and I have gotten a lot of help for myself. Now I am offering help to a larger audience of people through writing and running workshops. I give and get a lot of help from doing that too.

What I am trying to help people with these days is the terror and uncertainty of going sane. And, as has happened before, I am also currently undergoing a terrifying experience I need help with as much as the people I am attempting to serve: I think I am going sane. I am engaging people through writing and workshops and other conversations, to see what we can work out together, to support each other in being sane in an insane world. Please, either bring me back to normal or come with me. Lets do what we can to help each other. All the poor crazy people, driven to distraction out there, but pretending everything is O.K., need our help too. I'm going to participate in support groups for sanity from here on out. I have met the enemy and they are me.

Bibliography and Recommended Resources

Books

Aluna, Michael Dowd. *Earthspirit: A Handbook for Nurturing an Ecological Christianity*. 1991, Twenty-Third Publications.

Anderson, Sarah; Cavanaugh, John. *Top 200: The Rise of Global Corporate Power*. 1996, Institute for Policy Studies.

Anderson, Sarah; Cavanaugh, John; Lea, Thea. *The New Field Guide to the Global Economy*. 2000, The New Press.

Arendt, Hannah. *Eichmann in Jerusalem: A Report on the Banality of Evil*. 1994, Viking Penguin.

Arendt, Hannah. *Human Condition*. 1998, University of Chicago Press.

Berenstain, Stan; Berenstain, Jan. *Inside Outside Upside Down*. 1997, Random House Incorporated.

Blanton, Brad. *Radical Honesty: How to Transform Your Life by Telling the Truth*. 1996, Dell Publishing.

Bradshaw, John. *Creating Love*. 1993, Macmillan Library Reference.

Bradshaw, John. *Family Secrets*. 1996, Bantam Books.

Bradshaw, John. *Homecoming*. 1992, Bantam Books.

Breggin, Peter; Breggin, Ginger R. *The War Against Children*. 1994, Saint Martin's Press.

Breggin, Peter; Breggin, Ginger R. *The War Against Children of Color*. 1998, Common Courage Press.

Breton, Denise; Largent, Christopher, *The Paradigm Conspiracy: How Our Systems of Government, Church, School, & Culture Violate Our Human Potential*. 1996, Hazelden Foundation.

Brown, Norman O. *Life Against Death*. 1985, University Press of New England.

Brown, Norman O. *Love's Body*. 1990, University of California Press.

Cain, Albert C., ed. (Schneidman, Edwin S., contributor). *Survivors of Suicide*. 1972, Charles C.Thomas Publishers Ltd.

Campbell, Joseph. *Hero With a Thousand Faces*. 1996, Fine Communications.

Campbell, Joseph. *Inward Journey*. 1997, Donald I. Fine Books.

Campbell, Joseph. *Mythos*. 1999, Element Books Incorporated.

Cameron, Julia. *The Artist's Way*. 1995, Putnam Publishing Group.

Castaneda, Carlos. *Journey to Ixtlan*. 1994, Buccaneer Books Incorporated.

Castaneda, Carlos. *Teachings of Don Juan*. 1998, University of California Press.

Chodron, Pema. *Awakening Loving-Kindness*. 1996, Shambhala Publications, Incorporated.

Chodron, Pema. *Interview in Shambala Sun*, March 1997 and Utne Reader, June 1997.

Chodron, Pema. *Start Where You Are*. 1994, Shambhala Publications, Incorporated.

Chodron, Pema. *When Things Fall Apart.* 1996, Shambhala Publications, Incorporated.

Chodron, Pema. *The Wisdom of No Escape.* 1991, Shambhala Publications, Incorporated.

Chopra, Deepak. *Creating Affluence.* 1998, Amber-Allen Publishing.

Chopra, Deepak. *Dancing on the Razor's Edge.* 1998, Harmony Books.

Chopra, Deepak. *Everyday Immortality.* 1999, Crown Publishing Group Incorporated.

Chopra, Deepak. *Finding God.* 1999, Harmony Books.

Chopra, Deepak. *Healing the Heart.* 1998, Macmillan Library Reference.

Chopra, Deepak. *Journey Into Healing.* 1999, Crown Publishing Group Incorporated.

Chopra, Deepak. *Overcoming Addictions.* 1998, Three Rivers Press.

Chopra, Deepak. *Seven Laws of Spiritual Success.* 1999, Vedanta Press.

Covey, Steven. *The 7 Habits of Highly Effective People.* 1997, Covey Leadership Center.

Crosby, Bob; Scherer, John. *People Performance Profile.* 1985, Jossey-Bass, Incorporated Publishers.

cummings, e. e. *Eimi.* 1991, Reprint Services Corporation.

cummings, e. e.. *Poems 1923-1954.* 1954, Harcourt, Brace & World, Inc.

Dale, Stan. *Fantasies Can Set You Free.* 1980, Celestial Arts Publishing Company.

Dale, Stan. *My Child, My Self.* 1992, Human Awareness Publications.

Diamond, Jared M. *The Third Chimpanzee.* 1992, Harper Collins Publishers Incorporated.

Diamond, Jared M. *Why Is Sex Fun?* 1997, Harper Collins Publishers Incorporated.

Erhard, Werner. *Outrageous Betrayal.* 1993, Saint Martin's Press.

Farberow, N. *Suicide in Different Cultures.* 1975, University Park Press.

Ferguson, Marilyn. *The Aquarian Conspiracy.* 1987, The Putnam Publishing Group.

Ferguson, Marilyn. *The Brain Revolution.* 1973, Taplinger Publishing Co.

Ferguson, Marilyn. *Pragmagic.* 1990, Pocket Books.

Foundation for Inner Peace Staff. *A Course in Miracles.* 1996, Viking Penguin.

Francina, Suza. *The New Yoga for People Over 50.* 1997, Health Communications, Inc.

Fritz, Robert. *Corporate Tides.* 1996, Berrett-Koehler Publishers Incorporated.

Fritz, Robert. *Creating.* 1995, Butterworth-Heinemann.

Fritz, Robert. *The Path of Least Resistance.* 1989, Fawcett Book Group.

Gallwey, W. Timothy. *Inner Skiing.* 1998, Random House.

Gallwey, W. Timothy. *Inner Tennis.* 1998, Random House.

Gallwey, W. Timothy. *The Inner Game of Golf.* 1998, Random House.

Gallwey, W. Timothy. *The Inner Game of Tennis.* 1997, Random House.

Gallwey, W. Timothy. *The Inner Game of Work.* 1997, Random House.

Gatto, John Taylor; Mercogliano, Chris. *Challenging the Giant*. 1996, Down-to-Earth-Books.

Gatto, John Taylor. *Dumbing Us Down*. 1991, New Society Publishers, Limited.

Green, Barry; Gallwey, W. Timothy. *The Inner Game of Music*. 1986, Doubleday.

Heinlein, Robert A. *Stranger in a Strange Land*. 1961, 1991. G.P. Putnam's Sons.

Hendricks, Gay. *Conscious Breathing*.

Hendricks, Kathlyn; Hendrics, Gay. *The Conscious Heart*. 1997, Bantam Books.

Hendricks, Kathlyn; Hendrics, Gay. *Conscious Loving*.

Holt, John. *Escape from Childhood*. 1995, Holt Associates.

Holt, John. *Freedom & Beyond*. 1995, Boynton/Cook Publishers Incorporated.

Holt, John. *Growing Without Schooling*. 1997, Hold Associates.

Holt, John. *How Children Fail*. 1995, Addison Wesley Longman, Incorporated.

Holt, John. *How Children Learn*. 1995, Addison Wesley Longman, Incorporated.

Holt, John. *Kicking Up Trouble*. 1995, Wilderness Adventuring Press.

Holt, John. *What Do I Do Monday?* 1995, Boynton/Cook Publishers Incorporated.

Hubbard, L. Ron. *Child Dianetics*

Hubbard, L. Ron *Scientology : The Fundamentals of Thought*. 1997, Bridge Publishers

Hubbard, L. Ron *Dianetics : The Modern Science of Mental Health*. 1995, Bridge Publishers.

Hubbard, L. Ron *Clear Body Clear Mind*. 1990, Bridge Publishers.

Jones, Riki Robbins. *Negotiating Love*. 1995, Ballantine Books, Incorporated.

Kabat-Zinn, Myla; Kabat-Zinn, Jon. *Everyday Blessings*. 1998, Hyperion.

Kabat-Zinn, Myla; Kabat-Zinn, Jon. *Mindful Parenting: Nourishing Our Children, Growing Ourselves*.

Kabat-Zinn, Myla; Kabat-Zinn, Jon. *Soul Food: Stories to Nourish the Spirit & the Heart*. 1996, Harper San Francisco.

Keen, Sam. *Faces of the Enemy*. 1991, Harper San Francisco.

Keen, Sam. *Fire in the Belly*. 1992, Bantam.

Keen, Sam. *Hymns to an Unknown God*. 1994, Bantam.

Keen, Sam. *Inward Bound*. 1992, Bantam.

Keen, Sam. *Learning to Fly*. 1999, Broadway Books.

Keen, Sam. *The Passionate Life*. 1984, Harper San Francisco.

Keen, Sam. *Sacred Journey*. 1996, Simon & Schuster Trade.

Keen, Sam. *To Love & Be Loved*. 1999, Bantam.

Kelly, George A. *The Psychology of Personal Constructs*. 1992, Routledge.

Klein, Marty; Robbins, Riki. *Let Me Count the Ways: Discovering Great Sex Without Intercourse*. 1999, The Putnam Publishing Group.

Korten, David C. *The Post Corporate World.* 1998, CoPublications.

Korten, David C. *When Corporations Rule the World.* 1996, CoPublications.

Krishnamurti, Jiddu. *You are the World.* (out of print; other titles available)

Laut, Phil. *Money is My Friend.* 1999, Ballantine Publishing Group.

Liedloff, Jean. *The Continuum Concept.* 1990, Peter Smith Publisher Incorporated.

Llewellyn, Grace. *Freedom Challenge: African-American Homeschoolers.* 1996, Lowry House.

Llewellyn, Grace. *Real Lives: Eleven Teenagers Who Don't Go To School.* 1993, Lowry House.

Llewellyn, Grace. *The Teenage Liberation Handbook.* 1998, Lowry House.

Lore, Nicholas. *The Pathfinder: How to Choose or Change Your Career for a Lifetime of Satisfaction and Success.* 1998, Simon & Schuster.

McCarthy, Cormac. *Cities of the Plain.* 1998, B.E. Trice Publishing.

McCarthy, Cormac. *The Crossing.* 1996, Random House Value Publishing Incorporated.

Neill, A.S. *Freedom Not License.* 1978, Pocket Books.

Maharishi Mahesh Yogi. *TM.* 1998, NAL/Dutton.

Neill, A.S. *Summerhill.* 1984, Pocket Books.

Neill, A.S. *Summerhill For & Against.* 1978, Pocket Books.

Neill, A.S. *Summerhill School.* 1993, Saint Martin's Press, Incorporated.

Norretranders, Tor. *The User Illusion: Cutting Consciousness Down to Size.* 1998, Viking Penguin.

Ornish, Dean. *Eat More, Weigh Less.* 1997, Harper San Francisco.

Ornish, Dean, M.D. *Love & Survival: The Scientific Basis for the Healing Power of Intimacy,* 1998, HarperCollins Publishers Incorporated.

Parton, Dolly. *Coat of Many Colors.* 1996, Harper Collins Children's Books.

Patanjali's Yoga Sutras. 1995, Munshiram Manoharial Publishers Private, Limited.

Peck, M. Scott. *Gifts for the Journey.* 2000, Renaissance Books.

Peck, M. Scott. *The Road Less Traveled.* 1998, Simon & Schuster Trade.

Peck, Robert. *"Measuring the Mental Health of Normal Adults,"* Genetic Psychology Monographs, 1959-60.

Perls, Fritz. *The Gestalt Approach & Eye Witness to Therapy.* 1976, Bantam Books Incorporated.

Perls, Fritz. *Legacy From Fritz.* 1975, Science & Behavior Books, Incorporated.

Peters, Tom. *The Circle of Innovation.* 1999, Vintage Books.

Peters, Tom. *Heart & Soul of Excellence.* 1997, Random House Value Publishing Incorporated.

Peters, Tom. *Excellence in the Organization.* 1995, Simon & Schuster Trade.

Peters, Tom. *Liberation Management.* 1995, Random House Value Publishing Incorporated.

Peters, Tom. *The Pursuit of Wow!* 1995, Vintage Books.

Prather, Hugh; Prather, Gayle. *A Book For Couples.* 1998, Doubleday.

Prather, Hugh; Prather, Gayle. *I Will Never Leave You: How Couples Can Achieve the Power of Lasting Love*. 1995, Bantam Books.

Prather, Hugh; Prather, Gayle. *Parables from Other Planets*. 1992, Bantam Books.

Prather, Hugh; Prather, Gayle. *Spiritual Parenting: A Guide to Understanding and Nurturing Your Child*. 1997, Crown Publishing Group.

Robbins, Tom. *Another Roadside Attraction*. 1991, Bantam.

Robbins, Tom. *Even Cowgirls Get the Blues*. 1990, Bantam.

Robbins, Tom. *Half Asleep in Frog Pajamas*. 1995, Bantam.

Robbins, Tom. *Jitterbug Perfume*. 1990, Bantam.

Robbins, Tom. *Skinny Legs & All*. 1995, Bantam.

Robbins, Tom. *Still Life with Woodpecker*. 1990, Bantam.

Schiffmann, Erich. *Yoga: The Spirit and Practice of Moving into Stillness*. 1996, Pocket Books/Simon & Schuster, Inc.

Scherer, John; Shook, Larry. *Work & the Human Spirit*. 1993, John Scherer & Associates.

Schutz, Will; Turner, Evelyn. *Body Fantasy*. 1977, Harper Collins Publishing Incorporated.

Schutz, Will. *Leaders of Schools*. 1977, Pfeiffer & Company.

Schutz, Will. *The Human Element*. 1994, Jossey-Bass, Incorporated Publishers.

Schutz, Will. *Profound Simplicity*. 1982, Jossey-Bass, Incorporated Publishers.

Schutz, Will. *The Truth Option*. 1984, Ten-Speed Press.

Spock, Benjamin M. *A Better World for Our Children*. 1996, NTC/Contemporary Publishing Company.

Spock, Benjamin M. *Baby & Childcare*. 1997, Pocket Books.

Spock, Benjamin M. *Dr. Spock on Parenting*. 1998, Simon & Schuster Trade.

Spock, Benjamin M. *Raising Children in a Difficult Time*. 1985, Pocket Books.

Spock, Benjamin M. *Teenager's Guide to Life & Love*. 1971, Pocket Books.

Stevens, John O. *Awareness: Exploring, Experimenting, Experiencing*. 1973, Bantam Books, Incorporated.

Walsch, Neale Donald. *Conversations With God* series. 1999, Macmillan Library Reference.

Walsch, Neale Donald. *Friendship With God*. 1999, Putnam Publishing Group.

Williamson, Marianne. *Enchanted Love: The Mystical Power of Intimate Relationships*. 1999, Simon & Schuster.

Williamson, Marianne. *The Healing of America*. 1997, Simon & Schuster Trade.

Williamson, Marianne. *Healing the Soul of America*. 1999, Simon & Schuster Trade.

Williamson, Marianne. *Return to Love*. 1996, HarperCollins Publishers Incorporated.

Annotated Resources for Chapter 29

(Reviews by Michael Dowd)

Andruss, Van, Christopher Plant, et. al. *Home! A Bioregional Reader*. Philadelphia: New Society Publishers, 1990. An excellent introduction to bioregionalism, which is the North American equivalent to the Green movement in Europe. Presents an exciting vision and strategy for creating sustainable communities and cultures in harmony with the limits and regenerative powers of Earth.

Berry, Thomas. *The Dream of the Earth*. San Francisco: Sierra Club Books, 1988. This book is an enlightening and empowering presentation of our modern cosmology. Berry explores the implications of our common creation story with regard to energy, technology, ecology, economics, education, spirituality, patriarchy, bioregionalism, Christianity, and more. He also includes a very helpful annotated bibliography. A good introduction to perhaps the most prominent eco-theologian (or "geologian") alive today.

Bateson, Gregory. *Steps to an Ecology of Mind*. New York: Ballantine Books, 1972. Mind and Nature: A Necessary Unity. New York: Bantam Books, 1980. Bateson shows how we must think if we are to be reconciled to our true nature—how to "think as nature thinks," and regain our place in the natural world. Weighty reading, but well worth the effort.

Capra, Fritjof. *The Turning Point: Science, Society, and the Rising Culture*. New York: Bantam Books, 1983. A fascinating look at how discoveries in the sciences over the last century are ushering in a whole new way of being human. Capra, a physicist, compellingly shows how we have reached a time of dramatic change, a turning point for the planet as a whole.

Cogito. Alfred B. Starratt, Box 65190, Baltimore, MD 21209. Published twice a month, subtitled *A Journal Promoting the Healthy Human Spirit; Inspired by Love – Guided by Reason* Cogito is consistently excellent.

Devall, Bill, and George Sessions. *Deep Ecology: Living as if Nature Mattered*. Salt Lake City: Peregrine Smith, 1985. A fundamental exposition of the philosophy of deep ecology.

Devall, Bill. *Simple in Means, Rich in Ends: Practicing Deep Ecology*. Salt Lake City: Peregrine Smith, 1988. A good guide to embodying the deep ecology perspective in everyday life.

Dowd, Michael. *EarthSpirit: A Handbook for Nurturing an Ecological Christianity*. Mystic, Connecticut: Twenty-Third Publications, 1991. A resource for individual and group study. Thomas Berry says of this book, "A clear, delightful presentation of a Christianity that is alive, guides us, and evokes within us those spiritual energies that we need to assume our religious responsibilities for the fate of the Earth. Truly a handbook worthy of its subject, a guidebook for those who teach, a textbook for all of us who are learning."

Eisler, Riane. *The Chalice and the Blade: Our History, Our Future*. San Francisco: Harper & Row, 1987. A synthesis of feminist scholarship, archaeological research, and dynamic systems theory, this book draws heavily on what has been learned during this century about the neolithic cultures of Old Europe. Eisler insists that we must replace our present dominator model of human relationships with a partnership model, if we are to survive into the future.

Ferris, Timothy. *The Creation of the Universe* (90 minute videotape). PBS Home Video, 50 N. La Cienega Blvd., Beverly Hills, CA 90211; (800) 776-8300. Communicates what we know scientifically about the origin and nature of the universe in an exciting and understandable way.

Fox, Matthew. *Creation Spirituality*. San Francisco: Harper Collins, 1990. The Coming of the Cosmic Christ. San Francisco: Harper & Row, 1988. Original Blessing: A Primer in Creation Spirituality. Santa Fe, NM: Bear & Company, 1983. A Spirituality Named Compassion. San Francisco: Harper & Row, 1981. Fox, a controversial Roman Catholic theologian, explores the riches of the Christian tradition from the perspective of our new scientific cosmology. He breaks a lot of new ground.

Fox, Warwick. *Toward a Transpersonal Ecology: Developing New Foundations for Environmentalism*. Boston: Shambhala, 1990. An academic history and analysis of the deep ecology movement, with an exhausive bibliography. Suggests that the distinctive feature of deep ecology is the notion of an expansive identification with the natural world: Earth as our larger self.

In Context: A Quarterly Of Sustainable Culture. Context Institute, P.O. Box 11470, Bainbridge Island, WA 98110. A first-rate journal about thinking and living in harmony with nature.

Jantsch, Erich. *The Self-Organizing Universe: Scientific and Human Implications of the Emerging Paradigm of Evolution*. New York: Pergamon Press, 1980. This significant work examines the inner dynamism of the Universe from its origin through the development of humanity, and within human social systems. Jantsch refers to the fact that the entire Universe, at all levels, can be understood as an organic, developing whole; a living system.

LaChance, Albert. *Greenspirit: Twelve Steps in Ecological Spirituality*. Rockport, MA: Element Books, 1991. A practical guide to withdrawing from addictive consumerism and living a profoundly down-to-earth lifestyle. This book is a powerful synthesis of the new cosmology and a twelve-step recovery process.

LaChapelle, Dolores. *Sacred Land Sacred Sex — Rapture of the Deep: Concerning Deep Ecology and Celebrating Life*. Fine Hill Arts, Silverton, CO: 1988. Earth Festivals: Seasonal Celebrations for Everyone Young and Old. Fine Hill Arts, Silverton, CO: 1973. Earth Wisdom. Fine Hill Arts, Silverton, CO: 1978. PO Box 542, Silverton, CO. 81433; (303) 387-5729. Sacred Land Sacred Sex looks at how our Industrial Growth Society has brought the world to the brink of ecocide. It also points in the direction we must move to be saved from this fate. It may be the most provocative and comprehensive treatment of the topic anywhere. Earth Festivals is a wonderful resource for parents and teachers.

Laszlo, Ervin. *Evolution: The Grand Synthesis*. Boston: Shambhala, New Science Library, 1987. A very readable synthesis of new natural and social scientific perspectives on the nature of change within a self-organizing Universe.

Lovelock, James E. *The Ages of Gaia: A Biography of Our Living Earth.* New York: W.W. Norton & Company, 1988. Healing Gaia: Practical Medicine for the Planet. New York: Harmony Books, 1991. Lovelock, in 1972, was the originator of the Gaia hypothesis: the scientific understanding that the planet Earth, as a whole, is best understood as a living being; as a self-regulating organism. These books include the latest findings of scientists concerning Gaia. They also point in the direction of planetary health.

Macy, Joanna. *Despair and Personal Power in the Nuclear Age.* Philadelphia: New Society Publishers, 1983. World as Lover, World as Self. Berkeley: Parallax Press, 1991. Macy's work is a wonderful synthesis of experiential deep ecology, despair work, general systems theory and engaged Buddhism. Both of these books contain a wealth of wisdom and compassion essential for the healing of our world.

MacGillis, Miriam Therese. *Earth Learning and Spirituality* (5 hour videotape), New Earth Education (3 hour videotape), and The Fate of the Earth (90 minute audio tape). Global Perspectives, P.O. Box 925, Sonoma, CA 95476; (707) 996-4704. Each of these is an excellent popularization of the work of Thomas Berry.

Mander, Jerry. *In the Absence of the Sacred: The Failure of Technology and the Survival of the Indian Nations.* San Francisco: Sierra Club Books, 1991. A hard hitting critique of our modern technological society and the direction it is taking us, contrasted with the ongoing struggle for survival of the native traditions. A disturbing, enlightening and extremely important book.

Mills, Stephanie, ed. *In Praise of Nature.* Washington, D.C.: Island Press, 1990. A collection of essays, book reviews, and quotes from some of the leading nature writers of this century. A very helpful bibliographic source.

Plant, Christopher and Judith. *Turtle Talk: Voices for a Sustainable Future.* Philadelphia: New Society Publishers, 1990. A collection of interviews with some of the leading bioregionalists of our time.

Rifkin, Jeremy. *Biosphere Politics: A Cultural Odyssey from the Middle Ages to the New Age.* San Francisco: HarperCollins, 1992. A fascinating and most important look at how our changing notions of security have led us to the brink of ecological apocalypse. Rifkin also shows us how we must think and live if we are to survive into the future. A good companion volume to LaChapelle's Sacred Land Sacred Sex.

Sahtouris, Elisabet. *Gaia: The Human Journey from Chaos to Cosmos.* New York: Pocket Books, 1989. An excellent introduction to the Gaia theory—the scientific understanding that Earth itself is alive, rather than being merely a planet with life on it.

Seed, John, Joanna Macy, Arne Naess, et. al. *Thinking Like a Mountain: Towards a Council of All Beings.* Philadelphia: New Society Publishers, 1988. This collection of essays, group exercises, and poetry is an invaluable aid to personally experiencing the planet as one's larger self.

Shepard, Paul. *The Tender Carnivore and the Sacred Game.* New York: Scribner, 1973. Thinking Animals. New York: Viking Press, 1978. Nature and Madness. San Francisco: Sierra Club

Books, 1982. Shepard's work is important in understanding the historic and paleohistoric causes of our estrangement from nature. His writings are forceful and insightful.

Snyder, Gary. *The Old Ways*. San Francisco: City Light Books, 1977. Turtle Island. New York: New Directions, 1974. The Practice of the Wild. San Francisco: North Point Press, 1990. In both his essays and his poetry, Gary Snyder provides deep insight and inspiration regarding "living in place."

Spretnak, Charlene. *States of Grace: The Recovery of Meaning in the Postmodern Age.* This book is about reclaiming the core teachings and practices of Buddhism, Native American spirituality, Goddess spirituality, and the Semitic traditions (Judaism, Christianity, and Islam) for the well-being of the Earth community as a whole. Spretnak focuses on the wisdom of each of these traditions in light of the new cosmology.

Swimme, Brian. *The Universe is a Green Dragon: A Cosmic Creation Story.* Santa Fe: Bear & Company, 1984. Canticle to the Cosmos. Tides Foundation, NewStory Project, 134 Colleen St., Livermore, CA 94550. Swimme is a physicist who has studied extensively with Thomas Berry. The Universe is a Green Dragon is an alluring introduction to the new cosmology. Canticle to the Cosmos is a 12-part video lecture series designed to be used for academic classes, small group study, or for personal enrichment. It is excellent!

Swimme, Brian and Thomas Berry. *The Universe Story: From the Primordial Flaring Forth to the Ecozoic Era.* San Francisco: HarperCollins, 1992. This book is already being hailed as perhaps one of the most significant works of the twentieth century. It is a telling of the story of the Universe with a feel for its spiritual dimensions, and clearly indicates the role of the human in this sacred story of life. Must reading.

Movies/Videos

Bagdad Café

Courage Under Fire

The Englishman Who Went Up a Hill and Came Down a Mountain

Ikiru

The Karate Kid

Little Big Man

My Dinner With André

Secrets and Lies

Seven Samurai

Websites/Workshops

Arica Training/Arica Institute, Inc.
914-674-4091
145 Palisade St. #401
Dobbs Ferry, NY 10522-1617

Brad Blanton/Radical Honesty Enterprises
1-800-EL-TRUTH
646 Shuler Lane
Stanley, VA 22851
www.radicalhonesty.com

Conversations with God
www.conversationswithgod.com

Esalen Institute
831-667-3000 (CA)
www.esalen.org

The Landmark Forum
415-981-8850 (CA)
www.landmarkeducation.com

The Forum Graduate Association
703-971-3693
6008 Wendron Way
Alexandria, VA 22315-2656
fgainc@mnsinc.com

Hendricks Institute
805-565-1870
800-688-0772
1187 Coast Village Rd. Suite 1-416
Montecito, CA 93108
www.hendricks.com

The Learning Annex
212-371-0280 (NY)
310-478-6677 (Los Angeles, CA)
415-788-5500 (San Francisco, CA)
619-544-9700 (San Diego, CA)
New York
www.thelearningannex.com

Grace Llewellyn
541-686-2315
(homeschooling, *Teenage Liberation Handbook*)
PO Box 1014
Eugene OR 97440
http://hometown.aol.com/gracejanet/index.html

Omega Institute
800-944-1001
260 Lake Drive
Rhinebeck, NY 12572
http://eomega.org

Outward Bound
800-341-1744 (East Coast, US)
800-841-0186 (NC) (www.ncobs.org)
800-321-HIKE (Voyageur)
800-477-2627 (CO)
800-547-3312 (Pacific Crest, US)
www.outwardbound.org

Pathworks Centers
619-793-1246 (CA)
540-948-6544 (VA)
www.pathwork.org

The Pathwork Foundation
914-688-2211 (Northeast US)
13013 Colllingwood Terrace
Silver Spring, MD 20904-1414

Rockport Institute, Ltd.
(career counseling, coaching, life planning)
301-340-6600 (MD)
10124 Lakewood Drive
Rockville, MD, 20850
e-mail: pathfinder@rockportinstitute.com
www.rockportinstitute.com

Rowe Conference Center
413-339-4954 (New England)

Greg Small/The Human Element
916-985-8590 (CA)
www.startsmall.com

Thinking Allowed
http://spider12.lanminds.com/index.html

Footnotes

1 Korten, David, *When Corporations Rule the World*. 1996, CoPublications.

2 Ornish, Dean, M.D. *Love & Survival: The Scientific Basis for the Healing Power of Intimacy*, 1998, HarperCollins Publishers Incorporated.

3 Blanton, Brad. *Radical Honesty: How to Transform Your Life by Telling the Truth*. 1997, Dell Books Incorporated.

4 Berenstain, Stan (1923); Berenstain, Jan (1997). *Inside Outside Upside Down*. 1997, Random House Incorporated.

5 Breton, Denise; Largent, Christopher, *The Paradigm Conspiracy*, 1998, Hazelden Foundation.

6 Farberow, N. *Suicide in Different Cultures*. 1975, University Park Press.

7 Kelly, George A. *The Psychology of Personal Constructs*. 1992, Routledge.

8 Norretranders, Tor. *The User Illusion: Cutting Consciousness Down to Size*. 1998, Viking Penguin.

9 *Patanjali's Yoga Sutras*. 1995, Munshiram Manoharial Publishers Private, Limited.

10 Gallwey, W. Timothy. *The Inner Game of Tennis*. 1997, Random House.

11 cummings, e. e.. *Poems 1923-1954*. 1954, Harcourt, Brace & World, Inc. p. 370.

12 Robbins, Tom. *Skinny Legs & All*. 1995, Bantam.

13 Robbins, Tom. *Still Life with Woodpecker*. 1990, Bantam.

14 Robbins, Tom. *Another Roadside Attraction*. 1991, Bantam.

15 Britten, Crane. *The Anatomy of a Revolution*.

16 Scherer, John; Shook, Larry. *Work & the Human Spirit*. 1993, John Scherer & Associates.

17 Brown, Norman O. *Life Against Death*. 1985, University Press of New England.

18 Stevens, John O. *Awareness: Exploring, Experimenting, Experiencing*. 1973, Bantam Books, Incorporated.

19 Covey, Stephen. *The 7 Habits of Highly Effective People*, 1997, Covey Leadership Center.

20 Cameron, Julia. *The Artist's Way*. 1995, Putnam Publishing Group.

21 Fritz, Robert. *The Path of Least Resistance*. 1989, Fawcett Book Group.

22 Williamson, Marianne. *The Healing of America*. 1997, Simon & Shuster Trade.

23 Peck, Robert. *Genetic Psychology Monographs*, 1958.

24 Breton, Denise; Largent, Christopher, *The Paradigm Conspiracy*, 1998, Hazelden Foundation.

25 Anderson, Sarah. Cavanaugh, John. *Top 200: The Rise of Global Corporate Power*, 1996, Washington, D.C. Institute for Policy Studies

26 Salmon, Jacqueline L., *Intensive Child Care*, The Washington Post, Oct. 24, 1999, page A1.

27 Williamson, Marianne. *The Healing of America*. 1997, Simon & Shuster Trade.

28 Williamson, Marianne. *Return to Love*. 1996, HarperCollins Publishers Incorporated.

29 Korten, David C. *When Corporations Rule the World*. 1996, CoPublications.

30 Korten, David C. *The Post Corporate World*. 1998, CoPublications.

31 Walsch, Neale Donald. *Conversations With God* series. 1999, Macmillan Library Reference.

32 Walsch, Neale Donald. *Friendship With God.* 1999, Putnam Publishing Group.

Please send me information on Radical Honesty courses and publications.

Name: _____

Address: _____

_____

_____

Phone: _____

E-Mail _____

Please send me information on Radical Honesty courses and publications.

Name: _____

Address: _____

_____

_____

Phone: _____

E-Mail _____

Please send me information on Radical Honesty courses and publications.

Name: _____

Address: _____

_____

_____

Phone: _____

E-Mail _____

Radical Honesty Enterprises
646 Schuler Lane
Stanley, VA 22851

Radical Honesty Enterprises
646 Schuler Lane
Stanley, VA 22851

Radical Honesty Enterprises
646 Schuler Lane
Stanley, VA 22851